THE RHETORIC OF ECONOMICS

RHETORIC OF THE HUMAN SCIENCES

General Editors

David J. Depew

Deirdre N. McCloskey

John S. Nelson

John D. Peters

The Rhetoric of Economics

SECOND EDITION

DEIRDRE N. McCLOSKEY

THE UNIVERSITY OF WISCONSIN PRESS

The University of Wisconsin Press
2537 Daniels Street
Madison, Wisconsin 53718

3 Henrietta Street
London WC2E 8LU, England

5   4   3   2   1

Printed in the United States of America

Library of Congress Cataloging-in-Publication Data
McCloskey, Deirdre N.
    The rhetoric of economics / Deirdre N. McCloskey. — Second ed.
        248 pp.   cm. — (Rhetoric of the human sciences)
    Includes bibliographical references and index.
    ISBN 0–299–15810–1 (cloth: alk. paper).
    ISBN 0–299–15814–4 (pbk.: alk. paper).
    1. Economics. 2. Rhetoric.   I. Title. II. Series.
    HB71.M38   1998
    330—dc21   97–37740

Ad universitatem Iowae,
montuosam, humanam, urbanam,
quamvis in fustibus positam.

CONTENTS

Contents

PREFACE TO THE

SECOND EDITION

Why in 1985 did I write *The Rhetoric of Economics*? It was an odd book. An economic historian decides in the early 1980s to learn a little about philosophy, linguistics, literary criticism, the history of science, and other pieces of the literary culture. An odd thing to do. Then she feels she has to tell other economists the news—that the culture of economists itself is in large part literary, too. An odd thing to say.

Sometime in the late 1970s I stopped being a persuaded positivist. At the University of Chicago, where I taught for a dozen years from 1968 to 1980, the economists preached a simpleton's version of positivism. This version has by now entered the "philosophical" equipment of most economists. Nowadays you will find them repeating philosophical ideas that in 1968 on the lips of Milton Friedman and George Stigler seemed fresh (to simpletons like me), and seemed in 1918 revolutionary to some smart people in Vienna. At another graduate program they still hand out Milton's old essay of 1953 to every graduate student on the first day. Yet the brilliance of the actual scientific talk in seminar and lunchroom by my fellow Chicago economists—Chicago in the 1970s was the most creative department of economics in the world—contrasted strangely with the simpleton's science recommended by the methodology. I wondered. I got into some quarrels about it with George Stigler and Gary Becker.

I started again to read philosophy of science (I had stopped in graduate school, just short of the Karl Popper level). More important, around 1980 I came upon history and sociology of science that challenged the reigning philosophy. Scientists, these crazy radicals claimed, were not the macho saints that Popper said they were. The scientists, when you looked closely at what they did and wrote, were like other human beings, open to persuasion.

Most important of all, and on a big scale at Iowa in the 1980s, I discovered literary—and specifically "rhetorical"—criticism. It is a theory of how words persuade even scientists.

One could look on the book as a *philosophical* treatise. But that is to miss its main point, as many conscientious readers did. It was my fault.

Arrangement has never been my strong suit as a rhetorician, and I arranged the book badly. Specifically, I opened it badly. A lot of people thought that the main point of the book was contained in the opening complaint about positivism and its wider context, "modernism." After all, the first three chapters in the first edition were "philosophical." The article in the *Journal of Economic Literature* in 1983 that first announced the argument was essentially these chapters. If you took the 1983 article as a précis of the book you were going to miss the point.

What's the point? As I said: that economics is literary. My book was an early case study (not the first) in the rhetoric of science. That is, like earlier work by Maurice Finocchiaro on Galileo (1980), back through Thomas Kuhn and his master, Ludwick Fleck (1935), I was looking at science as persuasion. My own science of economics was literary, like physics (Feyerabend 1975, 1978, Bazerman 1981, 1983, 1984, 1988) or mathematics (Lakatos 1976; Steiner 1975) or biology (Gould 1977, 1981, 1984), a persuasive realm where the work was done by human arguments, not godlike Proof.

The point was obscured by the organization of the book. Most reviewers did not read beyond the third chapter, quite rightly—I mean, how much of this amateur philosophy are you supposed to put up with? (If you want more you can have all you want in my third book on the subject, *Knowledge and Persuasion in Economics* [1994], 396 pages of philosophical answers to critics and philosophical extensions of the first three chapters. Its contents are proof that most critics read the book as philosophical.)

I should have started *The Rhetoric* with the concrete readings of economic texts. I should have brought the practical rhetoric to a climax with the major case study, which shows that all this stuff does have some scientific payoff: my complaints about statistical significance. (Not about *statistics* understand. I am and remain a quantitative lady. Hurrah for statistics. Real science. But against that particular and dominant technique, declares Aunt Deirdre, the Marianne of modern economic science, *aux barricades*! Down with the boy's game in a sandbox called statistical "significance" and Student's-*t*!) *Then* I should have shown the wider cultural significance of The Case of Economics by showing it to be an instance of "modernism." I should *not* have started with this last, wider, and philosophical point.

So that's what I have done with the new edition. I have started with what I consider the most interesting and original ingredients of my stew, which is the close reading of economic writings. I've added an opening chapter that gets right down to work, "How to Do a Rhetorical Analysis of Economics, and Why," and later a detailed rhetorical study of a famous paper by Ronald Coase. I've rewritten the book where I can see small changes in expression that might make it clearer. I've tried to drop the boring passages, but you know how authors are about boring passages that *they* wrote. I've added a few more references, and have made two additional bibliographies, one a bibliography on the rhetoric of economics as I understand it and the other a list of the reviews of the first edition that I know of.

To get the whole picture of What I Now Believe, though, I ask you to read my other books, the *Knowledge* one, and the earlier *If You're So Smart: The Narrative of Economic Expertise* (1990), and then the fourth, *The Vices of Economists; The Virtues of the Bourgeoisie* (1997a). Buy them in bulk. They make excellent Christmas presents. The three down to 1994 are a trilogy (well, there are three of them aren't there?), with the 1997 one a sort of satyr play added on the end. *The Rhetoric* is, I see now, a poetics of economics, focusing on metaphor. See if you don't agree. *If You're So Smart* was more or less self-consciously a narratology of economics, focusing on its stories. I explain there why I regard metaphor and story as the two possibilities of thought. *Knowledge* was, as I have said, the philosophical finish to the trilogy, and explains where all this fits or fails to fit into philosophical traditions. And *The Vices* tries to draw the moral for the future of the field. In our charmless economic jargon, it contains the "policy prescription" following the first three books.

I have supplied in the present book a brief postscript, "Since Rhetoric: Prospects for a Scientific Economics." Its point is that a scientific economics can emerge through acknowledging the literary side. Not acknowledging it has by now made us economists stupidly unscientific. It's a feminist point: a human is stupid who acknowledges only his masculine side. A man is not weakened by being a whole human being. Likewise, an economist is not weakened by getting out of the sandbox he has played in since the 1940s.

I am hoping that the effect of the new edition is different from that of the first. The first confused a lot of philosophically oriented economists. They kept thinking they had me in various philosophical traps and were annoyed that I didn't seem to care, strolling around with bear traps clinging to my legs. I didn't care because the book was not primarily philosophical. It was rhetorical. The rest of the economist readers, or at any rate readers of the title of the book, grasped the bare idea that economists argue things—not much of a discovery, though worth having. The word "rhetoric" is more common in economics than before I wrote. (The power of the test is small, though: the word is more common everywhere, because we are seeing a revival of classical rhetoric.)

I hope the second edition will lead economists and noneconomists to see the field as it is, as part of the larger conversation of humankind. Economists are poets / But don't know it. Economists are storytellers without a clue. Economists are philosophers who don't study philosophy. Economists are scientists who don't know even now that their science has become a boy's game in a sandbox. Let's get serious, fellas. (The gals already know there's something wrong.)

ACKNOWLEDGMENTS

FOR THE FIRST EDITION

The germ of the book was presented as a talk to the old program in Politics, Economics, Rhetoric, and Law as I left the University of Chicago in 1979–1980. Wayne Booth asked me to talk on "The Rhetoric of Economics," and I said, "Sure. Glad to. Uh . . . What is it?" The prospect of a public hanging in the presence of Booth, Ira Katznelson, Edward Levi, Philip Kurland, and the like wonderfully concentrated my intellect. (The hanging proceeded as planned.) I had read Paul Feyerabend's *Against Method* a little earlier, picking it up by accident in a bookstore, and found it congenial. Booth's *Modern Dogma and the Rhetoric of Assent* and, on Booth's recommendation, Michael Polanyi's *Personal Knowledge* prepared me for the Chicago talk, and a little bit later I read the book of another Chicago colleague, Stephen Toulmin's *The Uses of Argument*, picked up again by chance in a bookstore. Glory be to bookstores.

In my first year at Iowa I discussed these matters with my new colleagues, and started with Alan Nagel a colloquium on rhetoric. Every two weeks, winter and summer, since 1980 it has met to discuss pieces of argument and the art of argument. There early in the 1980s I received from Nagel, and from Gerald Bruns, Evan Fales, Bruce Gronbeck, Paul Hernadi, John Lyne, Michael McGee, Allan Megill, Jay Semel, and above all John Nelson the elements of an education in literary theory, philosophy, and speech communication. The colloquium gradually expanded in ambition, though keeping its focus on what we came to call the "rhetoric of inquiry." It is a way of understanding and perhaps improving the conversations of scholarship, by listening to the "rhetoric" of a paper in mathematics or law or economics. In 1984 the colloquium led to a conference financed by the National Endowment for the Humanities, the Iowa Humanities Board, and the University of Iowa. Out of this came a book (Nelson, Megill, and McCloskey 1987) and the Project on Rhetoric of Inquiry (Poroi), with two book series, one here at Wisconsin and the other at the University of Chicago.

I had spent the summer of 1982 at the Institute for Advanced Studies at Australian National University thinking about this "rhetoric of economics." The intense intellectuality of the groups at Australian National in economic history, economics, philosophy, and history of ideas was wonderful, and I was especially fortunate to overlap for a month with Richard Rorty. Talking to him, and reading his book *Philosophy and the Mirror of Nature,* made many things clear.

I then dined out on the work for years. In the antipodes during 1982 seminars heard the paper at Australian National itself; Adelaide, Melbourne, Monash, New South Wales, and Western Australia; and Auckland and Victoria University of Wellington. Although everywhere I was startled at the warmth of the reception economists gave to a paper critical of their way of talking, the reception at the University of Tasmania was especially inspiriting. Back home in the United States one or another chapter was given to the Speech Communication Association's Third Conference on Argumentation at Alta, Utah, in 1983; to the Conference on Codes at the Humanities Center of Brooklyn College, CUNY, in 1983; to the Rhetoric of Economics conference at Middlebury College in 1984; to the Temple University/Speech Communication Association Conference on Kenneth Burke at Philadelphia in 1984; and to the American Economic Association convention at Dallas in 1984.

Seminars at the World Bank, the National Science Foundation, the Washington Area Economic History Workshop, the Columbia Economic History Seminar, and Miami University of Ohio heard pieces, as did groups at the universities of British Columbia, California at Davis, Chicago, Connecticut, Nebraska, the Pacific, Pennsylvania, Toronto, Virginia; Baruch (CUNY), Grinnell, Queens (CUNY), Union, and Williams colleges; and Ball State, Emory, Indiana, Iowa State, McMaster, North Carolina State, Princeton, Rutgers, Simon Fraser, Wesleyan, and Yale universities. Each audience raised points that had escaped me, which shows that even now I don't know what I am talking about. No wonder. Like oratory, argument depends for its virtues on the virtues of its audience, and develops as a conversation. Unlike machines, conversations are by nature surprising.

Fred Carstensen, A. W. Coats, Stanley Engerman, Arjo Klamer, Robert Higgs, Thomas Mayer, and Robert Solow wrote comments on the work early and often. Many other economists and economic historians have commented in writing on drafts of the chapters or on published papers, many at length and repeatedly. The commentary by economists— favorable or unfavorable—has been inspiring and enlightening. I am uneasily aware that this list misses some, but down to the date of publication it included Irma Adelman, Moses Abramovitz, J. D. Alexander, Edward Ames, Peter Bauer, M. Cristina Bicchieri, Mark Blaug, Richard Boltuck, Thomas Borcherding, William Breit, Martin Bronfenbrenner,

Acknowledgments

James Buchanan, Phillip Cagan, Bruce Caldwell, Rondo Cameron, Filippo Cesarano, Gregory Clark, Robert Clower, Ronald Coase, John Cochrane, Gordon Crovitz, Stephen De Canio, Arthur Diamond, J. E. Easley, Jr., Billy Eatherly, David Felix, Alex Field, Robert Fogel, Milton Friedman, Walter Galenson, Allan Gibbard, Claudia Goldin, Robert Goodin, Robert Gordon, Frank Hahn, Gary Hawke, Robert Heilbroner, Willie Hendersen, Abraham Hirsch, Albert Hirschman, A. B. Holmes, J. R. T. Hughes, Eric Jones, Charles Kindleberger, David Landes, Timothy Lane, Richard Langlois, John Latham, Edward Leamer, Nathaniel Leff, Harvey Leibenstein, Axel Leijonhufvud, Wassily Leontief, David Levy, H. G. Lewis, Peter Lindert, Rodney Maddock, Neil de Marchi, Terry Marsh, John Martin, Thomas McCaleb, Michael McPherson, Pedro Carvalho de Mello, Philip Mirowski, David Mitch, Richard Nathan, Charles Nelson, Richard Nelson, D. P. O'Brien, Avner Offer, Ian Parker, William Parker, Mark Perlman, Boris Pesek, Sidney Ratner, Joseph D. Reid, Jr., Robert Renshaw, Vernon Ruttan, T. W. Schultz, Amartya Sen, Martin Spechler, Frank Spooner, Paul Streeten, John Thorkelson, Thomas Ulen, Larry Westphal, Oliver Williamson, Gordon Winston, Gavin Wright, and Leland Yeager.

The implied reader of the book is an economist, but I have tried to make the argument intelligible and persuasive to noneconomists as well. On this score and others the detailed remarks by my staunch friends Wayne Booth and Richard Rorty on various versions, especially on the next-to-last draft, were immensely useful. Without their advice the book would have been even more obviously simpleminded about literary theory and philosophy.

The other noneconomists who wrote to me about drafts in one form or another include (here I suspect even more that I am overlooking some) Keith Baker, Charles Bazerman, Howard Becker, Robert Boynton, Bernard Cohn, Harry Collins, John Comaroff, Colin Day, Mary Douglas, Otis Dudley Duncan, Stanley Fish, James O. Freedman, Elizabeth Fricker, Clifford Geertz, Gerald Geison, Nelson Goodman, Allen Graubard, Stephen Graubard, Joseph Gusfield, Daniel Hausman, Martin Hollis, Martin Kessler, J. Morgan Kousser, William Kruskal, John Laffey, Laurence Lafore, Donald Levine, Leonard Liggio, Michael Mahoney, Donald Marshall, Laura McCloskey, William McNeill, Franklin Mendels, Denton Morrison, Peter Novick, Samuel Patterson, Amelie Oksenberg Rorty, Renato Rosaldo, Martin Rudwick, John Schuster, Herbert Simons, Donald Sutherland, Stephen Toulmin, and David Warsh. Humanists are less startled than economists by the message that technical economics involves literary, ethical, and rhetorical issues.

I owe financial debts for the final work on the book to the John Simon

Guggenheim Foundation, the Institute for Advanced Study at Princeton, the National Endowment for the Humanities (for its program in Humanities, Science, and Technology, and especially David E. Wright), and the University of Iowa. The time away from other duties during 1983–1984 brought the book substantially to its present form. My editor at Wisconsin, Gordon Massman, was encouraging well beyond the call of profit, exhibiting bourgeois virtue. He initiated at Wisconsin this series in the rhetoric of inquiry. Ginalie Swaim and Carolyn Moser exercised extraordinary care and intelligence on the manuscript and improved it. (My loving assistant Deborah Reese typed the second edition.)

Looking again at the writings most important to my thinking is embarrassing. Ideas and even forms of words that I had come to imagine were my own turn out to have been pillaged from Paul Feyerabend, Wayne Booth, Michael Polanyi, Stephen Toulmin, Richard Rorty, Thomas Kuhn, and Kenneth Burke (in order of the major pillagings, from 1980 to 1984). Later I stole from Michael Mulkay and Arjo Klamer. The only comfort is another phrase from Rorty (which he in turn borrowed from Michael Oakeshott) of intellectual life as a conversation, now in parts some three thousand years old. We *should,* after all, be influenced by our interlocutors, and should take over as our own their forms of words.

EXORDIUM

If translated into English, most of the ways economists talk among themselves would sound plausible enough to poets, journalists businesspeople, and other thoughtful though noneconomical folk. Like serious talk anywhere—among clothing designers and baseball fans, say—the talk is hard to follow when you have not made a habit of listening to it for a while. The culture of the conversation makes the words arcane. But the people in the unfamiliar conversation are not from another universe. Underneath it all (the economist's favorite phrase) conversational habits are similar. Economics uses mathematical models and statistical tests and market arguments, which look alien to the literary eye. But looked at closely they are not so alien. They may be seen as figures of speech—metaphors, analogies, and appeals to authority.

Figures of speech are not mere frills. They think for us. Says Heidegger, "*Die Spracht spricht, nicht der Mensch*": The language speaks, not the human speaker. Someone who thinks of a market as an "invisible hand" and the organization of work as a "production function" and her coefficients as being "significant," as an economist does, is giving the language a lot of responsibility. It seems a good idea to look hard at the language.

Finding that the economic conversation depends substantially on its verbal forms would not mean that economics is not a science, or just a matter of opinion, or some sort of confidence game. Economics is pretty successful as a science. In fact its failures over the past fifty years—they are boyish but correctable—can be related directly to its sleepwalking in rhetoric. Good scientists also use language. The best scientists, the Goulds and Feynmans and the like, use it with self-awareness. Using scientific language wide awake requires attention to the other minds present when you speak.

The paying of attention to one's audience is called "rhetoric," a word that I later exercise hard. You use rhetoric, of course, to warn of a fire in a theater or to arouse the xenophobia of the electorate. This sort of yelling is the newspaper meaning of the word, like the president's "heated rhetoric" in a press conference, or the "mere rhetoric" to which our enemies stoop. Since the Greek flame was lit, though, the word has also been used in a broader and more amiable sense, to mean the study of all the ways of accomplishing things with language: inciting a mob to lynch the accused, but also persuading readers that a novel's characters breathe, or bringing scientists to accept the better argument and reject the worse. The newspaper definition is Little Rhetoric. I am talking about Big Rhetoric.

In _Modern Dogma and the Rhetoric of Assent_ Wayne Booth gives many useful definitions. Rhetoric is "the art of probing what men believe they ought to believe, rather than proving what is true according to abstract methods"; it is "the art of discovering good reasons, finding what really warrants assent, because any reasonable person ought to be persuaded"; it is "careful weighing of more-or-less good reasons to arrive at more-or-less probable or plausible conclusions—none too secure but better than what would be arrived at by chance or unthinking impulse"; it is the "art of discovering warrantable beliefs and improving those beliefs in shared discourse"; its purpose must not be "to talk someone else into a preconceived view; rather, it must be to engage in mutual inquiry" (Booth 1974a, pp. xiii, xiv, 59, xiii, 137).

The question is whether the scientist—who usually fancies herself an announcer of "results" or a stater of "conclusions" free of rhetoric—speaks rhetorically. Does she try to persuade? I think so. Language, I just said, is not a solitary accomplishment. The scientist doesn't speak into the void, or to herself. She speaks to a community of voices. She desires to be heeded, praised, published, imitated, honored, loved. These are the desires. The devices of language are the means.

Rhetoric, to make a little joke with the definition of economics that helped make it narrow and sleepwalking, is the proportioning of means to desires in speech. Rhetoric is an economics of language, the study of how scarce means are allocated to the insatiable desires of people to be heard. It seems on the face of it a reasonable hypothesis that economists are like other people in being talkers who desire listeners when they go to the library or the computer center as much as when they go to the office or the polling booth. The purpose here is to see if this is true, and to see if it is useful: to study the rhetoric of economic science. The subject is science. It is not the economy, or the adequacy of economic theory as a description of the economy, or even mainly the economist's role in the economy. The subject is the conversation economists have among themselves, for purposes of persuading each other that the interest elasticity of demand for investment is zero or that the money supply is controlled by the Federal Reserve.

The purpose of thinking about how economists converse with each other is to help the field mature as a science, not to attack it. Economics is unsuccessful as social weather forecasting, a role forced on it by the rhetoric of politics and journalism. But it is strikingly successful as social history, or would be if it would stop sleepwalking in its rhetoric. Economics, like geology or evolutionary biology or history itself, is an historical rather than a predictive science. Economics is not widely regarded as an imposing creation of the human mind. But I think it is. It is social self-understanding (a critical theory, indeed, like Marxism or psychoanalysis), as remarkable as anthropology or history. All the more pity that economists have in the past fifty years become idiot savants of modernism. It's time for them to wake up and get serious about their scientific rhetoric.

The service that literature can do for economics is to offer literary criticism as a model for self-understanding. (It would not be a very good model for polite behavior or even, I am afraid, literary style.) Literary criticism does not merely pass judgements of good or bad; in its more recent forms the question of good or bad hardly comes up. Mainly it's concerned with making readers see how poets and novelists accomplish their results. An economic criticism of the sort exercised here is not a way of attacking economics, showing it to be bad because it is rhetorical. To repeat, everyone is rhetorical, from the mathematician to the lawyer. A literary criticism of economics is just a way of showing how economics accomplishes its results.

Not many economists think this way. A larger though small proportion of other social scientists do: literary thinking is common in anthropology and sociology. What the French call the "human sciences" generally—the disciplines, from English to paleoanthropology, that study humankind—can assemble nowadays quite a few people who think critically in a rhetorical sense. And many people in mathematics, physics, computer science, engineering, biology, paleontology, communication, political science, law, sociology, anthropology, archaeology, history, history of science, philosophy, theology, comparative literature, and English have done rhetorical criticism without realizing they are doing it.

I explore a rhetoric of inquiry in economics. I use and ancient rhetorical device, the figure *a fortiori*, "from the stronger": if even the economic study of hog farmers and railroads is literary as well as mathematical, if even the science of human maximization under constraints is part of the humanities as much as it is part of the sciences, then all the stronger is the hope for the rest.

THE RHETORIC OF ECONOMICS

1

HOW TO DO A RHETORICAL

ANALYSIS OF ECONOMICS,

AND WHY

It's Not Philosophical Reading,
It's Rhetorical

Start with an example taken from a book with which I mostly agree, the first edition of Richard Posner's *Economic Analysis of Law*:

> Our survey of the major common law fields suggests that the common law exhibits a deep unity that is economic in character. . . . The common law method is to allocate responsibilities between people engaged in interacting activities in such a way as to maximize the joint value . . . of the activities. . . . [T]he judge can hardly fail to consider whether the loss was the product of wasteful, uneconomical resource use. In culture of scarcity, this is an urgent, an inescapable question. (Posner 1972, pp. 98f.)

Posner is urging us to see the common law as economically efficient. That's the philosophical way of reading the passage, seeing through. But look at the surface, the rhetoric.

The argument is carried in part by the equivocal use of economic vocabulary. "Allocate," "maximize," "value," and "scarcity" are technical words in economics, with precise definitions. Here they are used also in wider senses, to evoke Scientific power, to claim precision without necessarily using it. The sweetest turn is the use of "uneconomical," which is not a technical word in economics, but encapsulates Posner's argument that in their courtrooms the judges follow economic models because to do otherwise would be "wasteful." The "economical/uneconomical" figure of speech supports the claim that economic arguments (arguments about efficiency) are pervasive in the law. The claim is hammered home by treble repetition (technically in classical rhetoric, *com-*

3

moratio): first in this word "uneconomical"; then in the reference to a culture of scarcity (a nice echo of "a culture of poverty," that, from the other side of the tracks); and finally in the repetition of "urgent, inescapable."

People involved mutually in automobile accidents or breaches of contract are said to be "engaged in interacting activities." That's on the surface of the words, yet the surface has philosophical importance. The "interaction" Posner talks about does not extend to the political or moral systems of the society. A rancher and a railroad "interact," but a judge does not "interact" with people who think that big enterprises like railroads are blameworthy or that people have inalienable rights. A vocabulary of "engaging in interacting activities" makes an appeal to the character of Scientist or Observer (technically, an "ethical" argument).

Again, on the surface the passage uses the metaphor of "deepness" in unity, as do other arguments trying to change the way we categorize the world. The left-wing radicals in American law, the critical legal theorists, will tell you that the "deep" structure of law is an apology for capitalism. The right-wing radicals, here Richard Posner, will tell you that the "deep" structure is on the contrary a celebration of capitalism.

As I say, I come down on Posner's side, though I have realized at last that a jurisprudence without a notion of rights is lunacy, a specifically Benthamite lunacy. But that I agree with many of Dick Posner's applications of economics to law does not make him, or me, or Milton Friedman immune from rhetorical scrutiny. The rhetorical reading is at least richer than the reading invited by the passage itself, which claims to represent the world. Posner wants us to read philosophically, which is good. But he does not want us to read rhetorically, which is bad. As the literary critic Richard Lanham has put it (1994), we need to do both, to be educated to "toggle" between philosophical and rhetorical readings, to know what the passage says but also how it achieves its end, persuasion.

The Old World "Rhetoric" Is a Good One

Science is an instance of writing with intent, the intent to persuade other scientists, such as economic scientists. The study of such writing with intent was called by the Greeks "rhetoric." Until the seventeenth century it was the core of education in the West and down to the present it remains, often unrecognized, the core of humanistic learning. A science like economics should be read skillfully, with a rhetoric, the more explicit the better. The choice here is between an implicit and naïve rhetoric or an explicit and learned one, the naïve rhetoric of significance tests, say, versus a learned rhetoric that knows what it is arguing and why.

Rhetoric could of course be given another name—"wordcraft," perhaps, or "the study of argument." The book that in 1987 began the "rhetoric of inquiry" was subtitled "Language and Argument in Scholarship and Public Affairs." Yet it revived the old "R" word in the main title, *The Rhetoric of the Human Sciences.* Why? The word "rhetoric" after all is used by newspapers as a synonym for the many words in English that sneer at speech: ornament, frill, hot air, advertising, slickness, deception, fraud. Thus the *Des Moines Register* headline: "Senate Campaign Mired in Rhetoric."

But the newspapers vulgarized, too, the word "pragmatism" shortly after its birth, by understanding it as unprincipled horse-trading. They defined "anarchism" as bomb-throwing nihilism. They defined "sentiment" as cheap emotionalism, "morality" as prudery, and "family values" as social reaction. They defined "science" as something no scientist practices. Not all usage should be decided by the newspapers, or else their views will be all we have. We need a scholarly word for wordcraft. The ancient and honored one will do.

The point of a rhetorical analysis is merely to read with understanding. Attending graduate school will somewhat educate an economist to read, supplying her with an implicit rhetoric for understanding. But the rhetoric in graduate school is incomplete and the understanding partial, a beginning but not the whole of economic science. What distinguishes good from bad economists, or even old from young economists, is additional sophistication about the rhetoric. It is the ability to read the depth and the surface of the text at the same time, to toggle. Robert Solow or Milton Friedman or Herbert Stein do not know anything of classical rhetoric—they grew up at the nadir of rhetorical education—but they can spot when a formal assumption is being used well or badly, and can sense when this or that verbal device is appropriate. And the wordcraft that the best economists exercise by instinct can be taught, at least a little.

Classical rhetoric was merely a list of terms with some thinking attached. A classical architecture without terms for architrave, echinus, guttae, mutule, quoin, and triglyph cannot see the Old Capitol in Iowa City (a Doric temple with Corinthian capital) as anything other than vaguely pretty (Summerson 1963, pp. 16, 47–52). Likewise we need terms to describe scientific argument, or else we are reduced to the vague and unexamined aesthetics of "deep," "rigorous," "elegant," "convincing." Gerard Debreu, for example, uses such terms to defend abstract general equilibrium analysis: it "fulfills an intellectual need of many contemporary economic theorists, who therefore seek it for its own sake"; "simplicity and generality" are "major attributes of an effective theory"; "their aesthetic appeal suffices to make them desirable ends in themselves for the designer of a theory" (Debreu 1984). The aesthetics here is vague, unlearned, inexplicit. Debreu's is a dress-designer's vocabulary for scientific argument. No, that's unfair: Debreu's rhetoric is less precise and less self-critical than that of the better dress designers.

A rhetorical vocabulary is more rigorous than airy talk about rigor, though really only a list with some thinking attached. Literary thinking is like that. The best introduction to the schools of criticism is called *Critical Terms for Literary Study* (Lentricchia and McLaughlin, eds. 1990), listing among others Structure, Narrative, Figurative Language, Author, Value/Evaluation, Determinacy/Indeterminacy, Canon, Ideology, and Rhetoric. The best way to understand the rhetorical school 427 B.C. to the present is to supply oneself with a copy of Richard Lanham, *A Handlist of Rhetorical Terms* (2nd ed. 1991), and another work that makes use of it on a familiar text, such as George A. Kennedy, *New Testament Interpretation Through Rhetorical Criticism* (1984). The best comprehensive modern treatments are Edward P. J. Corbett, *Classical Rhetoric for the Modern Student* (1971 and later editions), which is a thoughtful list of terms with readings attached, and Sharon Crowley's excellent *Ancient Rhetorics for Contemporary Students* (1994). An early and good use of rhetorical criticism to make an argument is Wayne C. Booth, *Modern Dogma and the Rhetoric of Assent* (1974a). Booth, too, works with the original handlists dating back to Aristotle and Quintilian.

That's encouraging for beginners like you and me. By contrast, to do a useful piece of *economic* analysis you need to have finished the course. The noneconomists imagine it's enough to have some first-week idea of what "oligopoly" means. Economics is in fact a good example of the "hermeneutic circle": you need to know the argument overall to understand the details, and the details to understand the argument. But many literary techniques, and in particular the techniques of rhetorical analysis, come piecemeal, item by item, and can be put to use at once even by tyros. In this they are like some of the empirical methods of economics, such as national income analysis. Obviously a master in literary study like Booth or Lanham (compare in economics Kuznets or Denison) is going to do a better job than you or me. But even you and I can start.

I am not suggesting that educated people come equipped to do a rhetorical analysis without study. The results of attempting to do so are as embarrassing as criticizing economics without knowing any. I can name some embarrassing examples of both. Come on, Professor, do the homework. The point is simply that in rhetorical analysis even students can do useful work almost immediately. A rhetorical analysis can start with any part of "writing with intent" and proceed. It's like unraveling a sweater: start with a loose bit of yarn and keep pulling. A student is unlikely to find a poem or novel that a professor of English cannot unravel blindingly quicker. But the writings in sciences like economics are frayed sweaters waiting to be unraveled, the better to be understood, and in some respects a professor of economics is likely to know better where to pull.

Here then is a partial and preliminary handlist of rhetorical terms for students of economic literature.

The Scientist Must Establish Her "Ethos"

Ethos, the Greek word simply for "character," is the fictional character an author assumes. It is the same as the Latin *persona* or the modern "implied author." No one can refrain from assuming a character, good or bad. An author without good character will not be credited. The exordium, or beginning, of any speech must establish an ethos worth believing. An established ethos is the most persuasive of scientific arguments, and scientists are therefore very busy establishing it.

Consider, for example, the implied authors created by these opening lines in the *American Economic Review*'s issue of March 1989: "Two decades of research have failed to produce professional consensus on the contribution of federal government civil rights activity to the economic progress of black Americans" (Heckman and Payner 1989, p. 138). The implied authors here are policy-oriented, precise but awkward (look at the nominal phrase "federal government civil rights activity"), aware of the longer trends in scholarship, scholarly (with a Latinate vocabulary), dignified yet decisive, men who will succeed where others have "failed." The reader has to be an economist for the sentence to have these effects, just as the listener had to be a fourth-century Athenian for Demosthenes's appeals to his good ethos to have their effects.

Or, "After a period of intensive study of optimal indirect taxation, there has been a renewed interest in recent years in the problem of optimal income taxation, with particular emphasis on capital income taxation and economic growth" (Howitt and Sinn 1989, p. 106). Here the implied authors are modest (contrast the ringing "Two decades of research have failed" above or the unconscious arrogance of "Consider . . . the setting" below), concerned to fill gaps rather than take on once more the great questions of the age, academic rather than political ("re-

How to Do a Rhetorical Analysis of Economics, and Why

newed interest," as there might be renewed interest in the satellites of Jupiter), but again Latinate in vocabulary, anonymous, American academic writers.

Or, "Consider the following stylized setting" (Lewis and Sappington 1989, p. 69). These two are mathematical, uninterested in facts, followers of a certain fashion, pretending to be direct but staying firmly in the lecture room, unaware of how funny the first sentence sounds to most economists, how pathetically stuck in blackboard economics. The writers of course need not be aware of every effect their writing has on the audience, no more than poets need be.

Finally, "There is good reason to think that the market for single-family homes ought to be less efficient than are capital markets" (Case and Shiller 1989, p. 125). These are candid, direct, practical, better writers than "After a period of intensive study," interested in explaining an empirical phenomenon, up-to-date in financial theory.

Everyone makes an appeal to ethos, if only an ethos of choosing never to stoop to such matters as ethos. No speech with intent is "nonrhetorical." Rhetoric is not everything, but it is everywhere in the speech of human persuaders.

It is a commonplace that formal complexity, for example, is a claim to the ethos of the Deep Thinker, a powerful appeal in modern economics. But any figure of speech can be pointedly reversed for ironic effect. Thus, complexity has been used in the literature on British economic "failure" as the opposite of an authoritative ethos, as evidence of disauthority. A paper by the historical economist Stephen Nicholas in 1982 tries to cast doubt on calculations of total factor productivity change in Victorian Britain. After a lucid prose survey of the debate on failure from Landes down to 1982, Nicholas "explains" the calculation of total factor productivity. He says, "It is assumed [note at once the style borrowed from mathematics] that the economic unit is a profit maximizer, subject to a linear homogeneous production function and operating in perfectly competitive product and factor markets. Given these limiting assumptions, the marginal productivity theory of distribution equates marginal products to factor rewards. It follows by Euler's theorem . . . ," etc., etc. (Nicholas 1982, p. 86).

To most of his readers he might as well have written "it is assumed that the blub-blub is a blub maximizer, blub-blub blub-blub-blub and blub in perfectly blub and blub blub. Given these limiting assumptions, the blub blub blub blub blub blub blub. It follows by blub blub . . ." The audience that can understand the argument is the audience of people who already understand it, leaving you to wonder why the argument was necessary in the first place. The people who do not understand it gain only the impression that "limiting assumptions" are somehow involved (they are not, by the way). The rhetorical form of the passage is explanation; its effect in the pages of the *Economic History Review* is to terrify the onlookers, convincing them that the "neoclassical" analysis makes a lot of strange and unconvincing assumptions. By the mere statement of the "assumptions" said to underlie the "neoclassical" calculation one can cast doubt on the calculation in the eyes of all historians and many economists.

In replying to a sharp rebuttal by Mark Thomas in a later issue of the *Review*, Nicholas repeats the turn. The last sentence of his exordium makes the argument explicit: "*The long list of restrictive assumptions* cautions the economic historians that, at best, the Solow index is a crude measure from which to draw conclusions about historical change" (Nicholas 1985, p. 577, italics supplied). The ethos here is of the Profound Thinker defending the innocents from other Profound (but Irresponsible) Thinkers.

Point of View Is a Scientific Choice

The implied author, in other words, chooses a vantage point, such as Huck in *Huckleberry Finn*, a first-person narrator who in this case is portrayed as not knowing what is happening beyond his sight; or the author in *Anna Karenina*, who can hear aloud what people are thinking and can travel from Moscow to St. Petersburg without a ticket. In the modern novel the suppression of the "authorial I" has resulted in a technique peculiar to literature, "represented speech and thought." Grammarians call it "unheralded indirect speech," the French *style indirect libre*. Any page or two of Jane Austen serves to illustrate, as in *Persuasion*: "Sir Walter had taken a very good house in Camdenplace, a lofty dignified situation, such as becomes a man of consequence" (1818, p. 107; Sir Walter's words ["dignified . . . a man of consequence"] in Austen's mouth). "Could Anne wonder that her father and sister were happy? She might not wonder, but she must sigh that her father should feel no degradation in his change" (p. 108; Anne's words ["sigh . . . no degradation"] in Austen's mouth.)

The parallel technique in science might be called "represented reality" or "unheralded assertion" or "*style indirect inévitable*." The scientist says, It is not I the scientist who make these assertions but reality itself (Nature's words in the scientist's mouth). When the audience applauded Fustel de Coulanges's inaugural lecture at the University of Paris long ago he put up his hand for silence: "Do not applaud me. It is not I who speak. It is the Voice of History speaking through me." Redoubled applause. Scientists, including economic scientists, pretend that Nature speaks directly, thereby effacing the evidence that they, the scientists, are responsible for the assertions. It's just there. The result is similar in fiction: "We (as readers) cannot question the reliability of third-person narrators. . . . Any first-person narrative, on the other hand, may prove unreliable" (Martin 1986, p. 142). Thus Huck Finn, a narrator in the first person, misapprehends the Duke and we the readers know he does. The scientist avoids being questioned for his reliability by disappearing into a third-person narrative of what really happened.

The sociologist Michael Mulkay notes in the epistolary arguments of biologists a Rule 11: "Use the personal format of a letter . . . but withdraw from the text yourself as often as possible so that the other party continually finds himself engaged in an unequal dialogue with the experiments, data, observations and facts" (1985, p. 66). The technique is similar in history: "The plot of a historical narrative is always an embarrassment and has to be presented as 'found' in the events rather than put there by narrative techniques" (White 1973, p. 20). It is widespread in economics, of course.

"Mere" Style Is Not Mere

The Greeks and Romans divided rhetoric into Invention (the finding of arguments), Arrangement, and Style (they included fourth and fifth categories, Memory and Delivery, less important in a literate and electronic culture). "Style versus content" is a rhetorical commonplace of our post-rhetorical culture, most common since the seventeenth century. But the modern premise that content can be split from expression is mistaken. The two are yoke and white in a scrambled egg. Economically speaking, the production function for thinking cannot be written as the sum of two subfunctions, one producing "results" and the other "writing them up." The function is not separable.

Tony Dudley-Evans and Willie Henderson, for example, have studied intensively the style of four articles from the *Economic Journal* over a century of publication. "Taxation Through Monopoly" by C. F. Bastable (1891), for example, "strikes one immediately as having been written for a highly educated reader [the implied reader] who happens also to be interested in economic matters" (1987, p. 7). And Bastable, they note, "frequently uses 'and,' 'but' and 'again' in initial position" (an ornament in modern English). Again he uses in initial position "elegant adverbial phrases," such as "So much is this the case" or "Alike in classical and medieval times" (p. 8). Alike in his scientific and his journalistic work, "Bastable based his writing not upon shared technical knowledge but on a shared understanding of an educated culture more widely defined" (p. 15).

Modern economics is quite different, obscure in style. The obscurity of the style is necessary to defend scientific ethos. St. Augustine, as the literary critic Gerald Bruns noted, viewed the obscurity of the Bible as having "a pragmatic function in the art of winning over an alienated and even contemptuous audience" (Bruns 1984, p. 157). Obscurity is not rare in religion and science. Bruns quotes Augustine (who might as well be justifying the obscurities of a mathematical economist proving the obvious): "I do not doubt that this situation was provided by God to conquer pride by work and to combat disdain in our minds, to which those things which are easily discovered seem frequently to be worthless" (p. 157).

Style Is Often an Appeal to Authority

Economic style appeals in various ways to an ethos worthy of belief. For example, a test claiming authority uses the "gnomic present," as in the sentence you are reading now, or in the Bible, or repeatedly in the historian David Landes's well-known book on modern economic growth, *The Unbound Prometheus* (1969). Thus in one paragraph on p. 562, "large-scale, mechanized manufacture *requires* not only machines and buildings . . . but . . . social capital. . . . These *are* costly, because the investment required *is* lumpy. . . . The return on such investment *is* often long deferred." Only the last sentences of the paragraph connect the rest to the narrative past: "the burden *has tended* to grow."

The advantage of the gnomic present is its claim to the authority of General Truth, which is another of its names in grammar. The gnomic present is Landes's substitute for explicit economic theory (of which he is innocent), a function the gnomic present serves in sociology and in much of the literature of economic development, too.

Note the tense in Landes's essay at p. 563, for example, after some *aporia* (rhetorical doubt) concerning whether it is true or not: "Where, then, the gap between leader and follower *is* not too large to begin with . . . the advantage *lies* with the latecomer. And the more so because the effort of catching up *calls* forth entrepreneurial . . . responses." That in general and as an economic law the advantage *lies* with the latecomer is offered as a deductive conclusion. And in truth it does follow deductively from the earlier assertions, themselves expressed in the gnomic present (for instance on p. 562, "There *are* thus two kinds of related costs").

The disadvantage is that it sidesteps whether it is asserting an historical fact (that in fact the return on "such investment" in 1900 was by some relevant standard long deferred) or a general truth (that in economies of the sort we are talking about most such returns will be long deferred), or perhaps merely a tautology (that the very meaning of "social capital" is investment of a generally useful sort with long-deferred returns). The one meaning borrows prestige and persuasiveness from the other. The usage says, "I speak as an historian, the Voice of History, who is telling you of the facts, this being one of them; but I am also an Economist in command of the best and timeless theorizing on the matter; and if you don't like that, consider that what I assert is anyway true by definition."

Economists Are Poets

The ancients spoke of "figures" as the surface of prose, dividing them into "figures of ornament" (such as the parallelism in the present sentence) and "figures of argument" (such as the metaphor of a "surface" of prose). The most well known of the figures of argument is metaphor, which, since the philosophers Max Black (1962a, 1962b) and Mary Hesse (1963) wrote on the subject, has been recognized as synonymous with the scientist's "model."

An example is a book, *The Zero-Sum Solution* (1985) by Lester Thurow, an economist and dean of the business school at M.I.T. The book is sporting. "To play a competitive game is not to be a winner—every competitive game has its losers—it is only to be given a chance to win. . . . Free market battles can be lost as well as won, and the United States is losing them on world markets" (p.59). One chapter is entitled "Constructing an Efficient Team." Throughout there is talk about America "competing" and "beating" the rest of the world with a "world-class economy." Thurow complains that more people don't appreciate his favorite metaphor, and calls it a "reality": "For a society which loves team sports . . . it is surprising that Americans won't recognize the same reality in the far more important international economic game" (p. 107). In more aggressive moods he slips into a military uniform: "American firms will occasionally be defeated at home and will not have compensating foreign victories" (p. 105). Foreign trade is viewed as the economic equivalent of war.

Three metaphors govern Thurow's story: the metaphor of the international zero-sum "game," a metaphor of the domestic "problem," and a metaphor of "we." *We* have a domestic *problem* of productivity that leads to a *loss* in the international *game*. Thurow has spent a long time interpreting the world with these linked metaphors. The we-problem-game metaphors are not the usual one in economics. The metaphor of exchange as a zero-sum game has been favored by anti-economists since the eighteenth century. Economists have replied that the metaphor is inapt. The subject after all is the exchange of goods and services. If exchange is a "game" it might better be seen as one in which everyone wins, like aerobic dancing. No problem. Trade in this view is *not* zero sum.

The example is not meant to suggest that metaphors are somehow optional or ornamental or unscientific. Although I disagree with Thurow's argument here, what is wrong about it is not that he uses a metaphor—no scientist can do without metaphors—but that his metaphor is inapt, as could be shown in various ways both statistical and introspective. The novice's mistake is to suppose that a rhetorical criticism is merely a way of unveiling Error. If we snatch away the veil of ornament, the novice thinks, we can confront the Facts and the Reality direct. The numerous books called "Rhetoric and Reality," such as Peter Bauer's collection of prescient essays (1984), commit this mistake.

True, devices of rhetoric such as metaphors can be veils over bad arguments. But they are also the form and substance of good arguments. I agree, for example, with most of Gary Becker's metaphors, from criminals as small businessman to the family as a little firm. Becker is an economic poet, which is what we expect of our theorists.

And Novelists

The word "story" is not vague in literary criticism. Gerald Prince used some ingenious mental experiments with stories and nonstories to formulate a definition of the "minimal story," which has

> three conjoined events. The first and third events are stative
> [such as "Korea was poor"], the second is active [such as "then
> Koreans educated themselves"]. Furthermore, the third event
> is the inverse of the first [such as "Then as a result Korea was
> rich"]. . . . The three events are conjoined by conjunctive features
> in such a way that (a) the first event precedes the second in time
> and the second precedes the third, and (b) the second event
> causes the third. (Prince 1973, p. 31)

How to Do a Rhetorical Analysis of Economics, and Why

Prince's technique isolates what is storied about the tales that we recognize as stories.

Is this a story? *A man laughed and a woman sang.* No, it does not feel like one—in the uninstructed sense we learned at our mother's knee. (Of course in a more instructed way, after Joyce and Kafka, not to speak of writers of French detective fiction, anything can be a "story.") The following sounds more like an old-fashioned story: *John was rich, then he lost a lot of money.* At least it has the claim of sequence of consequence, "then." And it has the inversion of status ("rich . . . poor"). But it doesn't quite make it. Consider, *A woman was happy, then she met a man, then, as a result, she was unhappy.* Right. If feels like a complete story, as "generally and intuitively recognized" (Prince 1973, p. 5). Contrast: *Mary was rich and she traveled a lot, then, as a result, she was rich.* Something is screwy. What is screwy is that her status is not inverted from what it was.

One can use Prince's examples to construct stories and non-stories in economics. Test the pattern:

> *Poland was poor, then it adopted capitalism, then as a result it became rich.*
> *The money supply increased this year, then, as a result, productivity last year rose and the business cycle three decades ago peaked.*
> *A few firms existed in chemicals, then they merged, and then only one firm existed.*
> *Britain in the later nineteenth century was capitalistic and rich and powerful.*

The pattern is story/nonstory/story/nonstory. Stories end in a new state. If a 5 percent tax on gasoline is said by some congressman or journalist to be "designed" to fall entirely on producers the economist will complain, saying "It's not an equilibrium." "Not an equilibrium" is the economist's way of saying that she disputes the ending proposed by some untutored person. Any descendant of Adam Smith, left or right, whether by way of Marx or Marshall, Veblen or Menger, will be happy to tell you a better story.

Many of the scientific disagreements inside economics turn on this sense of an ending. To an eclectic Keynesian, raised on picaresque tales of economic surprise, the story idea *Oil prices went up, which caused inflation* is full of meaning, having the merits that stories are supposed to have. But to a monetarist, raised on the classical unities of money, it seems incomplete, no story at all, a flop. As the economist A. C. Harberger likes to say, it doesn't make the economics "sing." It ends too soon, half-way through the second act: a rise in oil prices without some corresponding fall elsewhere is "not an equilibrium."

From the other side, the criticism of monetarism by Keynesians is

likewise a criticism of the plot line, complaining of an ill-motivated beginning rather than a premature ending: where on earth does the money
you think is so important come from, and why? Our jargon word for
this in economics is "exogenous": if you start the story in the middle the
money will be treated as though it is unrelated to, exogenous to, the rest
of the action, even though it's not.

There is more than prettiness in such matters of plot. There is moral
weight. Hayden White has written that "the demand for closure in the
historical story is a demand . . . for moral reasoning" (White 1981, p. 20).
A monetarist is not morally satisfied until she has pinned the blame on
the Federal Reserve. The economist's ending to the story of the gasoline
tax falling entirely on producers says, "Look: you're getting fooled by
the politicians and lawyers if you think that specifying that the refiners
pay the tax will let the consumers off. Wake up; act your age; look beneath the surface; recognize the dismal ironies of life." Stories impart
meaning, which is to say worth. A *New Yorker* cartoon shows a woman
looking up worried from the TV, asking her husband, "Henry, is there
a moral to *our* story?"

The sense of adequacy in storytelling works in the most abstract theory, too. In seminars on mathematical economics a question nearly as
common as "Haven't you left off the second subscript?" is "What's your
story?" The story of the gasoline tax can be put entirely mathematically
and metaphorically, as an assertion about where the gasoline tax falls,
talking of supply and demand curves in equilibrium thus:

$$w^* = -(E_d/(E_d+E_s))T^*$$

The mathematics here is so familiar to an economist that she will not
need explanation. In less familiar cases, at the frontier of economic argument, where we are arguing about what is important and what is not,
the economist will need more conversation. That is, she will need a
story. At the end of all the mathematics she will ask insistently *why*. In
seminars on economics the question "What's your story?" is an appeal
for a lower level of abstraction, closer to the episodes of human life. It
asks for more realism, in a fictional sense, more illusion of direct experience. It asks to step closer to the nineteenth-century novel, with its
powerful and nonironic sense of Being There.

Be Not Afraid of Deconstruction
and Other Terrors

When Richard Posner wanted in a recent book to ter-
rify his lawyer-readers about Reds in the English department, you can

imagine the school of literary criticism he began with: "Deconstruction and Other Schools of Criticism" (1988, p. 211). Deconstruction, by merest chance the most frightening version of literary criticism that could be brought before conservative readers, is "least well understood by lawyers, and . . . is therefore an appropriate starting point" (p. 211). Ho, ho.

Deconstruction, for all the calls to arms against it from the ignorant (and proud of it), constitutes only a tiny part of criticism. It is not even the most recent of fashions in literary theory (feminism and the new historicism are, with the new economic criticism on the horizon). It is merely one of a score of partially overlapping ways to do literary criticism. A partial list in historical order would include rhetorical, philological, Aristotelian, belletristic, hermeneutic, historical, new critical, psychoanalytic, neo-Aristotelian, archetypical, neorhetorical, Marxist, reader-response, deconstructive, linguistic, feminist, and new historicist criticism. In the same way you could divide economics into Good Old Chicago School, eclectic econometric macro, nouvelle Chicago, highbrow general equilibrium, and policy oriented micro.

But the journalistic interest in the word is so great that it cannot be ignored even in a brief list (a good treatment for economists is Rossetti 1990, 1992). One insight that the deconstructionists are properly credited with is the notion of verbal "hierarchy." The point is simply that words carry with them a ranking with respect to their opposites, as the word "infidel" calls to mind "Muslim," and "black" calls to mind "white." A sentence will achieve some of its effect through playing on these rankings. The hierarchies expose the politics (so to speak) in writing.

In economics long ago, for example, Wesley Clair Mitchell wrote, "it must never be forgotten that the development of the social sciences (including economics) is still a social process. Recognition of that view . . . leads one to study these sciences . . . [as] the product not merely of sober thinking but also subconscious wishing" (quoted in Rossetti 1992, p. 220). The passage contains at least these half-spoken hierarchies ready for liberating deconstruction (reading back to front, the terms in square brackets being those implied but not mentioned): sober/subconscious; thought/wishing; product/[mere ephemera]; sciences/[mere humanities]; study/[beach reading]; one/[you personally]; leads/[compels]; view/[grounded conviction]; sciences/[mere] processes; development/[mere chaotic change]; and must/[can]. The first term of each is the privileged one—except that in the pairs leads/[compels] and view/[grounded conviction] they are in fact polite self-deprecation, with ironic force: Mitchell is on the contrary claiming the commanding heights of compelling and grounded conviction, not the soft valleys of mere gently leading "views." Literary people speak of "deprivileging" the superior term in such pairs, which in economics would be, for example, "microfoundations/macroeconomics" or "general/partial" or "rigorous/informal."

In the vernacular, the economist Mitchell is playing mind games on us readers, and we'd better watch out. Mitchell, of course, is not special. It's easier to see the mind games played by writers long ago than in our own time, but you can depend on it that writing with intent has them.

The deeper point deconstruction makes is that among the mind games in which all writing participates is the claim that the writing *is* the world. The realistic novel is the plainest example, but scientific writing is another (for which see again Mulkay 1985). For example, the phrase "it is obvious that" conveys certitude in mathematics and in economics. One eight-page article in the *Journal of Political Economy* (Davies 1989) uses expressions such as "it is obvious that," "obviously," "it is evident," "doubtless," "easily seen," "needs no discussion," and "we may expect" some forty-two times. But nothing is "obvious" on a printed page except that certain marks have been made on a white field. The "easily seen" is evoked in the mind's eye.

Writing Is Performance

The point is not peculiar to deconstruction. In a way it is one of the chief findings of humanism. Books do not "reproduce" the world. They evoke it. Skillful fiction, whether in the form of *Northanger Abbey* or *The Origin of Species*, "stimulates us to supply what is not there," as Virginia Woolf remarked of Austen. "What she offers is, apparently, a trifle, yet is composed of something that expands in the reader's mind and endows with the most enduring form of life scenes which are outwardly trivial" (1925, p. 142). Commenting on her remark in turn, the critic Wolfgang Iser put it this way: "What is missing from the apparently trivial scenes, the gaps arising out of the dialogue—this is what stimulates the reader into filling the blanks with projections. [Iser's image is of the reader running a motion picture inside his head, which is, of course, why novels can still compete with television.] . . . The 'enduring form of life' which Virginia Woolf speaks of is not manifested on the printed page; it is a product arising out of the interaction between text and reader" (1980, pp. 110–11).

As Arjo Klamer (1987) has shown for the postulate of economic rationality, scientific persuasion, too, is like that. Persuasion of the most rigorous kind has blanks to be filled at every other step, whether it is about a difficult murder case, for example, or a difficult mathematical theorem. The same is true of a debate about economic policy. What is unsaid—but not unread—is more important to the text as perceived by the reader than what is there on the page. As Klamer puts it, "The student of the rhetoric of economics faces the challenge of speaking about the unspoken, filling in the 'missing text' in economic discourse" (1987, p. 175).

The running of different motion pictures in our heads is going to produce different texts as perceived. Tzvetan Todorov asks, "How do we explain this diversity [of readings]? By the fact that these accounts describe, not the universe of the book itself, but this universe as it is transformed by the psyche of each individual reader" (1975, p. 72). And, "Only by subjecting the text to a particular type of reading do we construct, from our reading, an imaginary universe. Novels do not imitate reality; they create it" (pp. 67f.). Economic texts also are made in part by the reader. Obscure texts are often therefore influential. The crafty John Maynard Keynes, for example, most influentially in *The General Theory of Employment, Interest and Money,* left many opportunities for readers to run their own internal motion pictures, filling in the blanks.

The argument can be pushed. An economist expositing a result creates an "authorial audience" (an imagined group of readers who know this is fiction) and at the same time a "narrative audience" (an imagined group of readers who do not know it is fiction). As the critic Peter Rabinowitz explains, "the narrative audience of 'Goldilocks' believes in talking bears" (1968, p. 245). The "authorial" audience realizes it is fiction.

The difference between the two audiences created by the author seems less decisive in economic science than in explicit fiction, probably because we all know that bears do not talk but we do not all know that the notion of "marginal productivity" in economics is a metaphor. The narrative audience in science, as in "Goldilocks," is fooled by the fiction, which is as it should be. But in science the authorial audience is fooled, too (and, incidentally, so is part of the literal audience, the actual readers as against the ideal readers the author seems to want to have). Michael Mulkay, again, has shown how important the inadvertent choice of authorial audience is in the scholarly correspondence of biochemists. Biochemists like other scientists and scholars are largely unaware of their literary devices, and become puzzled and angry when their literal audience refuses to believe in talking bears (Mulkay 1985, ch. 2). They think they are merely stating facts, not making audiences. Small wonder that scientists and scholars disagree, even when their rhetoric of "what the facts say" would seem to make disagreement impossible. Science requires more resources of the language than raw sense data and first-order predicate logic.

It requires what may be called the Rhetorical Tetrad (McCloskey 1994, pp. 61–63). Fact and logic also come into the economics in large doses. Economics is a science, and a jolly good one, too. But a serious argument in economics will use metaphors and stories as well—not for ornament or teaching alone but for the very science. Fact, logic, metaphor, and story.

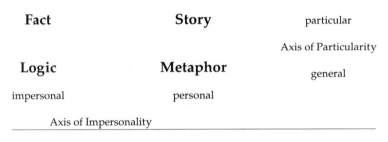

Figure 1. The Rhetorical Tetrad: The Four Human Arguments

The reasons to do a rhetorical analysis of an economic text are various: to understand it, to admire it, to debunk it, to set it beside other works of persuasion in science, to see that science is not a new dogma but is thoroughly and respectably part of the old culture. Rhetorical sophistication is an alternative to reading scientific texts the way the implied reader does, a reader who believes for example in talking bears. If we are to get beyond nursery school as scientific readers we need such a rhetoric applied to economic science.

2

THE LITERARY CHARACTER

OF ECONOMIC SCIENCE

Science Uses Literary Methods

[handwritten marginalia: What is science?]

[handwritten marginalia: reflection on English term for science]

The French and German triads that correspond to our plain English "natural sciences, social sciences, and humanities" are "les sciences naturelles, les sciences sociales, et les *sciences* humaines" and "die Naturwissenschaften, die Sozialwissenschaften, und die Geistes*wissenschaften.*" In both the term for studies of poetry, language, and philosophy—studies that are humanistic and decidedly literary in form—includes a "science" word. But in French and German, and in every other language I have looked into, the term is not properly understood as English "science." In Japanese, Finnish, Tamil, Turkish, Korean, and all the Indo-European languages, the science word means "systematic inquiry."

The German speaker has therefore less opportunity to use his word *Wissenschaft,* or the French speaker his *science,* as a club with which to beat on word folk. Nor, on the other side, can it be so easily used the way it is by the English-speaking literati, as a curse against that blackest art, the anti-art, the bane of sweetness and light. It means in all these other languages merely "disciplined inquiry," as distinct from, say, casual journalism or unaided common sense. It does not mean "quantitative," in the way Lord Kelvin used it in 1883: "When you cannot measure it, when you cannot express it in numbers, your knowledge is of a meagre and unsatisfactory kind"; and added, "It may be the beginning of knowledge, but you have scarcely in your thoughts advanced to the stage of *science.*" Outside of the English-speaking world nowadays the science word does not have epistemological clout.

The word "science" began to be used in the honorific sense by the English only in the late nineteenth century. The earliest citation in sense 5b of the *Oxford English Dictionary* is 1867, from W. G. Ward in the *Dublin Review* for April, p. 255n (italics supplied): "We shall . . . use the word 'science' in the sense *which Englishmen so commonly give to it;* as expressing physical and experimental science, to the exclusion of theological and metaphysical." (The later *Supplement* to the dictionary describes this definition 5b nowadays as of course "the dominant sense in ordinary use.") Earlier it meant "studies," as in "classical studies"—*Altertumswissenschaft* in German. In modern English you cannot imagine "classical science." The Wildhagen/Heraucourt German dictionary (1972) gives *die klassiche Wissenschaft* as "humanities" (clearly in the older sense of the English word) and *die philologischhistorische Wissenschaften* as "arts" (in the British academic usage, contrasted, again, with "science").

The point is that the foreigners have gotten it right. "Literary criticism is a science" or "Economics is a science" should not be the fighting words they are in English. The fighting lacks point because, as our friends across the water could have told us, nothing important depends on its outcome. Economics in particular is merely a disciplined inquiry into the market for rice or the scarcity of love. Economics is a collection of literary forms, some of them expressed in mathematics, not a Science. Indeed, science is a collection of literary forms, not a Science. And literary forms are scientific.

The idea that science is a way of talking, not a separate realm of Truth, has become common among students of science since Thomas Kuhn. The idea does not imply that science is inconclusive or that literature is cold-blooded. The point is that science uses art for urgent practical purposes daily. The aesthetic judgements necessary before one of the theories in particle physics is selected for the expensive experiment it requires for testing does not make science arbitrary or flimsy. As Steven Weinberg said about an experiment testing his piece of the physicist's art, "That experiment cost some $30 to $40 million dollars, not for the accelerator you understand, just for the experiment using the accelerator. This is an enormous commitment of your money and our time, one that can only be made when the judgement has been made that the theory is worth testing, and that judgment is very often entirely a matter of how beautiful we think the theory is" (1983, p. 20). From 1967 to 1971 Weinberg's theory was considered too ugly to test. He points out that no one would have financed the British expedition to the South Seas in 1919 to test Einstein's theory had it been thought ugly. The literary critic Kenneth Burke spoke of this persuasiveness of elegant forms: "A yielding to the form prepares for assent to the matter identified with it" (1950, p. 58).

And of course art, in turn, uses "scientific" figures of speech for urgent practical purposes, too. Statistics, for example, are figures of speech in numerical dress. Textual criticism since the Renaissance has depended on the logic of probability and the counting of frequencies. See, for example, Willis 1972, p. 24, on stemmatic theory, and p. 42 on the theory of errors. Anyone who believes the study of literature leads to a softening of the mind and mettle should be made to read this book, supplemented by Reynolds and Wilson (1974) and Housman (1922 [1961]). The height of this sort of thing is John G. Griffith, "A Taxonomic Study of the Manuscript Tradition of Juvenal" (1968).

Wayne Booth attacks the pretensions of Popperian falsifiability to be the very meaning of meaningfulness. Yet he notes that "the test is a powerful one, in dealing with certain problems; I use it myself in trying to test my own guesses about how literary works are put together" (1974a, p. 103).

The only point that Booth and Kuhn and I are making is that the statistical and falsificationist tests should not expand to take over all persuasions. As Booth puts it, "Stated as a universal dogma [falsifiability] is highly questionable" (1974a, p. 103). The only dogma worth promulgating is a broad-minded one, namely, that in a good argument the artistic and scientific modes of thought will interpenetrate each other. "Modernists" around 1950 (the term is explored later in the book, but roughly it means "positivist," "Bauhaus," "formalistic," "behaviorist") believed that the interpenetration of science and art is a contravention of God's law, likely to give birth to monsters. But in this they were mistaken.

The project here is to overturn the monopolistic authority of Science in economics by questioning the usefulness of the demarcation of science from art. To show that economics resembles literary criticism, philology, and social theory as much as particle physics and dam-building can either thrill economists with a wild surmise or leave them trembling from identity outraged.

If the project outrages some economists, noneconomists incline to fatigued indifference. Since the end of the nineteenth century they have not thought very much of the scientific claims of the subject anyway. All they know about economics is what they read in the papers, but they know what they don't like, and besides, it ain't Science.

The humanist's approach is wrong. It falls for demarcation, supposing without thinking about it much that science is easily demarcated from nonscience. Anyway, economics surely is science, a pretty successful sort at that, though with some peculiar problems coming from its rhetorical naïveté. Economics explains as much about business people and resources as evolution explains about animals and plants, for identical reasons. No one who knows the subject will deny it. Those who do not know it can become persuaded by reading Mancur Olson's *Logic of Collective Action* (1965) or Thomas Schelling's *Micromotives and Macrobehavior* (1978) or Albert Hirschman's *Exit, Voice, and Loyalty* (1970) or Robert Frank's *Passions Within Reason* (1988) or another of the accessible jewels of the discipline. The claim here is not the vulgar and modernist figure of logic that economics is mere humanism because it is a failure as a science. The claim is that all science is humanism (and no "mere" about it) because that is all there is for humans.

Proofs of the Law of Demand Are Mostly Literary

Economics is scientific, I am claiming, but literary too. Saying that something is "literary" is saying that you can talk of it in ways that sound like the things people say about drama, poetry, novels, and the study of them. Look for example at the performative character of the sentence "Economics is scientific." The sentence carries with it the implication that things can be said about economics and economies that use mathematics; the economists will emulate the rhetoric of controlled experiment; that the economists will have "theorems" from the mathematics and "findings" from the experiments; that it will be "objective" (whatever the word might mean); and even that the world it constructs, to use Nelson Goodman's way of talking, will have a certain character, of maximizing and equilibrium, captured in the perspicacious phrase, "the unreasonable effectiveness of mathematics." All these implications about economics are persuasive.

But equally persuasive are other implications, usually and erroneously thought to be antithetical to science, implied by the sentence "Economics is literary." The literary character of economics shows at various levels, from most abstract to most concrete, from methodology down to the selling of diamonds.

The workaday methods of economic scientists, for example, are literary, a pretty obvious remark when you recognize that the scientific paper is, of course, a literary genre with an actual author, an implied author, an implied reader, a history, and a form (see Bazerman 1981; Bazerman 1988; chapter 5 below). When an economist says, as she very frequently does, "The demand curve slopes down," she is using the English language; and if she is using it to persuade, as she very frequently is, she is a "rhetor," in Latin an orator, whether she knows or likes it or not. A scientific paper, and an assertion within it such as this Law of Demand (that when the price of something goes up the demand for something goes down), does literary deeds. The economic scientist is self-evidently a linguistic actress, and to her performance can be applied the dramatic notions of the literary critic Kenneth Burke, or of the philosophers J. L. Austin and John Searle. Scientific assertions are speech acts in a scene of scientific tradition by the scientist-agent through the agency of the usual figures of speech for purposes of describing nature or people better than the next scientist.

The error is to think that you are engaged in mere making of propositions, about which formal logic speaks, when in fact you are engaged— all day, most days—in persuasive discourse, aimed at some effect about which rhetoric speaks. The American pragmatist philosophers said this, too. Beliefs expressed in words are to be judged by their effects or, as it was put by William James with "disastrous felicity" (Burke), by their "cash value." Scientists are trying to persuade other scientists when they affirm a law.

The way they persuade others draws mostly on the usual arguments, arguments that you might see in *Areopagitica* or "A Modest Proposal for Preventing the Children of Ireland from Being a Burden to Their Parents or Country." Economists want to persuade themselves of the Law of Demand, that when the relative price of a good increases the quantity demanded of it declines. Consider the good reasons that economists believe the Law of Demand to be persuasive:

1. Sometimes, certain very sophisticated statistical tests of the law applied to entire economies, in which every allowance has been made for bias and incompleteness, have resulted, after a good deal of handwringing and computer-squeezing, in the diagonal elements of certain matrices being negative at the 5 percent level of significance. And sometimes they have not. Even the inventors of fully identified, complete systems of demand equations, such as Hans Theil, have no great confidence in the results. A shift of one metaphor here, a shift of one appeal to authority there, and the "proof" would be valid no longer.

2. Less comprehensive but more numerous demonstrations of the law have been attempted market by market. Agricultural economists, especially, have since 1924 been fitting demand curves to statistics on corn and hogs. Again, the curves sometimes give the right slope, and sometimes don't. The most elaborate of such studies—Houthakker and Taylor's study of all commodities in the American economy (1970)—found that the law was weak. In any case the thought before calculation that forces the law to work (in other words, the specification) contains elements of introspection, analogy, and other sorts of common sense embarrassing to the claims of mindless Objectivity. Econometricians have begun to take heed (Leamer 1978; Cooley and LeRoy 1981). But they need help in thinking about their before-calculation rhetoric.

3. Some economists have tried to subject the law to a few experimental tests. After a good deal of throat-clearing they have found it to be true for clearheaded rats and false for confused humans (Battaglio et al. 1981), an interesting result which no one worries about too much.

These three arguments are properly "scientific," in the strange modern English usage of the word, although only the third quite matches the received view of scientific method. The Scientific arguments yield mixed results.

Does this leave economists uncertain about the Law of Demand? Certainly not. Belief in the Law of Demand is the distinguishing mark of an economist, demarcating her from other social scientist more even than her other peculiar beliefs, such as that assets equal liabilities plus net wealth. Economists believe it ardently. Only some part of their ardor, therefore, is properly Scientific. The rest is below the demarcation line:

4. Introspection is an important source of belief. The economic scientist asks herself, "What would I do if the price of gasoline doubled?" If properly socialized in economics she will answer, "I will consume less." In similar fashion a poet might ask herself what she might do if she saw heather or a wave; a textural critic might ask himself how he would react to a line if "quod, o patrona virgo" were emended to "quidem est, patroni et ergo."

5. Thought experiments (common in physics) are persuasive too. The economic scientist asks in view of her experience of life and her knowledge of economics what other people might do if the price of gasoline doubled. A novelist, likewise, might ask how Huck would respond to Jim's slavery, or a critic might ask how an audience would react to the sacrifice of Coriolanus.

6. Cases in point, though not controlled experiments or large samples, persuade to some degree. A big triumph for the Law of Demand in modern economic history was the oil embargo of 1973–1974: the doubling of gasoline prices caused gasoline consumption to decline, although noneconomists predicted it would not. Likewise, the economist Julian Simon routed the ecologist Barry Commonor in a wager based in part on the Law of Demand (and the Law of Supply): that currently "scarce" resources would become cheaper, not more expensive. This is narrative, not statistical fit (although statisticians are moving toward a rhetoric that a literary person would recognize as narrative: Mosteller and Tukey 1977; Leamer 1978). The narrative tells. In the same way, Booth re-

The Literary Character of Economic Science

    marks, "The most sensitive book-length theological account we can imagine . . . lacks something that men know together when in answer to the question, 'What is the life of man?' they answer, 'There was once in Bethlehem.'" (1974a, p. 186).

7. The lore of the marketplace persuades. Business people, for instance, believe that the Law of Demand is true, for they cut prices when they wish to raise the quantity demanded. They have the incentive of their livelihood to know rightly. What mere professor would dispute such testimony? To do so would in fact contradict a fundamental conviction among professors of economics (and among professors of ecology and evolutionary biology, too) that opportunities for profit are not usually left lying about untaken. The argument is *ad hominem*, an argument from the character of its audience.

8. The lore of the academy persuades as well. If many wise economists have long affirmed the Law of Demand, what mere latecomer would dispute their testimony? All sciences operate this way, building on the testimony of forerunners. The argument from authority is not decisive, of course, but gives weight. Science could not advance if all questions were reopened every five years.

9. Commonly the symmetry of the law will be a persuasive argument, because, to repeat Kenneth Burke, "Yielding to the form prepares assent to the matter identified with it." If there is a Law of Supply—and there is ample reason to think there is—it is hard to resist the symmetrical attractions of a Law of Demand. At higher levels of the mathematical sciences the appeal to symmetry takes a higher percentage of conviction.

10. Mere definition is a powerful argument, and is more powerful the more mathematical the talk. A higher price of gasoline, for instance, leaves less income to be spent on all things, including gasoline (at least by one definition of income, or of the law).

11. Above all, there is analogy. That the Law of Demand is true for purchases of ice cream and movies, which no one would want to deny, makes it more persuasive also for gasoline. Analogy gives the law its majesty. If the law applied only to the trivial items for which it has been "proven" in modernist style, no one would care. That laboratory rats view cherry soda as a luxury good, though interesting, is not much of a basis for a human science. But if the law applies to gasoline (or to rats), then it is easier to believe that it applies to housing; and if to housing, then to medical care; and then to labor; and then to political power; and then to love. Anal-

ogy is essential for science, but is of course the quintessential literary device.

These are all good reasons for believing the Law of Demand, but only the first three, I repeat, are Scientific by the dichotomous definition of English modernism. The other eight are artistic and literary. The modernist might try to reduce the eight to the three. "Analogy is based on a series of earlier experiments," he might say. But it is easier to see how the efficacy of general equilibrium, simultaneous equation, three-stage least squares methods of fitting complete systems of demand equations (reason 1) depends on the authority of the traditions about error terms (reason 8) or the appeal of symmetry as an aesthetic principle of specification (reason 9) than to see how analogy and introspection can be reduced to econometrics.

The English modernist might say then, "Come, come: this introspection on which you rely for certain of the arguments would not be reliable unless our researchers had invisible lie detectors or perhaps mind-reading apparatus" (Machlup 1955). It is a postulate of modernism, largely unspoken and therefore unargued, that minds do not exist. The puzzle is that a modernist who examines his mind when getting dressed in the morning and assumes the existence of other minds when driving to work claims to deny both as soon as he flicks on the lights at his laboratory. On the job he no longer believes he has a headache when his head hurts, or that his son is sad when he cries.

The modernist might say in desperation, "These 'literary' arguments, as you call them, are in the end merely supportive and probable; the Scientific arguments are the decisive ones." The proper response is, "Who says?" Anyone who actually runs experiments or fits curves knows that they too depend on analogies (the market is just like this demand curve), metaphysical propositions (the time series is a sample from all possible universes), and traditional authority (we have always assumed finite variance of the error term). And she knows that they, too, are merely supportive and probable. There is no certitude to be had, with any methodology.

The arguments fitting a modernist methodology are not in any case the whole story of why economists believe the Law of Demand. As an empirical matter here they would be a rather small part of the story. Few economists would place more than 15 percent of their confidence in the Law of Demand on the first three reasons in total, leaving 85 percent to literary as against "scientific" rhetoric. You can test whether this is true by asking an economist, who will testify to its persuasiveness by introspection (then deny that persuasiveness comes sometimes from introspection). Or in properly modernist (i.e., behaviorist) fashion you can observe what arguments an economist uses when trying to persuade unbelievers, such as students. Much of her argument will rely on introspection, encouraging the students to examine theirs and improve it by critical thinking. She will exhibit the few cases in point she can remember, especially the more extreme cases such as the oil crisis, and will try to build on analogy with products that the students do believe follow the law. For the rest she will appeal to the identity of convex utility functions and the authority of the scientific tradition. No matter how sophisticated the class is, it will be a rare teacher, and a poor one, who relies much on the econometric results from the data mine and its miners.

Economic scientists, then, persuade with many devices, and as speakers have an audience. To repeat, they do not speak into the void: the rhetorical character of science makes it social. The final product of science, the scientific article, is a performance. It is no more separated from other literary performances by epistemology than pastoral poetry is separated from epic by epistemology. Epistemology is not to the point. Literary thinking is.

Linguistics Is an Appropriate Model for Economic Science

Here is a longer example of how economists can gain from looking at their subject with literary models in mind: linguistics. To quantitative intellectuals it is evident that the great achievement of the nineteenth and twentieth centuries was physics. To literary intellectuals [bracketing the perfection of the novel] it is equally evident that linguistics was. The styles of thought considered prestigious are determined by adherence to one or the other of these two models. Economics since Samuelson's *Foundations of Economic Analysis* (1947) has looked on nineteenth-century physics as its model. Perhaps it should try twentieth-century linguistics.

The founder of modern linguistics, Ferdinand de Saussure, devoted many pages of his *Course in General Linguistics* (1915, pp. 79ff., 115ff.) to the analogy between economics and his new linguistics. It is notable that a scientist as important for economics as Saussure was for linguistics, Léon Walras, flourished at the same time in the same nation, and had similar ideas about the salience of what economists would call cross-sectional and comparative static thinking. The motto of both was "Everything touches everything else, today."

Saussure distinguished two approaches to understanding societies, the diachronic and the synchronic. The diachronic (Greek for "through time") was the historical, dynamic, or (as economists would say) time-series approach typical of the linguistics of his day. It traced the history of words and grammar, showing how Latin *calidus* became by stages French *chaud*. Saussure noted, however, that a speaker of French in 1910 did not need to know any of this to communicate with other speakers: she needed to know only the system of oppositions and analogies extant in 1910 that allowed her to distinguish *chaud* from *froid*. A historical linguistics, in other words, interesting though it was in its own right, could shed no light on how people used language at any one time.

What was needed to understand the way a language worked at any one time was a *synchronic* ("same time") linguistics, an ahistorical, static, cross-sectional account of how one French speaker speaks to another. The two linguistics were, and had to be, distinct: it would make no difference to a French speaker if some historical chance had left her with the word *heiss* or *hot* instead of *chaud,* so long as she could keep the opposition of X against *froid* (and against various other things, such as *cabbage* or *cat*). Synchronic and diachronic linguistics, in Saussure's view, had to be separate sciences, one aligned along the "axis of successions" and the other along the "axis of simultaneties." Listen to how much Saussure sounds like an economist:

> For a science concerned with values the distinction is a practical necessity and sometimes an absolute one. In these fields scholars cannot organize their research rigorously without considering both co-ordinates and making a distinction between the system of values per se and the same values as they relate to time. The opposition between the two viewpoints, the synchronic and the diachronic, is absolute and allows no compromise. (Saussure 1915, pp. 80, 83)

The point, which Saussure himself made quite clear (p. 79), is that economics, especially neoclassical and Austrian economics, is synchronic. It fits his recommendation for a fresh organization of the linguistic sciences so closely that the economics of Menger and Jevons and Walras looks like his model. Both neoclassical economics and synchronic linguistics are theories of value—theories of psychological attitudes attached to things (whether lexical or woolen things, whether *chaud* the word or sweater/pullover the object). In such an economics, as in such a linguistics, the exact matching of material and person does not matter. It does not matter that a particular grain of wheat from the New Jersey farm of Patty Hersh finds its way to the dinner table of David Mitch

The Literary Character of Economic Science

in Baltimore, no more than it matters that *chaud* rather than *heiss* represents in French the character of stoves that makes them painful for a baby to touch; what matters is that a grain gets off the farm and onto the table, or that there is *some* sign for hotness.

Saussure's famous example of the 8:25 express from Geneva to Paris makes the point (p. 108). He observed that the 8:25 is for purposes of travel the same train every day, even though it is never the same in physical makeup. The cars, the personnel, even the exact time of departure, may vary (the last not very much in the Switzerland of Saussure's day), and of course a car a day older is not the same car it was. Yet the train is the same, defined by its opposition to other trains and its uses in the mental worlds of its passengers. In like fashion, economics is oriented away from such matters as the exact makeup of pairings in the marketplace or the origin of a particular product. It will not digest ideas of embodied labor, the history of institutions, the dependence of a particular demander on a particular supplier, or anything else along the axis of successions.

It keeps trying, and keeps failing. Economics has seen various projects to make the subject dynamic, to bring it into real time, to give it an historical perspective, to find out how much labor power is embodied in surplus value, to make it, in a word, diachronic. The comparison with synchronic linguistics suggests why the projects have failed to deflect economics from its static purity. Marxism, the German Historical School, Institutionalism new and old, have been trying to graft diachronic limbs onto a synchronic tree. The limbs keep falling off, to grow and flourish perhaps by themselves, but not as offshoots of the tree of analysis descended from Mandeville and Smith.

This does not mean that diachronic inquiries such as economic history are useless for economic studies as a whole, any more than historical linguistics is useless for linguistic studies as a whole. The same can be affirmed of the Marxist's political economy or the sociologist's history of institutions. Economic history is in this view the raw material for synchronic thinking. It becomes part of what the chemist and philosopher Michael Polanyi called the "tacit knowledge" about which the theorizing speaks. Synchronic theories such as neoclassical economics or Saussurean linguistics are suitable for mathematization. Polanyi wrote,

> A mathematical theory can be constructed only by relying on *prior* tacit knowing and can function as a theory only *within* an act of tacit knowing, which consists in our attending *from* it to the previously established experience on which it bears. Thus the ideal of a comprehensive mathematical theory of experience

which would eliminate all tacit knowing is proved to be self-contradictory and logically unsound. (Polanyi 1966, p. 21; tacit knowing is similar to Cardinal Newman's notion of the "illative sense" [the perception of that-ness], Newman 1870, ch. 9).

In other words, the chemist or economist must start with some interesting gunk in a test tube or some story about how a particular economy has developed—that is to say, with conceptions on which she has a tacit, experiential, diachronic grasp. The experience (in literary terms, the narrative, or in novelistic terms, perhaps, the dialogue) is the phenomenon to be theorized about. You have to have a direct grasp of the diachronic subject to have something to be synchronic about.

Literary Thinking May Improve Applied Economics

So, I've given a couple of instances of literary thinking applied to how economists talk. I have more and more and more. When confronted with the sentence "Economics is literary," however, only an economist would think first of applying it to the behavior of economists themselves or to the structure of economic theory. What occurs to a noneconomist is that it could be used to characterize the economy. Surely here is an opportunity to get rid of that great stick of a character, *Homo economicus* and to replace him with somebody real, like Madame Bovary.

It may be. The understanding of individual motivation in economics could use some complicating. The economist has from time to time inquired at the psychology shop for premises of behavior more complex than simple greed. She has not found much to her liking (though see Scitovsky 1976 and Akerlof and Dickens 1982). The experimental psychologists have stick figures of their own for sale, and few enough buyers. It would seem reasonable that the economist might inquire instead at the English or the communication shops. She might get them to sell a few behavorial assumptions on the sly, as for a while now they have been selling philosophy interdicted by the Department of Philosophy.

Some literary critics have been bold enough to begin. An economist hearing someone talking about "human action," distinct from "mere motion," such as the tides insensate have, attacking the behaviorist hallucination that man is a large rat, emphasizing the purpose-ness of human affairs and bringing this together with a declaration that "the resultant of many disparate acts cannot itself be considered an act in the

The Literary Character of Economic Science

same purposive sense that characterizes each one of such acts (just as the movement of the stock market in its totality is not 'personal' in the sense of the myriad decisions made by each of the variously minded traders)"—an economist hearing all this would think herself in the presence of an Austrian economist: Hayek, perhaps, or von Mises, or some approximation *sui generis* such as Frank Knight. But she would in fact be in the presence of the doyen of American literary critics, Kenneth Burke (1968, p. 447). The parallels between Burke's thinking and Austrian economics are notable, the more so because their politics otherwise do not match. (There do not seem to be any channels of mutual influence.)

The places where literature and economics overlap are not otherwise much explored. A pioneer from the literary side is Kurt Heinzelmann in *The Economics of the Imagination* (1980), which discusses at length how economic theory in the nineteenth century used language and how it, in turn, influenced the language of imaginative writers. Marc Shell has catalogued the use of (strictly) monetary metaphors in literature in his *The Economy of Literature* (1978). You can think of the possibilities.

Here's an instance. Both economists and literary critics talk about "preferences." Economists mean by this, of course, simply "what people want," in the sense of wanting some candy when the price is right. With a few other economists, Albert Hirschman has observed that stopping at mere wants causes economists to overlook higher-level preferences, wants about wants (1984, pp. 89f.). Elsewhere these are known as taste, morality, or (west of the Sierras) lifestyle. Hirschman's notion is that if you wish to be the sort of person who enjoys Shakespeare, you will sit through a performance of *Two Gentleman of Verona* as part of your education. You impose a set of preferences on yourself, which you then indulge in the usual way. You have preferences about preferences: metapreferences (cf. Elster 1979).

It would not be shocking if literary critics could teach economists a thing or two about metapreferences. Literary criticism, after all, is largely a discourse about them, and people like I. A. Richards, Northrop Frye, Wayne Booth, and Kenneth Burke are canny. You might think that the older line of critics—Sir Phillip Sydney, Johnson, Coleridge, Arnold— would have in fact the most to teach, being more concerned than the recent kind with matters of value (matters of how well, as against simply how). A passage from the younger line, though, can illustrate how literary notions might be used to understand the economy of taste. Richards wrote in 1925:

> On a pleasure theory of value [that is to say, a theory using only preferences, not metapreferences] there might well be doubt [that

good poetry is better than bad], since those who do enjoy it [namely, bad poetry, such as that collected in *Poems of Passion*] certainly appear to enjoy it in a high degree. But on the theory here maintained, the fact that those who have passed through the stage of enjoying the *Poems of Passion* to that of enjoying the bulk of the *Golden Treasury,* for example, do not return, settles the matter. . . . Actual universal preference on the part of those who have tried both kinds fairly is the same (in our view) as superiority in value of the one over the other. (Richards 1925, pp. 205f.)

An economist will notice that Richards's argument is the same as the economics of "revealed preference" or, on a national level, the "Hicks-Kaldor test of welfare improvements." To use the reasoning developed by Paul Samuelson, an early economic exponent of austere modernism in testing, one bundle of groceries is revealed preferred to another if you could buy either bundle (could afford to buy either) but in fact chose one. In your view, the bundle you could afford but did not take must be inferior.

The point is that Richards's test is a revealed preference test for (good) taste. It is a way of ranking metapreferences. You could have read the classic comic book, but in fact chose to read Dostoevski, because you wanted to be that sort of person. The Dostoevski-reading persona is revealed to be preferred by you. That someone passes through the stage of enjoying "The Love Boat" on television to that of enjoying the bulk of modern drama (and does not return) settles the matter. That someone passes through the stage of enjoying modern drama to that of enjoying the bulk of Shakespeare (and does not return) settles it again: Shakespeare is metapreferred to modern drama, which is in turn metapreferred to "The Love Boat."

The same applies to nonliterary preferences, which is why Richards's notion can be used by economists. To be sure, it's more complicated than that. We do drift slowly from one metapreference to another, and sometimes, gyrelike, return to elementary pleasures. But the notion is a good beginning. People who learn French cooking may never return to German. The style of life in Iowa City—that is, the preferences you choose to indulge—may be revealed to be preferred to those in Hyde Park, and those in Hyde Park to those in Stanford. It would be so if you observed people with free choice trekking from Stanford to Hyde Park and thence to Iowa City but never back again. In like fashion, a capitalist democracy may be revealed to be preferred to a workers' democratic republic in the old days by the direction in which the guns on the border point. Milton Friedman uses this very figure of speech to support his argument against conscription in peacetime: "I have observed many persons initially in favor of the draft change their opinions as they have looked into the arguments and studied the evidence; I have never observed anyone who was initially in favor of a volunteer force reverse his position on the basis of further study. This greatly enhances my confidence in the validity of the position I have taken" (1975, p. 188).

What is attractive about the test is that it replies in a suitably modernist way to the modernist argument that "you can't say anything about ranking tastes." The Richards test is similar to Rawls's test of political constitutions from behind a veil of prenatal ignorance; it is similar likewise to the tests of social preferences proposed before Rawls by the economists Harsanyi, Sen, and others; and these are, in turn, extensions from the individual to the society of the leading novelty in economic theory since the 1940s, expected utility. The Richards test, in short, may be literary criticism, but it is also economics. Even by the economist's narrow standard of sayability, there is nothing intrinsically can't-sayable about changes in preferences guided by taste. Or at any rate it is no more can't-sayable than ordinary remarks about ordinary choice, the usual sayings of economic theory.

Economics, then, can be seen as an instance of literary culture. That it can also be seen as an instance of scientific culture is no contradiction. It shows merely how the official rhetoric of science narrows the field, demanding that it honor the one and spurn the other. The unofficial, workaday rhetoric takes a broader view, and a more persuasive one.

3

FIGURES OF
ECONOMIC SPEECH

Even a Mathematical Economist Uses, and Must Use, Literary Devices: The Case of Paul Samuelson

Obscured by the official rhetoric, the workaday rhetoric of economics has not received the attention it deserves. Knowledge of it is therefore hidden in seminar traditions, advice to assistant professors, referee reports, and jokes. Economists can do better if they will look at their arguments.

Look at two pages (pp. 122–23), chosen at random from the beginning of modern economics, Paul Samuelson's *Foundations of Economic Analysis*. Published in 1947, it was a local maximum in economic scholarship. It reduced economics to the mathematics of nineteenth-century physics, and is brillant reading even now. And it laid down an official rhetoric. On the page preceding the selection, for example, Samuelson boasts that such and such "is a meaningful, refutable hypothesis which is capable of being tested under ideal observational conditions" (p. 121; cf. pp. 3–5, 84, 172, 221, 257).

But Samuelson does not persuade by testing, neither here nor anywhere in his writings.

1. To begin with, he gives a general mathematical form from which the results in comparative statistics can be obtained by reading across a row. The implication of the lack of elaboration is that the mathematical details are trivially easy (leading you to wonder why they are mentioned at all). An "interesting" special case is left "as an exercise to the interested reader," drawing on the rhetorical traditions of applied mathematics to direct the mind in the right direction. The mathematics is presented in an offhand way, implying that we can all read partitioned matrices at a glance (and fitting awkwardly with the level of mathematics in other passages).

Figures of Economic Speech

When speaking of mathematics Samuelson is "we," but when speaking of economics, "I." Mathematical results are to be laid out for inspection. They are impersonal. Their truth is apparent to "us," if we are not dunces. Economics, by contrast, is viewed as personal and arguable. (Samuelson is unusual among economists in the boldness with which he introduces "I"; most economists use in this case the passive voice.) Here as elsewhere in the book Samuelson's persona alternates between the cool stater of mathematical truth and the excited propounder of economic argument.

The air of easy mathematical mastery was important for the influence of the book, by contrast with the embarrassed modesty with which British writers at the time (J. R. Hicks most notably) pushed mathematics off into appendices. Samuelson's skill at mathematics in the eyes of his readers, an impression nurtured at every turn, is itself an important and persuasive argument. He presents himself as an authority, on good grounds. That the mathematics is sometimes pointless, as here, is beside the point. Being able to do such a difficult thing (so it would have seemed to the typical economist-reader in 1947) is warrant of expertise.

The argument is similar in force to that of a classical education conspicuously displayed. To read Latin like one's mother tongue and Greek like one's aunt's tongue is difficult, requiring application well beyond the ordinary. Therefore—or so it seemed to Englishmen in the 1890s—men who had acquired such a skill should have charge of a great empire. Likewise—or so it seems to economists in the 1990s—those who have acquired skill at partitioned matrices and eigenvalues should have charge of a great economy. The argument is not absurd or a "fallacy" or "mere rhetoric." Virtuosity *is* some evidence of virtue.

2. There are six *appeals to authority*—to C. E. V. Leser, Keynes, Hicks, Aristotle, Knight, and P. A. Samuelson (appeal to authority is a Samuelsonian specialty). It is often reckoned as the worst kind of "mere" rhetoric. Yet it is a common and often legitimate argument, as here. No science would advance without it, because no scientist can redo every previous argument. We stand on the shoulders of giants (or at least a big pyramid of midgets), and it is a legitimate and persuasive argument to point it out from time to time. In 1888 Francis Ysidro Edgeworth, an authority on economics, philosophy, and statistics worth paying attention to, justified appeal to authority on statistical grounds: "The Doctrine of [Offsetting] Errors supplies the *rationale* of the common-sense practice of defer-

ring to authority. All that authority can do is—what, according to Horace, all that philosophy can do—to get rid of a large portion of error" (quoted in Stigler 1978, p. 293; Edgeworth seems to have in mind *Epist.* 1.1.41–42).

3. There are several appeals to *relaxation of assumptions.* The demand for money, writes Samuelson, is "really interesting . . . when uncertainty . . . is admitted." Again, the implicit assumption in Hicks that money bears no interest is relaxed, unhitching the interest rate from the zero return on money. Relaxation of assumptions is the essay-maker of modern economics. In the absence of quantitative evidence on the importance of the assumption relaxed, mere speculation of this sort is not (for the kind of philosopher Samuelson claims to be) evidence at all. Samuelson is careful to stick to the subjunctive mood of theory (money "*would* pass out of use"), but he no doubt wants his strictures on a theory of the interest rate based merely on liquidity preference (that is, on risk) to be taken seriously, as comments on the world as it is. They are, but not on the operationalist grounds he articulates when preaching methodology.

4. There are in the two pages several *appeals to hypothetical toy economies*, constrained to one or two sectors, from which practical results are said to be derived. Since Ricardo this has been among the most common forms of economic argument, the Ricardian vice. The modern theory of international trade indulges in it the most; economic historical economics the least. It is no vice if done reasonably, but neither does it prove much in the narrow sense of proof. "It would be quite possible to have an economy in which money did not exist, and in which there was still a substantial rate of interest." Well, yes.

5. There is, finally, one explicit *appeal to analogy*, which is to be "not . . . superficial." Analogy pervades economic thinking, even when it does not think of itself as analogical: transaction "friction," yield "spread," securities "circulating," money "withering away," are inexplicit examples here from one paragraph in Samuelson of live or half-dead metaphors. Yet analogy and metaphor, like most of the other pieces of Samuelson's rhetoric, have no standing in his Official Rhetoric.

Two of the five devices are literary and rhetorical. The appeal to authority and the appeal to analogy are figures of speech that a poet would use. The other three are rhetorical alone—that is to say, figures of speech used to persuade. They are "figures of speech" because they are ways of talking. Such figures of speech are not, in strict Cartesian doctrine, persuasive at all. None prove by deduction or falsification. Yet *Foundations of Economic Analysis* used them all, with hundreds of others, in rich array.

Most of the Devices Are
Only Dimly Recognized

The practice of economic debate often takes the form of legal reasoning, because, as Booth put it, "the processes developed in the law are codifications of reasonable processes that we follow in every part of our lives, even the scientific" (1974a, p. 157). Economists might study jurisprudence with some aim other than subordinating it to economic theory. In his old book *What's Wrong with Economics?* (1972) Benjamin Ward examined the legal analogies of economic reasoning. They are many. Like jurists, for instance, economists argue by example, by what Edward Levi calls "the controlling similarity between the present and prior case" (1948, p. 7).

The details of the pleading of cases at economic law have little to do with the official scientific method. Without self-consciousness about workaday rhetoric they are easily misclassified. A common argument in economics, for example, is one from verbal suggestiveness. The proposition that "the economy is basically competitive" may well be simply an invitation to look at it this way, on the assurance that doing so will be illuminating. In the same way a psychologist might say "we are all neurotic": she does not mean that 95 percent of a randomly selected sample of us will exhibit compulsive handwashing; she merely recommends that we focus attention on the neurotic ingredient "in us all" (Passmore 1966, p. 438). To misunderstand the expression as a proper Hypothesis would invite much useless Testing. The case is similar to the monetarist equation $MV = PT$ understood as an identity. The equation is the same, term for term, as the equation of state of an ideal gas, and has the same status as an irrefutable but useful notion in economics as it has in chemistry. The identity *can* be argued against, but not on grounds of "failing a test." The arguments against it will deny its capacity to illuminate, not its Truth by a narrow and obsolete philosophical standard.

Another common argument in economics with no status in the official rhetoric is philosophical consistency: "If you assume the firm knows its own cost curve, you might as well assume it knows its production function too: it is no more dubious that it knows one than the other." The argument, usually inexplicit though signaled by such a phrase as "it is natural to assume," is characteristic of philosophical discourse (Passmore 1961; Warner 1989). It is analogous to symmetry as a criterion of plausibility and comes up in many forums. A labor economist tells a seminar about compensating differentials for the risk of unemployment, referring only to the utility functions of the workers. An auditor remarks that the value of unemployment on the demand side (that is, the value to the firm) is not included. The remark is felt to be powerful, and a long discussion ensues of how the demand side might alter the conclusions. The argument from "the other side is empty"—which is to say, an appeal to theoretical tidiness and symmetry is persuasive in economics. But economists are unaware of how persuasive it is.

Some of the rhetoric is aware of itself. Seminar audiences condemn "ad hoccery." An economist will cheerfully admit to having bad data if only she "has a theory" for the inclusion of such and such a variable in her regressions. "Having a theory" is not so open and shut as it might seem, depending, for instance, on what reasoning is prestigious at the moment. Anyone who before 1962 threw accumulated past output into an equation explaining productivity change would have been accused of ad hoccery. But after Arrow's essay "The Economics of Learning by Doing" (which, as it happened, had little connection with maximizing behavior or other higher-order hypotheses in economics), there was suddenly a warrant for doing it.

Economists are not completely aware of their rhetoric when they come to simulation. They will commonly make an argument for the importance of this or that variable by showing its potency in a model with back-of-the-envelope estimates of the parameters. In macroeconomics a spectacularly fine example is Cochrane (1989). In historical economics it is common. Common though it is, little writing is devoted to its explication (but see Zeckhauser and Stokey 1978). Students learn simulation entirely by studying examples of it, and by studying the examples without being told what they are examples of. The accidental teaching contrasts with the self-conscious way in which econometrics and theory are taught. Economists have developed few rhetorical standards for assessing simulation. Between A. C. Harberger's modest little triangles of distortion and Jeffrey Williamson's immense multiequation models of the American or Japanese economics is a broad range. Economists have no vocabulary for criticizing any part of the range. They can deliver summary grunts of belief or disbelief but find it difficult to articulate their reasons in a disciplined way.

Models Are Nonornamental Metaphors: The Case of Gary Becker

The most important example of economic rhetoric, however, is metaphor. Economists call them "models." To say that markets can be represented by supply and demand "curves" is no less a metaphor than to say that the west wind is "the breath of autumn's being." A more obvious example is "game theory," the very name being a metaphor. It is obviously useful to have in one's head the notion that an arms race is a two-person, negative-sum cooperative "game." Its persuasiveness is instantly obvious, as are some of its limitations. (A malicious wit remarked once that game theory has a nice name but no results.)

Noneconomists find it easier to see the metaphors than economists do, habituated as the economists are by daily use to the idea that of course production comes from a "function" and that of course business moves in "cycles." Some metaphors are perfectly self-conscious, as you can see for example from the exultation or irony with which the "invisible hand" is handled. And everyone understands that a metaphorical question is at issue when someone asks whether a mechanical or a biological analogy best suits the economy as a whole (Boulding 1975; Georgescu-Roegen 1975; Kornai 1983). Some economists, again quite self-aware, make their contributions to the field in metaphors used self-consciously: Albert Hirschman, for instance, with his exists and voices, or J. K. Galbraith with his countervailing powers.

But few economists recognize the metaphorical saturation of economic theories believed to be literal (one economist who does is Willie Henderson [1982]). Watchers of other fields are more aware of the metaphors they live by: an early volume of essays on metaphor by philosophers, linguists, and psychologists is entitled simply *Metaphor and Thought* (Ortony 1979). In the physical sciences the metaphors jump out. Jacob Bronowski noted that the scientist needs "the exploration of likenesses; and this has sadly tiptoed out of the mechanical worlds of the positivists and the operationalists, and left them empty. The symbol and the metaphor are as necessary to science as to poetry" (1965, p. 36). Even positivists and operationalists are tied to metaphor—the metaphor of "objectivity," for instance, and in any case the metaphors of their discipline. Richard Rorty had it more right: "It is pictures rather than propositions, metaphors rather than statements, which determine most of our philosophical [and economic] convictions" (1979, p. 12).

Each step in economic reasoning, even the reasoning of the official rhetoric, is metaphoric. The world is said to be "like" a complex model, and its measurements are said to be like the easily measured proxy variable to hand. The complex model is said to be like a simpler model for actual thinking, which is in turn like an even simpler model for calculation. For purposes of persuading doubters the model is said to be like a toy model that can be manipulated quickly inside the doubters' head as she listens to the seminar. John Gardner wrote,

> There is a game—in the 1950s it used to be played by the members of the Iowa Writers' Workshop—called "Smoke." The player who is 'it' [thinks of] some famous person . . . and then each of the other players in turn asks one question . . . such as "What kind of weather are you?" . . . Marlon Brando, if weather, would be sultry and uncertain. To understand that Marlon Brando is a certain kind of weather is to discover something (though something neither useful nor demonstrable) and in the same instant to communicate something. (1978, pp. 118–19)

In economics the comparable discovery *is* useful and demonstrable. What kind of a curve is a market? What king of a material is a worker?

Metaphor, though, is commonly viewed as mere ornament. From Aristotle until the 1930s even literary critics viewed it this way, as an amusing comparison able to affect the emotions but inessential for thought. "Men are beasts": if we cared to be flat-footed about it, the notion was, we could say in what literal way we thought them beastly, removing the ornament to reveal the core of plain meaning underneath. The attitude was, in 1958, common in philosophy, too: "With the decline of metaphysics, philosophers have grown less and less concerned about Godliness and more and more obsessed with cleanliness, aspiring to ever higher levels of linguistic hygiene. In consequence, there has been a tendency for metaphors to fall into disfavour, the common opinion being that they are a frequent source of infection" (Horsbaugh 1958, p. 231). Such suspicion toward metaphor is widely recognized by now to be unnecessary, even harmful. That the very idea of "removing" an "ornament" to "reveal" a "plain" meaning is itself a metaphor suggests why. Perhaps thinking is metaphorical. Perhaps to remove metaphor is to remove thought. The operation on the metaphoric growth would in this case be worse than the disease.

The question is whether economic thought is metaphorical in some nonornamental sense (Klamer and Leonard 1994). The more obvious metaphors in economics are those used to convey novel thoughts, one sort of novelty being to compare economic with noneconomic matters. "Elasticity" was once a mind-stretching fancy; "depression" was depressing, "equilibrium" compared an economy to an apple in a bowl, a

Figures of Economic Speech

settling idea; "competition" once induced thoughts of horseraces; money's "velocity," thoughts of swirling bits of paper. Much of the vocabulary of economics consists of dead metaphors taken from noneconomic spheres.

Comparing noneconomic with economic matters is another sort of novelty, apparent in the imperialism of the new economics of history, law, politics, crime, and the rest, and most apparent in the work of the Kipling of the economic empire, Gary Becker. Among the less bizarre of his many metaphors, for instance, is that children are durable goods, like refrigerators. The philosopher Max Black points out that "a memorable metaphor has the power to bring two separate domains into cognitive and emotional relation by using language directly appropriate to the one as a lens for seeing the other" (1962, p. 236). So here: the subject (a child) is viewed through the lens of the modifier (a refrigerator).

A beginning at literal translation would say, "A child is costly to acquire initially, lasts for a long time, gives flows of pleasure during that time, is expensive to maintain and repair, has an imperfect second-hand market. Likewise, a durable good, such as a refrigerator. . . ." That the list of similarities could be extended further and further, gradually revealing the differences as well—"children, like durable goods, are *not* objects of affection and concern"; "children, like durable goods, do *not* have their own opinions"—is one reason that, as Black says, "metaphorical thought is a distinctive mode of achieving insight, not to be construed as an ornamental substitute for plain thought" (p. 237). The literal translation of an important metaphor is never finished. In this respect and in others an important metaphor in economics has the quality admired in a successful scientific theory, a capacity to astonish us with implications formerly unseen.

But it is not merely the pregnant quality of economic metaphors that makes them important for economic thinking, and not mere ornaments. I. A. Richards was among the first to make the point, in 1936, that metaphor is "two thoughts of different things *active together,* . . . whose meaning is a resultant of their interaction" (1936, p. 93, italics supplied; cf. Black 1962, p. 46; Barfield 1947, p. 54). A metaphor is not merely a verbal trick, Richards continues, but "a borrowing between and intercourse of thoughts, a transaction between contexts" (p. 94). Economists will have no trouble seeing the point of his economic metaphor, one of mutually advantageous exchange. The opposite notion, that ideas and their words are invariant lumps unaltered by combination, like bricks (see again Richards 1936, p. 97), is analogous to believing that an economy is a mere aggregation of Robinson Crusoes. But the point of economics since Smith has been that an island full of trading Crusoes is different from and often better off than the mere aggregation.

Another of Becker's favorite metaphors, "human capital," invented at Chicago by Theodore Schultz, illustrates how two sets of ideas, in this case both drawn from inside economics, can mutually illuminate each other by exchanging connotations. In the phrase "human capital" the field in economics treating human skills was at a stroke unified with the field treating investment in machines. Thought in both fields was improved—labor economics by recognizing that skills, for all their intangibility, arise from abstention from consumption; capital theory by recognizing that skills, for all their lack of capitalization, compete with other investments for a claim to abstention. Notice by contrast that because economists are experts only in durable goods and have few (or at any rate conventional) thoughts about children, the metaphor that children are durable goods has, so to speak, only one direction of flow. The gains from the trade were earned mostly by the theory of children, gaining from the theory of durable goods (fertility, nuptiality, inheritance), not the other way around.

What is successful in economic metaphor is what is successful in poetry, and the success is analyzable in similar terms. Concerning the best metaphors in the best poetry, comparing thee to a summer's day or comparing A to B, argued Owen Barfield, "We feel that B, which is actually said, ought to be necessary, even inevitable in some way. It ought to be in some sense the best, if not the only way, of expressing A satisfactorily. The mind should dwell on it as well as on A and thus the two should be somehow inevitably fused together into one simple meaning" (1947, p. 54). If the modifier B (a summer's day, a refrigerator, a piece of capital) were trite—in these cases it is not, although in the poem Shakespeare was more self-critical of his simile than economists usually are of theirs—it would become, as it were, detached from A, a mechanical and unilluminating correspondence. If essential, though, it fuses with A to become a master metaphor of the science, the idea of "human capital," the idea of "equilibrium," the idea of "entry and exit," the idea of "competition." The metaphor, said a poet, is the "consummation of identity."

Few would deny that economists frequently use figurative language. Much of the pitiful humor available in a science devoted to calculations of profit and loss comes from talking about "islands" in the labor market or "putty-clay" in the capital market or "lemons" in the commodity market. The more austere the subject the more fanciful the language. We have "turnpikes" and "golden rules" in 1960s-style growth theory, for instance, and long disquisitions on what to do with the "auctioneer" in 1950s-style general equilibrium theory. A literary person with advanced training in mathematics and statistics stumbling into *Economet-rica* would be astonished at the metaphors surrounding her, lost in a land of allegory.

Allegory is long-winded metaphor (really, a combining of metaphor and story), and all such figures are analogies. Analogies can be arrayed in terms of explicitness, with simile ("as if") the most explicit and symbol ("the demand curve") the least explicit; and they can be arrayed by extent, from analogy to allegory. Economists, especially theorists, frequently spin "parables" or tell "stories." The word "story" has, as I've noted, come to have a technical meaning in mathematical economics. It is an allegory, shading into extended symbolism. A tale of market days, traders with bins of shmoos, and customers with costs of travel between bins illuminates, say, a fixed point theorem. "Tales well told endure forever," as an economist and poet named Robert Higgs put it.

Both Mathematical and Nonmathematical Reasoning in Economics Rely on Metaphor

The critical question is whether the opposite trick, modifying human behavior with mathematics, is also metaphorical. If it were not, you might acknowledge the metaphorical element in verbal economics about the "entrepreneur," for instance, or more plainly of the "invisible hand," yet argue that the linguistic hygiene of mathematics leaves behind such fancies. This was the belief of the advanced thinkers of the 1920s and 1930s who inspired the modernist conception of economic method. When engaging in verbal economics we are more or less loose, they said, taking literary license with our "story"; but when we do mathematics we put away childish things.

But mathematical theorizing in economics is metaphorical, and literary. Consider, for example, a relatively simple case, the theory of production functions. Its vocabulary is intrinsically metaphorical. "Aggregate capital" involves an analogy of "capital" (itself analogical) with something—sand, bricks, shmoos—that can be "added" in a meaningful way; so does "aggregate labor," with the additional peculiarity that the thing added is no thing, but hours of conscientious attentiveness. The very idea of a "production function" involves the astonishing analogy of the subject (the fabrication of things, about which it is appropriate to think in terms of ingenuity, discipline, and planning) with the modifier (a mathematical function, about which it is appropriate to think in terms of height, shape, and single-valuedness).

The metaphorical content of these ideas was alive to its nineteenth-century inventors. It is largely dead to its twentieth-century users, but deadness does not eliminate the metaphorical element. The metaphor got out of its coffin in an alarming fashion in the Debate of the Two Cambridges in the 1960s. The violence of the combat suggests that it was about something beyond mathematics or fact. The combatants hurled mathematical reasoning and institutional facts at each other, but the important questions were those you would ask of a metaphor: Is it illuminating, is it satisfying, is it apt? How do you know? How does it compare with other economic poetry? Do we want to talk this way? Why not? After some tactical retreats by Cambridge, Massachusetts, on points of ultimate metaphysics irrelevant to these important questions, mutual exhaustion set in, without decision. Daniel Hausman, a philosopher of economics, noted this in his book on the subject (1981) and nearly saw why. The reason there was no decision reached was that the important questions were literary, not mathematical or statistical (or philosophical). The debaters were answering the wrong questions, as though showing mathematically or statistically that a woman cannot be a summer's day. No one noticed. The continued vitality of the idea of an aggregate production function (in the face of mathematical proofs of its impossibility) and the equal vitality of the idea of aggregate economics as practiced in parts of Cambridge, England (in the face of statistical proofs of its impracticality), would otherwise be a mystery.

Even when the metaphors of your economics seem well and truly dead there is no escape from literary questions. The literary man C. S. Lewis pointed out in 1939 that any talk beyond the level of the-cow-is-in-fact-purple, any talk of "causes, relations, of mental states or acts . . . [is] incurably metaphorical" (1939, p. 47). For such talk, he pointed out, the escape from verbal into mathematical metaphor is not an escape: "When a man claims to think independently of the buried metaphor in one of his words, his claim may . . . [be] allowed only in so far as he could really supply the place of that buried metaphor. . . . This new apprehension will usually turn out to be itself metaphorical" (p. 46). If economists forget and then stoutly deny that the production function is a metaphor, yet continue talking about it, the result is mere verbiage. The phrase "production function" will be used in ways satisfying grammatical rules, but will not signify anything.

The charge of meaninglessness applied so freely by old-fashioned philosophers to forms of argument they do not like or understand sticks in this way to themselves. Lewis notes that "the meaning in any given composition is in inverse ratio to the author's belief in his own literalness" (1939, p. 27). An economist speaking (she believes) literally about the demand curve, the national income, or the stability of the economy

Figures of Economic Speech

is engaging in "mere syntax." "The percentage of mere syntax masquerading as meaning may vary from something like 100 percent in political writers, journalists, psychologists, and economists, to something like forty percent in the writers of children's stories. The mathematician, who seldom forgets that his symbols are symbolic, may often rise for short stretches to ninety percent of meaning and ten of verbiage" (p. 49). If an economist is not comparing a social fact to a one-to-one mapping, thus bringing two separate domains into cognitive and emotional relation, she is not thinking:

> I've never slapped a curved demand;
> I never hope to slap one.
> But this thing I can tell you now:
> I'd rather slap than map one.

Unexamined metaphor is a substitute for thinking—which is a recommendation to examine the metaphors, not to attempt the impossible by banishing them. Richard Whately, D.D., archbishop of Dublin, publicist for free trade as for other pieces of classical political economy, and author of the standard work in the nineteenth century on the elements of rhetoric, drew attention to the metaphor of a nation being like an individual and therefore benefiting like an individual from free trade. He devoted some attention to the aptness of the figure:

> To this it is replied, that there is a great difference between
> a Nation and an Individual. And so there is, in many
> circumstances. . . . [He enumerates them, mentioning, for
> instance, the unlimited duration of a nation] and, moreover,
> the transaction of each man, as far as he is left free, are regulated
> by the very person who is to be a gainer or loser by each—the
> individual himself; who, though his vigilance is sharpened by
> interest, and his judgment by exercise in his own department,
> may chance to be a man of confined education, possessed of
> no general principles, and not pretending to be versed in
> philosophical theories; whereas the affairs of a State are regulated
> by a Congress, Chamber of Deputies, etc., consisting perhaps of
> men of extensive reading and speculative minds. (Whately 1846,
> pp. 101–2)

The case of intervention cannot be better put. The metaphor is here an occasion for and instrument of thought, not a substitute.

Metaphors evoke attitudes that are better kept in the open and under the control of reasoning. This is plain in the ideological metaphors popular with parties: the invisible hand is so very discreet, so soothing, that we might be inclined to accept its touch without protest; the contradictions of capitalism are so very portentous, so scientifically precise, that we might be inclined to accept their existence without inquiry.

But even metaphors of the middling sort carry freight. The metaphors of economics often carry in particular the authority of Science and often carry, too, its claims to ethical neutrality. It's no use complaining that we didn't *mean* to introduce moral premises. We do. "Marginal productivity" is a fine, round phrase, a precise mathematical metaphor that encapsulates a powerful piece of social description. Yet it brings with it an air of having solved the moral problem of distribution facing a society in which people cooperate to produce things together instead of producing things alone. It is irritating that it carries this message, because it may be far from the purpose of the economist who uses it to show approval for the distribution arising from competition. It is better to admit that metaphors in economics can contain such a political message than to use the jargon as an innocent.

A metaphor, finally, emphasizes certain respects in which the subject is to be compared with the modifier; in particular, it leaves out the other respects. Max Black, speaking of the metaphor "men are wolves," notes that "any human traits that can without undue strain be talked about in 'wolf-language' will be rendered prominent, and any that cannot will be pushed into the background" (1962b, p. 41). Economists will recognize this as the source of the annoying complaints from nonmathematical economists that mathematics "leaves out" some feature of the truth or from noneconomists that economics itself "leaves out" some feature of the truth. Such complaints are often trite and ill-informed. The usual responses to them, however, are hardly less so. The response that the metaphor leaves out things in order to simplify the story only temporarily is disingenuous, occurring as it often does in contexts where the economists is simultaneously fitting fifty other equations. The response that the metaphor will be "tested" eventually by the facts is a stirring promise, seldom fulfilled.

A better response would be that we like the metaphor of, say, the selfishly economic man as calculating machine because of its prominence in earlier economic poetry or because of its greater congruence with introspection than alternative metaphors (of men as religious dervishes, say, or as sober citizens). In *The New Rhetoric* (1958, p. 390), Perelman and Olbrechts-Tyteca note that "the acceptance of an analogy . . . is often equivalent to a judgment as to the importance of the characteristics that the analogy brings to the fore." What is remarkable about this unremarkable assertion is that it occurs in a discussion of purely literary matters but fits easily into economic science.

Economists and other scientists are less isolated from the civilization than you might think. Their modes of argument and the sources of their conviction—for instance, their uses of metaphor—are not very different from Cicero's speeches or Hardy's novels. This is a good thing. As Black wrote (1962b, p. 243), discussing "archetypes" as extended metaphors in science, "When the understanding of scientific models and archetypes comes to be regarded as a reputable part of scientific culture, the gap between the sciences and the humanities will have been partly filled."

The Master Tropes Rule Economics: The Case of Robert Solow

The best way to show the metaphorical character of economics is to show it working in the economics apparently most far removed from literary matters. A good instance is a famous essay of 1957 on the production function and productivity change by Robert Solow, a president of the American Economic Association, a Nobel laureate, and in other ways eminent in the field (most surprisingly in the dismal science for his fluency and wit).

The paper has been important, as any economist knows from her knowledge of the conversation. Solow's paper, together with some related ones he wrote about the same time, inaugurated a new field of economics. If introspection or questionnaire does not persuade, the importance of the paper is plain in the statistics of citations in other economic papers. Ten years after its publication it was still receiving over twenty-five citations a year on average, and still over twenty a decade and a half later (Table 1).

Solow was trying to understand the rising income of Americans from 1909 to 1949. He wished to know in particular how much was caused by more machinery, buildings, and other physical "capital" and how much by other things—chiefly, perhaps, the increasing ingenuity of people. He began,

> In this day of rationally designed econometric studies and super input-output tables, it takes something more than the usual "willing suspension of disbelief" to talk seriously of the aggregate production function. The new wrinkle I want to describe is an elementary way of segregating variations in output per head due to technical change from those due to the availability of capital per head. Either this kind of aggregate

Table 1. Annual Citations, 1966–1982, of Solow's 1957 Article

1966	25
1967	22
1968	28
1969	28
1970	30
1971	21
1972	23
1973	24
1974	24
1975	25
1976	30
1977	19
1978	14
1979	16
1980	27
1981	25
1982	17

Source: *Social Science Citation Index.*

economics appeals or it doesn't. Personally I belong to both schools. It is convenient to begin with the special case of *neutral* technical change. In that case the production function takes the special form $Q = A(t)f(K,L)$ and the multiplicative factor $A(t)$ measures the cumulated effect of shifts over time. (Solow 1957, reprinted in Zellner 1968, pp. 349–50, to which reference is made)

He then uses a mathematical twist and the assumption of perfect competition to derive a measure of $A(t)$.

The four master tropes discussed at length by literary theorists such as Kenneth Burke (e.g., 1945, pp. 503–17) are here at work: metaphor, metonymy, synecdoche, and irony. The argument depends at once on a metaphor. The "aggregate production function" that Solow diffidently introduces (he is not really diffident: he is pretending to be for rhetorical effect) says that the making of our daily bread is like a mathematical function. The jumble of responsibility, habit, love, conflict, ambition, intrigue, and ceremony that is our working life is supposed to be similar to a chalked curve on a blackboard. Economists are used to such figures of speech, as I have said, to the point of not recognizing that they are, but noneconomists will agree that the figures are bold. No wonder Solow says this one requires willing suspension of disbelief.

The K and the L in the equation are metonymies, letting another thing merely associated with the thing in question stand as a symbol for it, as the White House does for the presidency. The L reduces the human attentiveness in making bread to an hour of work. The hour is a mere emblem, no more than substance of the matter than the heart is of emotions, or a bottle is of the wine. The K reduces the material inheritance of the workplace to a pile of shmoos. Solow is aware of the boldness of this figure, too. Though defending it as conventional, he "would not try to justify what follows by calling on fancy theorems on aggregation and index numbers," and refers in a footnote to Joan Robinson's exploration of "the profound difficulties that stand in the way of giving any precise meaning to the quantity of capital" (quoted in Zellner 1968, p. 350 and note; the Debate of the Two Cambridges was just beginning).

The identification of $A(t)$ with "technical change" is another of the master tropes, a synecdoche, taking a part for the whole; and on it the paper turns. The notation says that the multiplier A depends on time, rising as technologists get smarter. But as Solow admits (p. 350), "slowdowns, speedups, improvements in the education of the labor force, and all sorts of things" will also cause it to rise. Critics of the calculation—such as Evsey Domar, Theodore Schultz, and Solow himself—have called it a mere "measure of our ignorance." Calling it "technical change," as Solow does apologetically though persistently, is a bold synecdoche, taking the part for the whole and running with it.

Solow runs with it into a paragraph containing a little simple mathematics and a clever exploitation of the conventions of the economic conversation. By the second page of the article he has made his main point and persuaded most of the economists listening. He persuades them with the symmetry of the mathematics and the appeal to the authority of scientific traditions in economics, and with the perspectival tropes: metaphor, metonymy, and synecdoche.

Especially he persuades them with irony, the "perspective of perspectives" (Burke 1945, p. 512). Observe his ironical bow to "rationally designed econometric studies" (he knew, as did part of his audience, that their rationality was in doubt, though in 1957 the econometricians were humorlessly unaware.) He describes his notion as a mere "wrinkle" and as "elementary," so elementary a wrinkle that no one had thought of it before, and after Solow an intellectual industry arose to exploit it. (Literally speaking it had in fact been thought of before, in its price-dual form, by G. T. Jones in 1933 in his *Increasing Returns.* Solow was not aware of Jones, an economic historian, though he was aware of several attempts in the 1950s by historically oriented economists such as Valavanis-Vail, Schmookler, and Abramovitz to measure the same thing. The others were less influential because they did not use the metaphor of the production function as explicitly as Solow did.) He protects himself from criticism by mocking the sobersides: "Personally

I belong to both schools" (p. 350). The synecdoche of "technical change" is protected when in doubt by ironical quotation marks, though the marks fall away as the doubt fades.

Irony is the most sophisticated of the master tropes. Hayden White, an historian who has treated the master tropes in the writing of history in the nineteenth century, put the matter of the sophistication of irony this way:

> It presupposes that the reader or auditor already knows, or is capable of recognizing, the absurdity of the characterization of the thing designated in the Metaphor, Metonymy, or Synecdoche used to give form to it. Irony is in one sense metatropological, for it is deployed in the self-conscious awareness of the possible misuse of figurative language. Irony thus represents a stage of consciousness in which the problematical nature of language itself has become recognized. It points to the potential foolishness of all linguistic characterizations of reality as much as to the absurdity of the beliefs it parodies. It is therefore "dialectical," as Kenneth Burke has noted. (White 1973, p. 37)

The most sophisticated economists, like the most sophisticated novelists, favor irony (Booth 1974b). Irony presupposes an existing conversation off of which you can score; in this and in other ways it is mature. George Stigler, for instance, the constant intellectual companion and ally of Solow, wrote of the guiding metaphor of consumer preferences: "It would of course be bizarre to look upon the typical family—that complex mixture of love, convenience, and frustration—as a business enterprise. Therefore, economists have devoted much skill and ingenuity to elaborating this approach" (1966, p. 21).

Economic metaphors, then, are important for economic rhetoric, and not mere frills. No economist could speak without metaphor and the other master tropes. Economists make more appeals to their audience than simply their appeals to The Facts or The Logic, though facts and logic, of course, figure in from time to time as well.

4 THE RHETORIC OF SCIENTISM

HOW JOHN MUTH PERSUADES

Muth's Article Was Ill-Written but Important

Consider another example in detail, less charming than Solow's but as important. In 1961 John Muth published a paper in *Econometrica* (the leading journal of statistical and mathematical economics, and the very embodiment of modernism in economics) entitled "Rational Expectations and the Theory of Price Movements." For years economists ignored it. Robert Lucas and Thomas Sargent, who were chiefly responsible for its later fame, wrote in 1981 (p. xi) that the paper had "a remarkably quiet first decade," which is no rash assessment. Although early accorded, like Solow's paper, the honor of inclusion in Arnold Zellner's *Readings in Economic Statistics and Econometrics* (1968), it was for a long time little read. The pattern of citations to the paper is unusual in a field that models itself so self-consciously on the urgent bustle of physics (Table 2). Seventy-four citations in 1982: even such an important paper as Solow's reached, at most, thirty in a year. There was a tiny flash, and long afterwards a boom.

Table 2. Annual Citations, 1966–1982, of Muth's 1961 Article

1966	5	1975	20
1967	3	1976	33
1968	2	1977	41
1969	2	1978	47
1970	4	1979	44
1971	2	1980	71
1972	9	1981	56
1973	10	1982	74
1974	10		

Source: *Social Science Citation Index*. The index begins in 1966.

The paper took a long time to be recognized as important because it was badly written. It is a good bet that most of the citers of the article have never laid eyes on it, and would not understand it if they did. The case illustrates, by an argument from contraries, the importance of good writing in successful science. Galileo was a master of Italian prose; Poincaré, Einstein, and Keynes influenced science and society almost as much with their pens as with their mathematics.

Even by the undemanding standards of American academic life Muth's prose was not masterful or influential. It was badly organized, with ill-motivated digressions and leaps from large claims to lame examples. Little distinction was made between minor points of form and major revisions of economic thinking. Though no reader of *Econometrica* would have stumbled over the inelegant mathematics involved, she probably did wonder what exactly it was supposed to prove.

The paper bore some of the marks of professional excellence, such as an easy familiarity with mathematical statistics at a time when not many economists could claim it, and a wide-ranging bibliography. But even a serious reader of the journal could easily have dismissed it as mere muttering. Apparently most did. While richer in invention even than it seemed, it was too obviously clumsy in arrangement to warrant much investment by its readers.

Yet Muth was making an important argument. The trouble with the prevailing explanation of hog cycles or inventory accumulation and other dynamics was that it implied that economic actors are less perceptive than economics professors. The actors were supposed to be slow to change, but the professors were said to know the actors' slowness, and to be able to trace their slow adjustment. The audience claimed to know the lines better than the players. Before Muth's theory the prevailing explanation was that people get a more or less correct idea of what the future will bring and then gradually adjust to it. Muth's notion was that the professors, even if correct in their model of man, could do no better in predicting than could the hog farmer or steelmaker or insurance company. The notion is one of intellectual modesty. The professors declare themselves willing to attribute to economic actors at least as much common sense as is embodied in professional theories. The common sense is "rationality": therefore Muth called the argument "rational expectations."

What made Muth's version of the argument especially important was its application, at first by Stephen Turnovsky and Robert Lucas and later by many others, to the matter of macroeconomics. Muth's paper became the holy writ for one of the sects that sweep macroeconomics every five years. In the Keynesian or monetarist models of the 1960s and before the economic actor was perpetually astonished, the perfect rube: [Seizes newspaper.] "My word! The government has just reduced taxes in depression!" [Eyes bug out.] "Holy cow! The government has

trimmed the growth of money after a long period of inflation! Gosh!"
[Faints.] It would be easy to manipulate such a dunce, from which grew
the conviction in the 1940s and 1950s that it was easy to manipulate the
economy—to "fine-tune" it, as the journalists said. The models of rational expectations in the 1970s went to the opposite extreme. They
viewed the economic actor as a man of the world: "Oh, yes, a tax cut."
[Yawns, lights cigarette in a golden holder.] "Hmm: I see that inflation
has been going on for some months." [Settles into club chair.] "About
time for the Fed to do its tight money act." [Calls broker, sips scotch,
dozes off under his copy of *Barron's*.]

Muth's Main Points Can
Be Expressed in English

By what means does Muth persuade? The question is a
critical not an historical one. The critical issue doesn't depend on the
usual questions in the history of economic thought—who influenced
Muth's paper, how it circulated in draft, what circumstances in macroeconomics made it an idea whose time had come, and whether it was
anticipated in Austrian economics, Chicago-school finance, or growth
theory. Its history is relevant only to the extent that the history illuminates the way it achieves its effect now. In Saussure's jargon, the issues
here are synchronic not diachronic.

Below are reproduced the crucial sentences in the paper. It would be
easy to persuade economists that the selection here is the core.

Muth:

Translation:

[A] The objective of this paper is to
outline a theory of expectations and
to show that implications are—as a
first approximation—consistent with
the relevant data. (Muth 1961, as
cited in Zellner, 1968, p. 536)

The paper asks how people guess
about what the future will bring. The
answer is tested against some of the
facts in agricultural markets.

[B] I should like to suggest that expectations, since they are informed
predictions of future events, are essentially the same as the predictions
of the relevant economic theory. At
the risk of confusing this purely de-

The guesses people make are probably no better or worse than the
guesses economists would make. I'll
call such guesses "rational," to distinguish them from the irrational—
that is, unreasonable, foolish—

scriptive hypothesis with a pronouncement as to what firms ought to do, we call such expectations "rational." It is sometimes argued that the assumption of rationality in economics leads to theories inconsistent with, or inadequate to explain, observed phenomena, especially changes over time (e.g., Simon 1959). Our hypothesis is based on exactly the opposite point of view: that dynamic economic models do not assume enough rationality. (p. 537)

guesses that present theories posit. Hostility to "rationality" is common among the critics of economics. I wish to go in the other direction: to see how far one can get by supposing that people are as rational in guessing about the future as in buying bread in the present.

[C] The hypothesis asserts three things: (1) Information is scarce, and the economic system generally does not waste it. (2) The way expectations are formed depends specifically on the structure of the relevant system describing the economy. (3) A "public prediction," in the sense of Grunberg and Modigliani (1954), will have no substantial effect on the operation of the economic system (unless it is based on inside information). This is not quite the same thing as stating that the marginal revenue product of economics is zero, because expectations of a single firm may still be subject to greater error than the theory. (p. 537)

In other words, I'm saying that people take appropriate care with their guesses, and economists should credit them with such caretaking. If people take care in guessing, talk about the future will be pointless: people will have allowed for the effects being talked about. For instance, declarations that prosperity is just around the corner will have no impact, unless the declarer really does know something we all don't know. Economists do know something, though not as much as their present notions about guessing imply: they know that a bunch of guesses by individuals average out over a large group to less quirky guesses.

[D] It does *not* assert that the scratch work of entrepreneurs resembles the system of equations in any way; nor does it state that predictions of entrepreneurs are perfect or that their expectations are all the same. (p. 537)

Business people do not have to be trained in mathematical economics to do about as well as economists can do in guessing the future. Nor do they have to guess perfectly or all in the same way.

[E] If the prediction of the theory were substantially better than the ex-

The notion of rational guessing makes a lot of sense. If economists

pectations of the firms, then there would be opportunities for the "insider" to profit from the knowledge—by inventory speculation if possible, by operating a firm, or by selling a price forecasting service to the firms. The profit opportunities would no longer exist if the aggregate expectation of the firms is the same as the prediction of the theory: . . . The expected price equals the equilibrium price. (p. 539)

[F] It is rather surprising that expectations have not previously been regarded as rational dynamic models, since rationality is assumed in all other aspects of entrepreneurial behavior. From a purely theoretical standpoint, there are good reasons for assuming rationality. First, it is a principle applicable to all dynamic problems (if true). Expectations in different markets and systems would not have to be treated in completely different ways. Second, if expectations were not moderately rational there would be opportunities for economists to make profits in commodity speculation, running a firm, or selling the information to present owners. Third, rationality is an assumption that can be modified. Systematic biases, incomplete or incorrect information, poor memory, etc., can be examined with analytical methods based on rationality. (p. 550)

[G] The only real test, however, is whether theories involving rationality explain observed phenomena any better than alternative theories. In this section we shall therefore compare some of the empirical im-

could do better than business people, the economists would be rich. They are not. A farmer guessing about the price of hogs will arrive on average at the price the market does: he'd better.

It is asymmetric for economists to treat people as rational economic men in buying bread or building ships but not in guessing the future. On aesthetic grounds it would be better to use one principle of rationality. As I said, if economists were smart enough to know how business people were failing to be rational, the economists would be rich. Furthermore, rationality is usually a good place to start thinking about human affairs, especially economic affairs. You can add later whatever allowance for ignorance or foolishness seems justified in each case.

But these arguments I've made so far are just frosting, and are not good scientific method. The cake is the ability of my notion to make better sense of the world than some competing notion. In agricultural mar-

plications of the rational expectations hypothesis with those of the cobweb "theorem." The effects of rational expectations are particularly important because the cobweb theorem has often been regarded as one of the most successful attempts at dynamic economic theories (e.g., Goodwin 1947). Few students of agricultural problems or business cycles seem to take the cobweb theorem very seriously, however, but its implications do occasionally appear. For example, a major cause of price fluctuations in cattle and hog markets is sometimes believed to be the expectations of farmers themselves. As a result, the prediction of the cobweb theory would ordinarily have the sign opposite to that of the firms. (p. 551)

kets especially (though also in the study of general booms and busts) the competing notion is called the "cobweb theorem." No one actually takes the "theorem" very seriously, perhaps because they recognize without thinking about it much that it's not rational. In any event, it says that each single farmer thinks prices will stay high when they are high, and that he will therefore raise lots of hogs to take advantage of the high price. By the time the little hogs become big hogs, however, every other farmer has also raised lots of hogs; the price is in fact low, contrary to what he expected. The farmer, poor fool, never learns.

[H] There is some direct evidence concerning the quality of expectations of firms. Heady and Kaldor (1954) have shown that for the period studied, average expectations were considerably more accurate than simple extrapolation. (p. 552)

Heady and Kaldor showed that the firms do learn, or at least that they learn better than this.

[I] It often seems that reported expectations underestimate the extent of changes that actually take place. . . . Such findings are clearly inconsistent with the cobweb theory, which ordinarily requires a negative coefficient. (p. 553)

Other writers have found that farmers do not expect prices to move as much as the prices actually do move, but that they at least predict the right direction: the cobweb theorem says they would predict the wrong direction.

[J] The evidence for the cobweb model lies in the quasi-periodic fluctuations in prices of a number of commodities. The hog cycle is perhaps the best known, but cattle and potatoes have sometimes been cited as others which obey the

The whole notion of the cobweb is based on the ups and downs of, say, hog prices. But hog prices take much longer to go up and down than it takes to raise hogs. Something is wrong. What is wrong, I'll venture, is that the irrational theory of how

"theorem.". . . That the observed hog cycles were too long for the cobweb theorem was first observed in 1935 by Coase and Fowler (1935, 1937). The graph of cattle prices given by Ezekiel (1938) as evidence for the cobweb theorem implies an extraordinarily long period of production (5–7 years). The interval between successive peaks for other commodities tends to be longer than three production periods. (pp. 553–54)

farmers make guesses about the future is mistaken.

Muth's Article Engages in the Usual Appeals to Scientific Method

The question is how such a wretchedly expressed argument achieves credence. Its obscurity of course became a rhetorical advantage once it had been made into holy writ. It is composed in a foreign language, but the language is a sacred one, like Old Church Slavonic.

Its style is the key to its rhetorical appeal, because it is the style of scientism. Lucas and Sargent, the most prominent users of the argument, are persuaded that it is "one of the most carefully and compactly written papers of recent vintage: every sentence in the introduction [not reproduced here] counts, and many have since been expanded into entire articles. Muth introduces the hypothesis at a general, verbal level, motivating it as a corollary of the general principles of economic equilibrium, and then turns to specific, certainty-equivalent examples" (1981, p. xvii). The praise is itself scientistic and draws on the stylistic rhetoric of modernism. The language of "introduc[ing] the hypothesis at a general, verbal level, motivating it as a corollary of . . . general principles" is undiluted modernism. You deduce lower-level hypotheses from general principles, and the test of the lower hypothesis is therefore an indirect test of the principles. The talk of corollaries is part of the same tradition (and so too, incidentally, is the special virtue attributed to care and compactness, the virtues of mathematics in the Math Department, not in Engineering). The hypotheses come from the context of discovery, before the rigor of justification. You "motivate" a proof in mathematics—the language used here—by stepping for a little while outside the rigorous mode of proof-making to show the groundlings what's afoot.

Muth himself makes similar remarks, also couched in modernist language, about what should warrant belief. In the first sentence of the selection he implicitly declares that most of his arguments to follow in the paper are, by his own standards, epistemologically lame. Showing that "the implications are . . . consistent with the relevant data" (paragraph A) is indeed the positivist criterion of truth in science, but little of the paper does it. He does show that if he is careful his notion does not lead to manifest absurdity, such as a condition that speculators in hogs entered the business to lose rather than to gain money. These are the quality of the "data" he shows "consistent" with his argument. Toward the end, after much argument that would find no place in the epistemology of positivism, he turns impatiently on himself with a positivist *ukase*: "The only real test, however, is whether theories involving rationality explain observed phenomena any better than alternative theories" (paragraph G). The words are redolent of the received view. The richness of scientific persuasion is to be reduced to a crucial experiment, a "real test" *(pace* Duhem and the dilemma that no test is crucial). Since the alternative views are "theories," the job of science is to upend or uphold them *(pace* Kuhn and the history of normal science fitting fact to invariant theory). The relevant test depends on "observed phenomena," the hard, objective data so much to be desired *(pace* Polanyi and the truth that scientific knowledge is not epistemologically special).

The appeals to the method of science in Muth's paper are mainly matters of style, arising out of a modernist conversation. The paper does not achieve credence by axiomatic proof or statistical curve-fitting, though written in the genre recommended by modernism. What is modernist in it is not the turns of argument but the style.

The conflict between the "nonrhetorical" ideology of modernism and the actual practice of modernists has been apparent from the beginning, showing up repeatedly in matters of style. Amelie Oksenberg Rorty observes of Descartes that "despite his austere recommendations about the methods of discovery and demonstration, he hardly ever followed those methods, hardly ever wrote in the same genre twice" (1983, p. 548). She notes that his attacks on the common topics of argument, such as authority or the appeal to common knowledge, have an ironic air, for he "found himself using the very modes he intended to attack" (p. 548). Since Bacon and Descartes and the creators later in the seventeenth century of the scientific paper, any scientist who wished to persuade had to adopt the modernist style, as Muth did. Darwin is the leading case. The student of rhetoric John Campbell has argued that Darwin took "care to redescribe his path to discovery so that it appeared to conform with conventional standards of Baconian induction-ism" (1984, p. 15); and Edward Manier writes that "the early drafts of the theory do not conform to the 'hypothetico-deductive model' of scientific explanation, although they indicate Darwin's intent to represent his views as if they did conform to that model" (Campbell 1984, p. 77, and p. 76, where Manier is quoted).

The style of Muth's article makes an ethical and emotional appeal, an appeal to his character as a Scientist and to the self-image of his audience as fellow scientists. The word "I" occurs twice only (once in the selection), in keeping with the convention that kings, editors, people with tapeworms, and honest-to-goodness scientists are permitted to use the more dignified "we" instead. The style is often indirect in other ways, as suits a Scientist (one can make insecure scientists still more insecure by violating such stylistic conventions). Ten of the thirty sentences in the selection have their main clauses in the passive voice. Amidst much that is self-confident and even cocky there are soothing words of proper scientific modesty: "as a first approximation" (A) the theory works; "I would like to suggest" (B), not assert; "it is rather surprising" (F) that the theory has been overlooked; "it often appears" (I) that behavior is inconsistent with the alternative theories. And throughout the essay the reader is treated to dollops of scientific vocabulary from the classical languages: "purely descriptive hypotheses," "observed phenomena," "objective probability distributions of outcomes," "analytical methods," and the like. Northrop Frye observes that "much of the difficulty in a philosophical [and scientific] style is rhetorical in origin, resulting from a feeling that it is necessary to detach and isolate the intellect from the emotions" (1957, p. 330). He examines a characteristically opaque sentence from James Mill, translates it in the style of the translation of Muth above, and wonders, as you do about Muth, "why, if James Mill meant that, he could not have said it." The answer is that "the style is motivated by a perverse, bristling intellectual honesty. _He_ will not condescend to employ any of the pretty arts of persuasion, sugar-coated illustrations or emotionally-loaded terms; he will appeal only to the cold logic of reason itself—reinforced, to be sure, by a peculiarly Victorian sense that the more difficult the style, the tougher the moral and intellectual fibre one develops in wrestling with it" (p. 330). On the page before he remarks, "All of these are clearly at least in part endeavours to purify verbal communication of the emotional content of rhetoric; all of them, however, impress the literary critic as being themselves rhetorical devices" (p. 329).

Well, of course. The form of Muth's article seeks to persuade. Not to fool: to persuade. Put clearly or modestly or, above all, unscientifically, it would not have been in the end a success as a scientific paper. If he had written in the plain style I have translated it into, no one would have made it into a holy text. In a word, the article, like any other piece of scientific work, is rhetorical, even in its stylistic appeal to a rhetoric of not having a rhetoric.

Muth's Appeal Is in Fact to the Community of Scholars

The theory of knowledge put forward by the objective, data-respecting, sober style of modernism in Muth's paper is that the privileged form of knowing is knowing by the lone person himself, *solus ipse*. That is, real knowing is said to be individual and solipsistic, not social. No one needs to *say* anything to you, the Cartesian says, to persuade you of the ancient proof of the irrationality of the square root of two. There is nothing social about your assent to it.

But on the contrary, persuasive knowledge is social. It is a social event that Muth's arguments came to be credible. The arguments were not written in the heavens or, as Descartes imagined, in the soul of the self-regarding man. The astronomer relies for his convictions on "a sequence of instrument makers and astronomers and nuclear physicists, specialist in this and that, each of whom he must trust and believe. All this knowledge, all our knowledge, has been built up communally. The fallacy which imprisons the positivist and the analyst [in philosophy] is the assumption that he can test what is true and false without consulting anyone but himself" (Bronowski 1965, p. 57).

The evidence for the social character of knowledge is that not everyone of Muth's society has been persuaded. A particular society of economists, not the ages, was to be persuaded. Not all were persuaded, and those who were have identifiable characteristics. His arguments, to use the modernist word, were not altogether "compelling." They did not compel assent the way some (but not all) of the simplest and oldest proofs in mathematics do, or the way some (but not all) of the simplest and most dramatic controlled experiments in physics do. This may be seen in the refusal of such intelligent economists as Robert Gordon, James Tobin, and Benjamin Friedman, among many others, to give their assent to Muth's arguments.

The official rhetoric of the paper allows no room for anything but unanimous assent, since the paper claims to be a certified piece of positivism "consistent with the facts." But noncompulsion in scientific argument is, of course, commonplace. When honest and well-informed biologists disagree about the strength of a tendency to inherited altruism among human blood relatives or when honest and well-informed physicists disagree about the significance of Bell's Theorem, they must be using arguments that do not compel assent in the conclusive way required by modernist method.

Muth's paper has in fact few modernist certitudes. The main argument, as I have said, is that rational expectations applies more widely a principle of entry used daily by economists elsewhere. The usual models "do not assume enough rationality" (B); "rationality is assumed in all other aspects of entrepreneurial behavior" (F), so why not here? It is an appeal to a figure of speech discussed earlier, philosophical consistency. Muth is simply pointing to an oversight in the application of economic theory. It is as though for some reason astronomers who grasped Newton's theory had not noticed that the motions of the earth's moon could be brought under it. A paper pointing out that this too could be fitted into a theory that explained the motions of the earth, Jupiter, and Mars, and even of Ganymede and Phobus, would be instantly plausible to many. Likewise in Muth's case.

The analogy was not persuasive to all economists, I have noted. Yet it had magical power over others. Some of Muth's audience were persuaded as much as they were ever going to be as soon as they understood the argument, that is to say (if they were among the tiny group who saw through its "compactness"), by about the second page. Compare the rapidity with which Solow persuaded his audience, or at least the part of it that believed anyway the metaphor of the production function. There is nothing unscientific about such ready if partial assent.

Nor did Muth break with the traditions of science when he turned to little mathematical simulations that seemed to behave well—not simulations that "predict well" in properly modernist style, but that compute and fit and lie still beside the existing theory without exploding. Thomas Kuhn, in contrasting his views on the "logic of discovery or psychology of research" with Popper's, argued that for the most part a scientist is concerned rather with evaluating his "best guesses about the proper way to connect his own research problem with the corpus of accepted scientific knowledge. The scientist must *premise* current theory as the rules of the game" (Kuhn 1977, p. 270, his italics). Science, to repeat, is not "testing" its theories against predictions. The attempts at simulation are mostly puzzles the scientist poses which are "like crossword puzzles, challenges only to his ingenuity. *He* is in difficulty, not current theory" (p. 271n, his italics).

The role of simulation in science is evident in the conversation about the extinction of the dinosaurs. The new explanation argues that a comet hit the earth scores of millions of years ago, creating a natural version of the nuclear winter. As a reviewer of a book on the subject wrote, "The chief difficulty is in rendering it quantitative. We must hope that someone will now produce a numerical simulation that extinguishes/perpetuates all the right species in all the right numbers" (McCrea 1983). A related conversation has been taking place in astronomy since the early 1980s, using identical rhetorical devices. One astronomical argument, beginning with the observation that there are regular mass extinctions, is that the sun has a mate, a star called Nemesis, whose orbit periodically disturbs the comet fields surrounding the sun, causing comets to rain into the solar system. Or perhaps the disturbing body is a Planet X:

> Although the Planet X model also appears to explain the periodic mass extinctions adequately, Mr. Whitmire says he does not consider it to be better than the Nemesis model. Nemesis, he noted, has so far withstood many detailed calculations. But if the Planet X model can withstand similar calculations, "I think it will be a better model than Nemesis" for two reasons, he added. The most important reason, he said, is that the existence of Planet X has long been postulated, so scientists "would not be inventing anything new." The second reason is that the orbit of the planet is closer to the sun than that proposed for Nemesis, which means it would be much more likely to be stable. (*Chronicle of Higher Education,* February 20, 1985)

When the puzzle is solved, the scientific community applauds, but it is not applauding an event in the hypothetico-deductive model of science. The situation is similar in economics and in Muth.

The Explicit Arguments
Are Rhetorically Complex

Having shown that his instance can be simulated without gross violation of the facts, Muth is ready to make more direct arguments for it. Early on he remarks that "information is scarce, and the economic system generally does not waste it" (paragraph C; compare the remark on the "marginal revenue product of economics" in the same paragraph, which makes the same point). Such remarks are common in economics: economists delight in posing deep but tough little examination questions for their colleagues, just as classicists delight in posing for theirs apt but difficult quotations from *The Greek Anthology.* The correct reaction is a show of effortless understanding.

The Rhetoric of Scientism

In Muth's case the understanding is that he is comparing information about the future of hog prices with any other good that can be bought and sold. If the analogy persuades, then you will believe that business people buy information to the optimal extent—or at any rate to the extent of optimality that they exhibit in their other and more ordinary purchases. Their purchases of trucking services or space in feedlots do not leave any gaps between the cost of the last units of such things and the marginal value in use. There is no waste, no misallocation. Nor, Muth is saying, is there misallocation in purchasing information about the future, which implies that there is no gap for mere economists to exploit. When business people have done their jobs, the future will in fact bring what *on average* they had expected it would bring. The argument does not "state that the predictions of entrepreneurs are perfect" (C). They do not hit the bull's-eye every time. But at least their hits are distributed around the bull's-eye in such a way that no economist could profitably advise them to aim higher in shooting (E, F near the middle).

His three further arguments "from a purely theoretical standpoint" (F) are revealing. They are purely aesthetic, which is what economists mean when they call an argument "theoretical." As I have noted, when economists are asked why almost all of them believe in free trade, they will say that it is a "theoretical" argument that persuades them. Further inquiry will reveal that it is in fact a pretty diagram that persuades them. Evidence that would persuade a consistent positivist is absent. So here, which probably explains why Muth immediately turns on himself with the stern injunction to seek positive virtue and "explain observed phenomena."

The arguments are arguments from symmetry and suitability and personal character, distant from the rules of modernism. His notion of rational expectations would be a unified theory of expectations, Muth argues, symmetrical in all its applications. The appeal is to a uniformity in social nature—or, more accurately, to a desire to understand social nature uniformly. He argues again that economists would be rich if they were as smart as alternative theories posit (E again). The argument is practically *ad hominem* and has the reflexive character that the Frankfurt School of philosophers associates with critical, as against scientific, theories.

He argues finally that rational expectations can be conveniently modified to fit the imperfections of the social world. Flexibility is frequently praised in scientific theories and of course should be. But flexibility is simply a promise that the theory will be able to evade crucial tests, surviving unscathed from positivist tortures. Nothing could be further from naïve falsification. All the arguments he uses are, as Muth

says, "good reasons"; but they do not fit with the narrowing epistemology that many scientists still believe.

Even when he has jerked himself back to "real tests," Muth cannot
follow the modernist line. His "observations" (H, I, J) are all reports of
other people's work, once removed from the virtue of primary experiment. They are, in fact, mainly attacks on the plausibility of one among
the infinite number of possible alternatives to rationality, not the full,
fair horse race among alternatives imagined in positivist folklore. The
Heady and Kaldor paper cited by Muth used self-reporting of expectations by the farmers themselves, which is forbidden in the economist's
version of positivist method. The regression coefficients discussed in
paragraph I are open to numerous objections, as Muth well understood.
And the observation in J that cycles in Hog prices are in fact much
longer than the gestation period of hogs (the gestation period is important to the other theories of expectation) is hardly decisive, as Muth
himself remarks: "Positive serial correlation of the exogenous distur-
bances" means that farmers may have a series of several bad years in a
row, lengthening the apparent cycle beyond the period it takes to raise
a hog. The rejection of the nonrational hog cycle may be merely apparent. The test Muth proposes, to put it technically, is underidentified.

To say that Muth's "observations" would not persuade consistent
modernists is not, however, to say that they do not persuade reasonable
economists. Economists cannot be consistent modernists and remain
reasonable. The persuasiveness of Muth's paper comes from the richness
and catholicity of its unofficial arguments, well beyond the official narrowness. Among economists an argument from axiomatic demonstration, statistical test (regression in particular), or appeal to the competitive model all have prestige. None is logically compelling, nor even
very persuasive by itself. You can object to each that garbage in implies
garbage out. Yet the most hostile economist, if properly socialized, will
want to yield to the form. She will be pleased by their success at a formal level—"Gosh, what a clever argument that is: What a neat proof/
statistical test/appeal to the intellectual traditions of economics"—
even if she wants to disbelieve their substance.

To claim that Muth persuades by rhetorical means is not of course a
criticism. Quite the contrary: it is inevitable, and even good. Outside of
a rather small group of specialists in speech communication, theatre
arts, and related fields the study of the rhetoric of a text is usually a
preface to debunking it. There is a rhetoric of the analysis of rhetoric.
An outsider reading "Sweet Talk: The Moral Rhetoric Against Sugar"
by Elizabeth Walker Mechling and Jay Mechling, published in 1983 in the
Central States Speech Journal, aches for the demonstration that the dia-

tribes against sugar, analyzed rhetorically in the paper, are in fact misled. But the demonstration does not come. The expectation that it must come is naïve. Critical thinking is not necessarily "critical" in the common sense.

Muth's article is typical of the literature of economics, with its rich and unexplored rhetoric. That is the point: economists are not aware of the rhetorical riches buried in their style of talk. The richness is not astonishing, of course. That economists persuade the way other professional arguers do is no more astonishing than that arguers now use much the same common topics as were current in Cicero's time (Burke 1950, p. 56). True, you might be equally astonished by both facts, and study them with wondering respect. An anthropologist, for instance, would do well, as some have, to study rhetoric among the Sherpas or the Ilongot, to see if the same figures of argument carry conviction there as with us. In any case a study of rhetoric among the Econ need not encourage bad rhetoric any more (or less) than the study of econometrics encourages bad econometrics.

Muth's Rhetoric Is Indistinguishable from That in Other Fields

Muth's rhetoric ought to be familiar, because it uses figures of speech common to our civilization. Different fields of study pick from the same list of figures of speech. The list is issued with an education.

Imagine the figures of speech stuffed into a storeroom: twelve dozen appeals to authority here, a gross of syllogisms there, 157 metaphors (few of them fresh) on the top shelf, a dozen urn models stuck in behind the metaphors, and one argument from design, apparently secondhand, over by the window. These and others are available for use. A field such as economics will at one time make large use of the argument from design, say, and little use of appeals to the character of Scientist; at another time it will use a different bundle, having put the used ones back in the storeroom. None of the items are epistemologically privileged. To be proud that you achieve human persuasion by using existence theorems as against analogies does not make much sense, especially considering that the bundle of figures used is not permanent. Today's user of an argument from experiment will be tomorrow's user of an appeal to authority.

In short, any field, such as economics, differs from another, such as history or physics, in two respects. It uses for a while a somewhat different selection from the common store of figures of speech. Much over-lap can be expected. And it studies different objects. A science is a class of objects and a way of conversing about them, not a way of knowing truth.

The overlap of argument especially requires factual demonstration. You do not after all see engineers using the metaphor of the invisible hand every day or theologians using Brouwer's fixed-point theorem (though each could). You can see the overlap by getting down into the details of argument in fields different from economics, showing the similarity point by point to Muth's argument.

Three fields that among them must surround economics, whatever coordinates you might use, are paleontology, pure mathematics, and the study of Latin literature. If we accept the modernism that correlates what is out there with how we know, these surely will be the realms of plain fact, indubitable proof, and mere opinion. It will develop that they are not.

For paleontology I have already remarked on how the conversation about mass extinctions uses simulation, a figure of speech whose use in economics has grown as the price of computer time has fallen. Even when away from their computers the economists use it, to think about the effect of withholding the grain crop on prices, for example. It is mathematical analogizing. In this, unsurprisingly, economists are not different from other scientific poets. Another case is described by Stephen Jay Gould. The sudden proliferation of species at the begin-ning of the Cambrian period, one of the great puzzles in evolution, was explained by Steven Stanley in 1973 by positing the sudden arrival of forms of life that fed on other forms of life, single-celled herbivores, as it were, in a grassy sea. Their grazing on the dominant forms allowed the new forms to survive the competition from the previously domi-nant ones, which in turn resulted in new grazers. For the similarity of Stanley's explanation to the analysis of Muth, Gould's description is worth quoting at length:

> Stanley did not develop his theory from empirical studies of
> Precambrian communities. It is a deductive argument based on
> an established principle of ecology that does not contradict any
> fact of the Precambrian world and seems particularly consistent
> with a few observations. In a frank concluding paragraph,
> Stanley presents four reasons for accepting his theory: (1) "It
> seems to account for what facts we have about Precambrian life";
> (2) "It is simple, rather than complex or contrived"; (3) "It is
> purely biological, avoiding *ad hoc* invocation of external controls";

and (4) "It is largely the product of direct deduction from an established ecological principle."

Such justifications do not correspond to the simplistic notions about scientific progress that are taught in most high schools and advanced by most media. Stanley does not invoke proof by new information obtained from rigorous experiment. His second criterion is a methodological presumption, the third a philosophical preference, the fourth an application of prior theory. Only Stanley's first reason makes any reference to Precambrian facts, and it merely makes the weak point that his theory "accounts" for what is known (many other theories do the same). But creative thought in science is exactly this—not a mechanical collection of facts and induction of theories, but a complex process involving intuition, bias, and insight from other fields. Science, at its best, interposes human judgment and ingenuity upon all its proceedings. (Gould 1977, p. 125)

That the theory "accounts for what [few] facts we have" (as Stanley put it, in the usual phrase) is exactly Muth's claim too, buttressed immediately—lest we pause too long over the paucity of these facts and become depressed—by appeals to the traditions of reasoning in the field and the aesthetic pleasure of the simpler argument. It is not strange to find evolution and economics using identical rhetorical devices, for they are identical twins raised separately. In any case, Muth's and Stanley's theories are similar in the rhetorical appeals they make.

In pure mathematics the case is one described by Mark Steiner in 1975, suggested in turn by George Polya's book on the rhetoric of number and quantity, *Induction and Analogy in Mathematics* (1954). The great Swiss mathematician Leonhard Euler wished to find a simple expression, supposing one existed, for the infinite sum $1 + 1/4 + 1/9 + 1/16 + \ldots$ and so forth forever, the sum of the reciprocals of successive squares of the positive integers. To those unfamiliar with infinite sums, the logic of which was not developed in full rigor until long after Euler wrote, there is no obvious reason why the sum should exist (although a little calculation makes it very plausible that it does and is somewhere around 1.64). What Euler showed is typical of the rabbits that eighteenth-century mathematicians were always pulling out of hats: that the sum is exactly $(\pi)^2/6$. To nonmathematicians it is astonishing that π turns up so often in expressions apparently unrelated to circles.

The argument that Euler developed depended on many things, among them, as Steiner puts it, precisely that "he knew that a constant like π on the basis of past experience, was likely to show up in such a context" (1975, p. 105). Likewise, Muth knew on the basis of past experience that rational models were easy to manipulate and likely to give especially simple results. Euler felt his result to be "simple and esthetic" (Steiner's words, p. 105), as Muth did. Euler could see no alternative, as Muth could see no merit and many demerits in the cobweb theorem. Euler, a famous calculator, showed the formula to be empirically correct to twenty decimal places. Muth had less precise material, but made an identical argument, dressed up for purposes of modernist epistemology as "the only real test."

The most important strand in Euler's web of persuasion was an algebraic derivation of the equality. But the derivation depends on a crucial "inductive 'leap'. . . unjustified by anything so far presented" (Steiner 1975, p. 103). The leap was an analogy between finite equations like $0 = 3 + 4x - 10x^2$, of the second degree, and equations like

$$0 = x/1 - x^3/(3)(2) + x^5/(5)(4)(3)(2) - x^7/(7)(6)(5)(4)(3)(2) + \dots.$$

Euler explained that these should be viewed as equations of the "infinite" degree, yet as Steiner notes, "no axiomatization, or even formalization, of 'infinite addition' existed at the time" (1975, p. 106). It was "Euler's genius and his painstaking verifications" by numerical simulation that made fruitful this notion of "exploiting the analogy between finite and infinite" (p. 106). Even by the standards of eighteenth-century mathematics "Euler had not proved his results." But—and this is the crucial point—"we must admit that Euler had a right to be confident in his discovery, beyond any doubt" (p. 106).

So too Muth. His discovery, though clearly more doubtful than Euler's, also rested on an unproven analogy, between ordinary goods and information about the future. He claimed, with approximately as much prior warrant as Euler, that both were objects of production, allocation, and lucid plan. The analogy, like Euler's, carried much of the weight of persuasion. Like Euler, Muth had a warrant for using the analogy that in other applications a similar analogy "yields other results that are also verified to many decimal places," and that it is "an analogy that brings forth previously proved theorems" (Steiner 1975, p. 107). This is the burden of Muth's use of the word "rational." He is pointing out that other applications of the analogy between human action and methodical calculation have proven fruitful in understanding. And of course they have. The mathematician, like the paleontologist, does not argue in a way much different from the economist.

Another theorem of Euler was the subject of Imre Lakatos's experiment in the rhetorical study of mathematics (Lakatos 1976; it would have irritated Lakatos and the Lakatosians to describe it as a "rhetorical study"). The conversation about the Descartes-Euler theorem on polyhedra witnessed many correct but contradictory proofs, though a purely modernist line would demand only one. As the Teacher in Lakatos's dialogue says, "Proofs, even though they may not prove, certainly do help to improve our conjecture" (Lakatos 1976, p. 37). Muth's demonstrations do not "prove" the theorem of rational expectations in any final, ultimate, modernist sense, any more than Euler's proved his theorem: they illuminate it and improve it, with an audience in mind.

In Latin literature the example is a striking new understanding of the arrangement of poetry books in the late republic and early empire. Helena R. Dettmer (1983 and later works) has discovered that the poets arranged their books with methodical care (one might say rationally), going so far as to impose numerical patterns on the sums of lines in corresponding sections. Her treatise on the structure of Horace's *Odes*, for instance, discovers in them an immense structure of nested rings, linking poems hundreds of lines distant from each other. *Odes* 1.1 corresponds (as has long been known) to *Odes* 3.30 in theme and meter, *Odes* 1.2 to *Odes* 3.29 in theme (as had not been suspected, significant though it is for understanding Horace's attitude to the peace-giver and liberty-taker Octavius Augustus Caesar). Likewise, 1.3 corresponds to 3.27 (a slight irregularity), 1.4 to 3.28, 1.5 to 3.26, and so on and on in dazzling and unsuspected symmetry.

Certain poems stand out by their tightness of symmetry in the arrangement as "structural," and for these Dettmer discovered dozens of astonishing arithmetical truths: the fourteen structural poems in the first half of the book have in sum (not individually) exactly the same number of lines as the fourteen corresponding ones in the second half (348 lines); the five structural poems on one side of the midpoint have in sum 124 lines, as do the five corresponding ones on the other side. As Dettmer says, difficult though it may be to believe, "The mathematical symmetry is highly significant because it furnishes clear and compelling evidence that all the structural poems have been identified" (1983, pp. 525, 531; note that Dettmer, with no training in statistics, here uses the word "significant" in exactly its statistical sense, as a low probability of rejecting the hypothesis of no symmetry if it were true).

Other Latin poets of late republican and early imperial times used similar artifice. In Catullus's little book, for example, Dettmer has discovered a series of numerical theorems no less astonishing than Euler's and more precise than Muth's (Dettmer 1984a). Divide the middle (long) poems on the basis of theme and evident verbal echoes into sets labeled A (which is poem 64), B (poems 61 and 62), B' (68a and 68b), A' (65 and 66), C (63), and C' (67). Note a lemma (which, like Euler's algebra, Stanley's cropping theory, and Muth's rationality, "yields other results that are also verified") that Roman poets arranged their poetry in balanced rings, as Dettmer has shown to be true of Horace, Vergil, Propertius, Ovid, and others. Signify the number of lines in a section by its letter. THEOREM: A - B + A' - B' = C + C'

It takes the breath away. You can believe almost anything about π, precambrian organisms, or hog farmers, but had imagined that poets were of different stuff. This and many scores of other instances detailed by Dettmer change the conception of Latin poets, increasing admiration for their artfulness, if not their art. The embedding of the poetry in verified structures can resolve numerous textual and interpretative doubts, from the validity of the conjecture *"o patrona virgo"* in line 9 of *"Cui domo lepidum novum libellum"* to the understanding of how the Romans thought.

What is chiefly important here is the character of the argument. Dettmer's book on Horace is 550 pages long and assesses methodically hundreds upon hundreds of verbal echoes and thematic clues, embedding them in the two-thousand-year-old conversation of scholarship about Horace. It is wholly "scientific" if the word means "precise, numerical, thorough, crushingly persuasive." Dettmer realizes that she will have trouble making the numerical symmetries believable to many classicists, who identify as dogmatically with the literary side of the cultural chasm between literature and science as most economists identify with its mathematical side:

> Whether one likes numbers or not (and many do not), the fact remains that they exist. It is true that numbers and their implications, the [poet indulging in] addition or deletion of verses to make patterns, do indeed destroy our romantic illusions of a poet posed with stilus and wax tablet sitting beneath a spreading plane tree, invoking the Muse for inspiration. [But numerical patterns] furnish an invaluable tool for the literary critic. (Dettmer 1983, pp. 7–8)

Their use can be denied only by an epistemological theory that forbids numerical figures of speech in the study of poetry. The official epistemology gets in the way of the science. Few classicists have understood or believed Dettmer's work, though she has by now demonstrated overwhelmingly that similar structures appear in the books of Catullus and other Latin poets. Her discovery is in her own field comparable to genetics or plate tectonics, yet most classicists have never heard of it. That Dettmer is right does her no good in a rhetorical community in which people can get away with dismissing numbers because they are not words. Similarly, on epistemological grounds economists like Muth deny official status to arguments from introspection and authority, and dismiss words because they are not numbers.

Dettmer's scientific precision, though expressed more in "numbers" than most, is characteristic of the best classical scholarship. Steele Commager in "Notes on Some Poems of Catullus" (1965) or Ronald Syme on "Piso and Veranius in Catullus" (1956) argue in a similarly exact way. They argue, to be sure, about literary and historical matters, such as the impression that a certain line of poetry makes in view of the linguistic evidence on usage in republican Rome or the identity of a certain governor of Macedonia in 60–59 B.C. in view of the political evidence on families and parties. But in their use of figures of speech they might as well be arguing about the usages of hog farmers in A.D. 1950 or the identity of a herbivore in 600,000,000 B.C. Subjects do not entail epistemologies. If "science" means "indubitable," then there is no science in science. If it means "very persuasive," then much clear and honest thinking is scientific.

The contrary notion, shared by literary and scientific modernists, is that only certain subjects can be scientific, and that their study will always depend on certain invariant figures of speech. Modernist methodism, exhibited in Muth's paper, asserts that only experiment, statistical procedures, or axiomatization are "scientific."

Methodism infects classical textual criticism, too, and is as unhelpful there as it is in economics. One methodological rule in textual criticism, for example, embodied in various Latin maxims, is to honor the text. Every surviving manuscript of Macrobius's *Saturnalia* 1.6, line 14, speaking of an article of clothing, reads *totam*. A thoughtless scientism, of the sort that measures regardless or axiomatizes regardless, would therefore resist the emendation *togam*, the well-known article of male clothing, even though this other, alleged *totam* would be the sole occurrence of such a word in Latin literature (James Willis 1972, p. 7, who is eloquent on the point).

Such voluntary imbecility in the application of rules of methodology infuriated the poet and textual critic A. E. Housman. On the rule that "The More Sincere Text Is the Better" (even if erroneous and senseless), he wrote,

> The best way to treat such pretentious inanities is to transfer them from the sphere of textual criticism . . . into some sphere where men are compelled to use concrete and sensuous terms, which force them, however reluctantly, to think. I ask him to tell me which weighs most, a tall man or a fat man. *Tall* and *fat* are adjectives that transport even a textual critic from the world of

humbug into the world of reality, a world inhabited by
comparatively thoughtful people, such as butchers, grocers, who
depend on their brains for their bread. (Housman 1922, p. 1063)

The best way to treat such pretentious inanities as that economics is distinct from other fields by virtue of a unique methodology is to translate
them into comparatively concrete and sensuous terms. Which is the
more persuasive evidence, a correlation coefficient of .90 or an uncontroversial piece of introspection? A rule of methodology claims to say,
in general. But there is no point in knowing such a thing in general. An
economist does not do economics in general. She does it in particular.
Surely if she does it well she uses particular figures of speech from the
common store.

THE PROBLEM OF AUDIENCE

IN HISTORICAL ECONOMICS

ROBERT FOGEL AS RHETOR

Classically and properly, to repeat, rhetoric is critical inquiry, not merely "giving effectiveness to truth but . . . creating truth" (Scott 1967, p. 9). The writing of history has a rhetoric (Hexter 1971; White 1973; Novick 1988), no small matter: it limits the historian in what sorts of evidence and what sorts of logical appeals she can make if she wishes to retain an audience. And economic history has a rhetoric, too.

The Text Was Important

Railroads and American Economic Growth, published in 1964, was a revised version of Robert Fogel's Ph.D. dissertation in economics at Johns Hopkins. It is relevant to the book's rhetoric that Fogel had started the advanced study of economics late, at thirty years of age, after a youth devoted to radical politics. By his own account the events of 1956, a year of rethinking by the left, turned him toward the academic as against the political study of economic-historical problems. The book was his second: he had published his M.A. thesis from Columbia as *The Union Pacific Railroad: A Case in Premature Enterprise* (1960). He was by 1964 well known among "cliometricians," a then-tiny band of economists such as Brinley Thomas, Alexander Gerschenkron, Anna Schwartz, Walt Rostow, Robert Gallman, Douglass North, William Parker, Lance Davis, and J. R. T. Hughes attempting to reinvent economic history as economics. His 1964 book made him more widely known to historians and economists, although the center of its argument had already stirred specialists in economic history at conferences and had been published by itself two years before (Fogel 1962). What stirred them was its powerfully argumentative form and its startling conclusion: that railroads did not have very much to do with American economic growth.

The conclusion was in the air. Albert Fishlow published the next year his own Ph.D. dissertation, from Harvard, which made a point for the 1850s very similar to the one Fogel made for his year, 1890. The simultaneous discovery came from a simultaneous stimulus, namely, Rostow's claim a few years earlier that railroads had begun America's "take-off into self-sustained growth." Fogel wrote his dissertation under the premier student of national income, Simon Kuznets, and began the study, as can be seen from his preliminary thesis proposal, expecting Rostow's enthusiasm for the railroads to be confirmed. It was not, and Fogel turned to attacking it.

To an audience of a certain kind of professional economist the point of Fogel's book comes down to a three-line proof:

1. Railroads are supposed to have been a large factor in American growth.
2. From the railroad, canal, and wagon rates for transportation, however, you can see that railroads were about half as costly as the alternatives and carried half the transport; further, transport is 10 percent of national income.
3. If Adam Smith is in heaven and all is right with the world, then a 50 percent cost saving times a 50 percent of transport times a 10 percent of national income equals 2.5 percent of national income, no large factor.

The three-line proof of smallness (known to some economists as Harberger's Law) was crafted in virtually this form by Peter McClelland (1975) to apply to the economic history of the Navigation Acts, and it has become a cliometric routine. For example, Gary Hawke's replication of Fogel's calculation for England and Wales in 1865 also gives the three-line proof (1970, p. 173).

Fishlow's book made effectively the same point, was better written than Fogel's, used techniques of persuasion more familiar to historians, and was reviewed more genially, yet was in the end less influential. Fogel's novelty of argumentative form attracted the attention of the young and the anger of the old. The attention and anger inspired methodological declarations and denunciations, and in 1993 the Nobel Prize.

Fogel's book is the archetype of "cliometrics." Through thirty years it has worn well and still inspires imitators and respectful critics. It was more than a methodological advance. The theme that one innovation cannot explain much of economic growth has converted many from romanticism about the Iron Horse or the Big Steel Mill.

The Problem of Audience in Historical Economics

Its argument was largely concentrated in a brilliant display in the first fifty pages of the book. The enemy is the "axiom of indispensability," that is, the notion that the railroad could not be dispensed with. The assault proceeds so: Fogel on pages 10 and 11 translates the axiom into an assertion that the coming of the railroad increased national income. He points out on page 12 that if there were good substitutes for the railroad then its coming might have increased income very little. A good substitute—say a canal—might still have required a big shift in the location of production, Denver declining and St. Louis rising. But if it was indeed a good substitute the impact on the whole would have been small.

On pages 19 and 20 he labels the increase of income from the railroad as against the next best alternative, the "social saving." On page 20 and in a long footnote he argues that forcing hypothetical canals to carry goods in the same pattern as on the railroads would make his measure an upper bound on the truth. That is, his measure of social saving would always have to be *higher* than the true but unmeasurable amount. By an argument *a fortiori*, then, if he finds the measured social saving from the railroad to be small, the true social saving would be smaller still. On pages 22, 23, and 24 he examines the substitutes for rail—namely, wagon and water—arguing that if water was widely feasible the social saving would be small. After a diversion into linear programming (p. 26), and another repetition of his *a fortiori* argument that his procedure gives a lower bound (p. 28), he turns to estimating the costs of water (pp. 44–47), breaking the cost into its parts. The costs of the higher stocks of grain and meat that would be required when the canal water froze in winter, for instance, is only a small amount (pp. 44–46). Page 47 modestly describes these ruminations as "casual," yet puts forward a sharp conclusion: on this score railroads increased national income by only 0.6 percent.

The figure relates to transport among the major regions of the nation, most particularly between the granary of the Midwest and the cities of the East and Europe. In Chapter 3 Fogel calculates the amount that was saved within the Midwest. It too was small. In Chapter 4 he argues (contra Rostow again) that the secondary effects of railroad construction were small, not large. In Chapter 5 he attacks in particular the Rostovian idea that the demand for railroad iron greatly stimulated the iron industry. Chapter 6, finally, is a concluding movement allegro, with crescendo and cymbal clash, drawing wide conclusions about the role of theory and statistics in history.

The core of the book is the first fifty pages: it was this exercise that most stimulated the imagination of imitators and most infuriated the critics. In a few pages Fogel showed to the satisfaction of some that the railroad did not dominate American economic growth, and to the satisfaction of most that the question needed rather more study than was earlier believed. It is a characteristic bit of Fogeliana, and of cliometrica.

It Is a Most Rhetorical Book

Fogel's rhetoric is unusually aware of itself as rhetoric. The prose has above all force: no urbane indirection here; just bang, bang, bang. It announces its purpose repeatedly, signaling the use of this or that argumentative form. "The implicit assertion" is one thing; the "crucial aspect" is another; such and such "is beyond dispute"; "but the axiom is not primarily about" X, "it is about" Y; and "if the axiom ... merely asserted" Z "there would be no reason to question it." These remarks *about* the argument and its enemies occur in one paragraph on page 10. Right to the last the arguments keep this self-referential character: the author's calculation is "casual" and "subject to considerable error," a self-deprecating description (compare Solow's irony) which readies the reader to believe that "there are grounds for having confidence in the result" (p. 47); the estimates "may be too low," but even if they were raised, they would not amount to much; "indeed"—an argumentative word itself, like "in fact" or "nonetheless"—even an absurdly generous concession to the opposition leaves the estimate low.

The heavily rhetorical rhetoric of the book on railroads inaugurated a new style of economic history, a forensic style that has become important in cliometrics. The book made it fashionable and persuasive in economic history to use the argument *a fortiori* (itself an aggressive rhetorical figure), to which Fogel returns again and again. Along with this self-consciously methodological innovation came a style more suited to the courtroom than to the study, and widely imitated by younger scholars.

Fogel brought to American economic history, a distinctly right-wing and *goyisch* field, the traditions of flamboyantly Talmudic disputation characteristic of New York Jewish intellectuals, especially left-wing intellectuals. The combination of a somewhat heated tone and the methodical treatment of every imaginable point—known anciently as *indignatio, diasyrmus, digestion,* and *diallage*—was invented by Marx himself and attached by him to self-conscious scientism. In the 1940s you see it in the cases prepared by labor union intellectuals about such mundanities as the construction of cost-of-living indices—pieces of science, but tough, disputatious, lawyerly science. So in Fogel.

Fogel wears the garb of Scientist self-consciously. All his methodological papers have promoted what he calls scientific history, though he graciously sees merit in other kinds (cf. Fogel and Elton 1983, pp. 65–70). The language of his book, like Muth's paper, is filled with scientisms: "the hypothesis can now be stated" (Fogel 1964, p. 19) and "tested" (p. 22); "the objective standard for testing the hypothesis stated above" is X (p. 20); we have, in a properly scientific way, some "estimates" (p. 22 and throughout), an "inference" (p. 22), "available evidence" (p. 22), an "order of magnitude" (p. 23), a "method" requiring "the following data" (p. 26), and so forth. The talk of hypothesis-testing uses words appropriate to rolling balls down inclined planes (or, it would seem, claiming to have rolled balls down inclined planes without actually having done so). The appeal is "I am a Scientist: give way."

Fogel addresses audiences that have two different notions of what constitutes good scholarly character, economists and historians. The appeal to the Scientist has some force to both, or to anyone participating in our science-loving civilization. Fogel appeals to historians in particular with his conspicuously displayed mastery of government documents and trade publications relevant to railroads, no trivial feat (see his pp. 44–45 nn. 53, 55). The soothing words of caretaking that he sprinkles around each number are part of an ethical appeal to the character of an historical scholar: "the preceding argument is based on a [merely] hypothetical case" (p. 12); "the calculation is very crude" (p. 23); the estimate is "subject to considerable error" (p. 47). Some historians are suspicious of numbers and are pleased to be told of their frailties. All are impressed by scrutiny of the methods used to construct them, which Fogel delivers in quantity. The sheer length of the book is an ethical appeal in historical circles.

But Fogel mainly appeals to economists, presenting the ethos of the Sharp Economist. Economic history in 1964 was on the defensive in American Departments of Economics, dismissed as antique by the new technocrats strutting about the camp in their gleaming armor (they hadn't yet done any fighting in it and hadn't therefore discovered that it didn't cover much). It was essential that young economic historians prove themselves technically able. Fogel repeatedly displays the brightness of his economic armory. On page 44, for instance, he expresses false doubt (*aporia* in Greek rhetorical terminology) that the value of time lost in winter on waterways can be calculated. Then he shows elegantly and quickly in the next two paragraphs how it in fact can. The most bizarre case is the proposal to apply to the problem of simulating a counterfactual system of canals "a relatively new mathematical technique—linear programming" (p. 26; the technique was some twenty years old at the time). The proposal is made, discussed as a proposal for two pages, then suddenly and permanently dropped without any calculations, having served its function of establishing the scientific ethos of the writer. His rhetoricity irritates, undermining the ethos he seeks to portray by an excess of enthusiasm. Irony, distance, humor: these work better, though not always in making a new field.

It Uses Intensively the Common Topics

Take two pages or so of Fogel's book and compare them sentence by sentence with a list of the classical figures of rhetoric. The pages 10–12 are chosen to match the length of the selection from Muth, to draw a contrast in their rhetorical richness. They are the two most important pages in the book, arguing for its central point in a preliminary way, before the empirical work to follow. The list against which Fogel is compared appears in Lanham 1991. Of the classically recognized figures of speech, Fogel uses in these two pages nearly twenty:

- The whole is *diallage*, the piling up of arguments on one point, the point being that what matters is how good the substitutes for railroads were. Within his diallage he uses these:
- Repeatedly, *paramologia*, that is, conceding a minor point the better to achieve a larger: "If the axiom of indispensability merely asserted [X] . . . there would be no reason to question it" (first paragraph). "Although the evidence demonstrating that the eruption of a boom psychology . . . is considerable . . ." (third paragraph). "Even the demonstration that railroads produced effects that were both unique and important" (fourth paragraph). The concession is part of his most characteristic rhetorical figure, in which he says, in effect, "Even if I concede to my opponents such-and-such a point, my argument wins."
- Repeatedly, he draws attention to what he claims is the important aspect of a case. At the end of the first paragraph, the importance of substitution is emphasized by the figure of *anaphora* at the beginning of the next sentence: "The crucial aspect . . . The crucial aspect." The two alternative expressions of the same idea are repeated for effect: *commoratio*. Each of the two sentences has internally a strongly parallel structure, balancing the phrases in the first sentence *(isocolon)*, leaving off phrases in the second *(ellipsis,* as this sentence left off the second occurrence of "sentence"). The beginning of the second paragraph repeats the point again; the second sentence still again: four repetitions of the point in different words *(tautologia)*, bordering on *pleonasm*. But it is the main point

of the book, and one difficult for much of his implied audience to grasp. If any point warranted emphasis, this one—*a fortiori*—did. The third and fourth paragraphs draw attention to the central point by attacking its alternatives, that is to say, alternative definitions of what it might mean for railroads to have been "indispensable": the figure is *apophasis*, the orderly rejection of all the alternatives except one.

- Repeatedly, he disparages opposing arguments *(diasyrmus)*—a technique so obviously forensic that historians use it gingerly if at all. Fogel, with other economists, has no such scruples. In the second half of the second paragraph, for instance, he is scandalized by the lack of scientific evidence concerning the allegedly unique contribution of the railroad. You can see the indignation by examining the words that impart it: "almost exclusively"; "systematic"; "virtually"; "questionable"; "rather than on demonstrated fact." In the fourth paragraph (p. 11), again, he adopts an ironic tone to disparage the indispensability of block signals and track walkers, by *reductio ad absurdum.*

- Repeatedly, he notes the absence of decisive evidence. He appeals again to the ideally modernist historian/scientist, who does not carry an umbrella without a scientifically certified prediction of light rain. The "evidence" so often mentioned is quantitative. The figure is therefore a modern one, little used in the nonquantitative civilization that thought most carefully about the means of persuasion.

- A derivative of the modernist enthusiasm for properly modernist evidence is the figure in the third paragraph (pp. 10f.): "No evidence has been supplied. And it is doubtful such evidence can be supplied" (note the parallel construction). This is one of the common topics of modern intellectual life, carrying conviction among all who pretend to intellectuality. The example at the end of page 11 is simulation (a Fogelian favorite, occurring throughout, as at pp. 23, 24, and 47), one of the special topics in economics and in other quantitative subjects. These carry conviction only among experts.

One can fit the argument of a paper like Muth's much less readily than Fogel's into the classical categories. Muth, with most economists, seems seldom able to carry a rhetorical turn to its conclusion. He says, "It is rather surprising that X is so," but this promising beginning of a good old-fashioned bout of ironic *thaumasmus* (expression of wonder), which Fogel would have teased out to a paragraph, is immediately abandoned in favor of an appeal to "theoretical reasons." They turn out in the next sentence to be appeals to aesthetic standards, Ockham's razor in particular. And in the next the American Question is asked. The argument is *ad hominem*, that is to say, suitable only for persuading economists, by their very character. But Muth drops quickly even this use of the common topics crucial to his case: he indulges in no fourfold repetition and elaboration, no *commoratio, tautologia,* or *apophasis* here.

What divides the rhetoric of Fogel from the mainstream of economics is Fogel's heavy use of the standard issue, *common* topics of argument. Using these heavily will inspire a charge of "mere rhetoric," such as Fogel faced for his trouble; by contrast, using mainly the uncommon, *special* topics that appeal mainly to economists or historians will inspire a commendation for eschewing mere rhetoric, the rhetoric disappearing from view behind the mask of the economic or historical Scientist.

By far the most important of Fogel's rich array of common topics was his argument from lower or upper bounds. The book consists of an attempt to find the least upper bound on the benefit from railroads. If the upper bound is small, *a fortiori* the true effect is small. He draws on the argument very frequently (for instance, on pp. 20, 23, 28, 45, and 47), biasing the case against himself. The argument is widely used. Rogue Riderhood in *Our Mutual Friend,* for instance, used it in attempting to frame Gaffer Hexam by perjured affidavit: "He says to me, 'Rogue Riderhood, you are a man in a dozen'—I think he said in a score, but of that I am not positive, so take the lower figure, for precious be the obligation of an Alfred David" (an affidavit; thanks to Barry Supple for the quotation).

Technically speaking, the argument from upper and lower bounds combines elements of *paramologia* (conceding a smaller point to gain a larger) and the argument *a fortiori*:

a. *Paramologia:* Even if I admit as influencing the True magnitude a factor X, which runs against my case, the case that the Truth is small is true.

b. *Least upper bound:* Even if I take a very large overestimate, call it Erroneous, of the Truth, Erroneous is small, and therefore the Truth is bound to be small.

c. *A fortiori:* The estimate Erroneous is bound to be larger than the Truth; Erroneous is small; all the more reason to believe *(a fortiori)* that the Truth is small.

In other words, the figure of speech here *(paramologia)* is a version of a much-used mathematical figure; the mathematical figure is a version of a much-used figure of reasoning.

Fogel's use of such figures of speech and reasoning led many graduate students to take up careers of under- and overestimating things. The usual rhetoric of history in such matters (and of economics, though less prominently displayed) demands "accuracy." An estimate of the population of fifth-century Athens must be "accurate"; a description of the American economy as competitive is to be judged for "accuracy." A physicist would attest that the word is meaningless without bounds on the error; and a literary critic would attest that the accuracy necessary to the argument depends on the conversational context. There is no absolute sense of "accuracy," as Oskar Morgenstern once argued to economists in a neglected classic drawing on the rhetoric of applied mathematics, *On the Accuracy of Economic Observations* (1963).

The Book Also Uses the Special Topics of Economics

Fogel's contribution to economic method, then, is classically rhetorical, drawing on the common topics. But of course, like any economist—indeed, partly to make the ethical appeal that he was like any other economist—Fogel used also the special topics of economic discourse. Special topics are potted thoughts for specialists, ready in the storeroom marked "Economists Only" to be used prettily for some argumentative purpose. The common topic appeals to reasons that most people can appreciate; the special topic to reasons only the specialist can. Fogel speaks for example on page 11 of the "opportunity to profit from unexpected changes in the value of land" consequent on an improvement in transportation. An historian reading this, unless a genius of untutored perspicacity like Frederick Maitland or Marc Bloch, is unlikely to realize that profits in the sense of capital gains must be unexpected if they are to exist. Few without training in economics will realize that if a rise in land values is widely expected it is no longer an opportunity for profit, because the value of the land will have risen already. The force of the word "unexpected" escapes the noneconomist entirely. Here Fogel is speaking to his economist colleagues, as though in an aside.

Again, he speaks on page 10 of the "incremental contribution over the next best alternative." To an economist the phrase is familiar poetry, bringing to mind an apparatus of thought in handsome graphs. He accedes to the metaphor. The noneconomist, on the other hand, does not understand why the "next best alternative" would be especially relevant. Even if he understands it, to believe it he needs to believe that people do things for good reasons. But the noneconomist believes he knows they often do not: he can easily believe they would sometimes pick walking, or carts, rather than the relatively more efficient canals if deprived of their beloved railroads. And "incremental" is equally foreign to a noneconomist's way of thinking, which sees the railroad as immense and lumpy, no "increment" at all. The special topics evoke special responses in the economist.

The opportunity cost of enchanting one's fellow economists is alienating noneconomists. There is no such thing as a free argument. A desire to speak to economists explains the sudden turn of the argument at the top of page 13, a pretty pirouette. Fogel speaks to historians when patiently explaining just before the turn why manipulations of rates by railroads did not necessarily cause a loss of income to the whole nation. The economist asks, But what if the manipulation leads to monopoly? Another economist shoots back (dropping Schumpeter's name: *commemoratio*), Monopoly can be good for you. Speculation is met with counterspeculation.

Some of the special topics are so special that they are not topics. That is, they are not intelligible even to most economists on first reading. If repeated enough in a scholarly conversation they would take on a topical character. Fogel anticipates criticism and wards it off with many such cryptic little arguments (the figure is *procatalepsis*). A comparatively lengthy example is the talk without evidence in paragraph 16 about the marginal cost of canals. Canals have to be able to take easily the extra burden imposed on them in Fogel's counterfactual world without railroads. "The available data" is supposed to imply that they could take it easily. The "data" turns out to be unelaborated common knowledge, but seeing the implications of the common knowledge in this case is not easy even for an economist.

Another argument forestalling criticism is embodied in a dependent clause on page 12: "given the historical stability of the aggregate saving and capital-output ratio." Like the argument about the marginal cost of canals, it later grew into a substantial literature. Both have to do with the three-line proof of the small social saving of railroads. The alleged fact of stability in the savings rate was announced by Fogel's mentor, Simon Kuznets. Fogel claims implicitly here that if true (it is not if human capital is included), it parries a possible thrust. The thrust was delivered some years later by Jeffrey Williamson, who argued that the railroad caused a big rise in savings rates. Williamson's argument fails if during the coming of railroads the savings rates did not in fact rise.

Fogel crams a good deal of economics into each page, more than is usual even in densely argued theoretical works.

The Text Invented an Audience

The talk of special and general topics presupposes a division in the audience between specialist and generalist. Rhetoric emphasizes the audience. The writer does more than merely choose an audience from the existing population: in his mind's eye, or his writing's tone, the readers become not merely his choice but his creation. The idea is that of Kenneth Burke, Walker Gibson, Wayne Booth, Louise Rosenblatt, and other exponents of rhetorical criticism (Burke 1950; Gibson 1950; Booth 1961, p. 138; Booth 1974b; Booth 1979, pp. 268ff.; Rosenblatt 1978). The author of *Emma*, to take Booth's favorite example, creates an authorial persona, an "implied author," who speaks to another of her creations, the "implied reader." The actual reader must adopt the role of the implied reader if he is to enjoy or believe the book (see Figure 2). The author's domain is everything within the lines. The reader comes along for the ride: the actual readers "assume, for the sake of the experience, that set of attitudes and qualities which the language asks us to assume." "A bad book," continues Walker Gibson, "is a book in whose mock reader we discover a person we refuse to become, a mask we refuse to put on, a role we will not play" (Gibson 1950, pp. 1, 5). The implied author in this little drama, of course, has the floor. He delivers an oration to the implied reader. That's why it is a matter of rhetoric.

Actual Author	Jane Austen; Robert Fogel
Actual Reader	Wayne Booth; Deirdre McCloskey
Implied Author	A perfectly witty and perceptive Austen; a perfectly scientific and historical Fogel
Implied Reader	A cultivated listener c. 1810; a counterfactual cliometrician c. 1964

Figure 2. The Author Creates an Implied Reader and an Implied Author

Fogel would seem to require two implied readers, both close to contradictions in terms, the historically interested economist and the economically sophisticated historian. Fields under dispute between two methods, as American economic history was during the 1960s, cannot have one reader. Yet much writing, Fogel's included, presupposes one alone, able to appreciate every nuanced remark about fixed capital/ output ratios or the wisdom of the Joint Traffic Association, *Proceedings of the Board of Managers,* 1896. At the time Fogel wrote there were few actual readers who could take on the role of his ideal implied reader.

But the excellence of his work, and the work of other pioneers, created in time actual ideal readers for Fogel's books, the cliometric movement. Fogel was an orator setting up his soapbox in Hyde Park, gathering after a while a crowd capable of appreciating his speech. This is how scholarly discourse changes: the crowd gathers bit by bit around a different orator with a different implied audience. The audience is not so much selected as trained, trained by repeated attempts to imagine itself as the implied reader. Something of the sort seems to have occurred in modern mathematics. Hilbert's program of formal rigor has been pushed so far that some present-day mathematicians only understand formal rigor of a Hilbertian sort. An audience of such mathematicians is merely puzzled, even confused, by attempts to give physical or other motivation to mathematical argument. An audience deaf to certain forms of talk has been assembled.

Fogel created an implied reader more definite than merely a generalized historical economist. His reader is an earnest fellow, much impressed by science, in love with figures and the bottom line, a little stubborn in his convictions but open to argument and patient with its details. Such an implied reader is less attractive than the more common one in successful academic prose. Albert Fishlow's book, by contrast, creates an implied reader more distant and disengaged, one sensitive to ironies, amused by verbal rotundities, impatient with closely argued economics but very patient indeed with narrative indirection. It is something like the implied reader of the best history.

Fogel, though well aware that to the right audience his point could be made in three lines, felt it necessary to write nine thousand more. The three-line proof draws on all the peculiarities of the implied reader of modern economics. It translates a literary remark about the indispensability of railroads into algebra, then draws on the logic of markets to make the simplest available inference. Fogel gives it on page 11, repeating it in a slightly different form on pages 23 (where he states the opposite case the better to knock it down: *exadversio)* and 24. But it could not persuade the reader Fogel wished to create, and whom by his eloquence he did in time create.

Fogel, then, accomplished a good deal with his rhetoric. Style, the genre, the audience, are not "mere matters of form." Hayden White remarks that "the link between a given historian and his potential public is forged on the pretheoretical, and specifically linguistic, level of consciousness" (1973, p. 429). Amelie Oksenberg Rorty again said it well. In economic scholarship, as in philosophical scholarship, it is a good part (not all) of the substance:

> Conviction is often carried by a charismatic, authoritative style:
> its clarity and condensation, the rhythms of its sentences, and

> its explosive imagery. But often the form of a work assures its
> legitimation: a dedication indicating continuity of descent, a *nihil
> obstat*, the laying on of hands by footnotes acknowledging the
> advice of established authorities, the imprimatur of publication
> by a major university press. The apparatus of footnotes,
> appendixes, graphs, diagrams, formulas, used with measure
> and discretion, indicate a proper sobriety. Sobriety, attention to
> detail, care without obsession, the right balance of generality
> and attention, an easy rather than a relentless use of imagery
> and metaphor—these are integral to philosophical legitimation.
> (Rorty 1983, p. 546)

Fogel was doing more than working within an existing scholarly genre
and existing audiences. He made new ones.

William Robinson remarked long ago, in *Forensic Oratory: A Manual for
Advocates:* "Every oration is in reality a dialogue, in which the doubts
and objections of the auditor are so many silent interrogatories to
which the orator audibly replies" (1893, p. 29). It is sometimes a new
style of conversation, a new way of speaking. Fogel (to use a distinction
drawn by Roland Barthes) was an author rather than a writer, a creator
of a new genre, a Max Planck or a Gerard Manley Hopkins, an author
of a new way of conversing rather than a user of a preexisting genre.
Even the science of the counting house and the railroad station draws
on the rhetoric of poets and mathematicians.

6 THE LAWYERLY RHETORIC

OF COASE'S "THE NATURE

OF THE FIRM"

Coase Solved His Problem of Ethos
by Appeal to Axiom and Proof

An author, twenty-seven years old in 1937, of an essay called imposingly "The Nature of the Firm," an author who had not published a line when he drafted the article (early summer 1934; see Coase 1988c, p. 19; it was based closely on a lecture he gave in October 1932, at age twenty-one), "a young man who knew virtually no economics" (Coase 1988d, p. 35), had a problem. The problem was to establish in the reader's mind a character worth listening to. In 1960, by contrast, forty-nine years old and well-known if not yet famous in economics, he had no such problem, and could start in a more offhand, self-deprecating way, using even the deadly beginning "This paper": "This paper is concerned with those actions of business firms which have harmful effects on others" (Coase 1960, p. 95).

For his exordium Ronald Coase declared that "Economic theory has suffered in the past from a failure to state clearly its assumptions" (Coase 1937, p. 32). He was drawing on the rhetoric of axiomatization, the French claim since Descartes that we know what we mean only if we know what axioms we have started with. Such claims were helpful for a young economist even in 1937, and have since become compulsory. Coase acknowledged with a citation to Nicholas Kaldor (among appeals in the paragraph to the authority of five other well-known economists) "a trend in economic theory towards starting analysis with the individual firm and not with the industry" (Coase 1937, p. 32), a tendency pronounced in Hicks's *Value and Capital* (1939) and brought to perfection as the main method of economics by Paul Samuelson. Assume a maximizing individual self-aware of his constraints and tastes, and proceed. You will then know what you mean. Many economists cannot now understand an argument unless it is expressed axiomatically.

But Coase did not in the article or in his later work actually carry out the Cartesian program of his exordium. In the event, his was a British, empirical, and nonmathematical approach, altogether scrappier and less formal. He got into economics, he has said, through courses in "works and factory management" in 1930–1931, "for which I was singularly ill-suited, but what else was there for someone to do who did not know Latin and did not like mathematics?" (Coase 1988b, p. 5; at Coase 1998d, p. 45, he remarks, "fortunately for me, 1932 saw the height of the Depression, there were no jobs in industry, and I went to Dundee [School of Economics and Commerce] and became an economist"). Coase has never been an economist in the Samuelsonian mode, in love with rigor of a mathematical kind. He was as enthusiastic as any young economist in the 1930s about the new apparatus, which "has the advantage that one could cover the blackboard with diagrams [later with equations] and fill the hour in one's lectures without the need to find out anything about what happened in the real world" (Coase 1988c, p. 22). But he outgrew it. When George Stigler started in the 1960s calling his misunderstanding of one of Coase's propositions in the celebrated article of 1960 "Coase's Theorem," Paul Samuelson snorted, "Where's the theorem"? Where is the axiom system from which an if-then statement can be rigorously derived, the only way of knowing what we mean? Not in "The Problem of Social Cost," nor in "The Nature of the Firm."[1]

Coase also speaks the language of highbrow economic science, establishing an ethos worth believing, when late in the paper he ponderously generalizes: "Other things being equal, therefore, a firm will tend

1. I should mention my longstanding conviction that the misnamed "Coase's Theorem" (it is Smith's or Edgeworth's or Arrow-Debreu's Theorem, misnamed by that fine student of economic thought, George Stigler) is not the point of Coase's article in 1960 (see McCloskey 1985, pp. 335–40; and the full argument in McCloskey 1997b). The article was *not* meant to show that we live already in the best of all possible worlds (as Stigler was inclined to assume in this and other cases) but, on the contrary, that if we did live in such a world there would of course be no need for policy, as economists have been pointing out since Smith. In fact, as Coase argued also in the 1937 article, transaction costs put our world far away from the blackboard optimum. But I have given up hope of persuading any other economist of this interpretation, since the only economist who shares it is R. H. Coase (Coase 1988a, pp. 15, 174), and we know how unpersuasive he has been. Coase's chief contribution to economics has been to remind economists, as he does when complaining about Kaldor assuming "all relevant prices" are known, "but this is clearly not true of the real world" (Coase 1937, p. 38n. 18). The misunderstanding of the Coase Theorem arises from economists thinking that Coase is trying, like them, to flee the world.

to be larger: (a.) the less the costs of organzing" and so forth. The "other things being equal," "therefore," and "tend" are careful and conventional boilerplate in the contract between reader and economic Scientist. When claiming the ethos of Scientist the young Coase was especially fond of "tend to," the phrase becoming virtual anaphora on p. 46 (Coase 1937), repeated in all six of the complete sentences on the page and once in the footnotes.

Such a treatise-rhetoric was popular in economics at the time. Likewise Coase indulged in outlining, anticipation, and summary, the curse of modern prose, borrowed from the Germanic textbooks of an earlier age: phrases like "The point has been made in the previous paragraph" (Coase 1937, p. 44); "The problem which has been investigated in the previous section" (p. 47); "This point is further discussed below" (p. 51n. 41); and "The factors mentioned above" (p. 53) litter the essay. Economics had developed a rhetoric of close outlining, treatise-like, the better to win the victory on the blackboard, which may be seen in works like Marshall's *Principles* (1920) or in its most tedious form in Irving Fisher's *The Theory of Interest* (1930): "First Summary," "Introduction," "The Theory in Words," "The Theory in Mathematics," "Further Discussion," "Second Summary," "The Theory in Words," "The Theory in Mathematics," . . . "First Approximation in Geometric Terms," "Second Approximation in Geometric Terms," "Third Approximation," and so forth (Fisher 1930, pp. xiii–xiv). Economists regard Fisher's great but unreadable book as a masterpiece of exposition, which is a measure of the discipline's understanding of exposition.

But Coase Was an Advocate, Not a Prover

Coase's core rhetoric, however, as becomes apparent after a page or two, is not really Cartesian or Scientific or Treatise-like. It is lawyerly. That's the main point about Coasean rhetoric: it takes as much from the Law School as from the Department of Economics, and promises therefore a new style of economic science.

The paper reads like a brief. Unusually for an economist trained in the English-speaking world (it was commonplace on the Continent), Coase was immersed from the beginning in the study of the law. He testified that during his two years in residence as an undergraduate at the London School of Economics, 1929–1930, "I took no course in economics, and although some of the courses had an economic content, most did not. The courses to which I devoted the most time were those on law, particularly industrial law. I was fascinated by the cases and by legal reasoning" (1988b, p. 6). The lawyerly rhetoric was no youthful fancy. It has defined the Coasean approach.

One lawyerly feature of his rhetoric, for example, is its disputatiousness. Coase repeatedly and firmly rejects this or that line of argument, after thorough enumeration of the possibilities (called *diallage* in Greek rhetoric), as when he turns back the claims of Frank Knight (an economist similar to Coase in many ways), "But those [like Knight] . . . would appear to be introducing a point which is irrelevant to the problem" (Coase 1937, pp. 40–41). Or, "The reason given by [the Marxist] Maurice Dobb is therefore inadmissable" (p. 47). The essay is filled with such sharp disputation, usually with a name attached: "This is surely incorrect" (p. 50); "Austin Robinson's conclusion . . . would appear to be definitely wrong" (p. 51n. 44); and so forth. The definiteness cannot have endeared the young man to the establishment in British economics, skewered thus in lawyerly cross-examination.

The adversarial rhetoric shows in the details, such as Coase's fondness for starting sentences with "But." "But . . . why is such organization necessary?" (p. 35); "But this is clearly not true in the real world" (p. 38n. 18); "But he does not develop the idea" (p. 39n. 19); "But it is difficult to believe that it is measures such as those . . . which have brought firms into existence" (p. 41). Three more times on p. 44, twice on p. 50 contradicting Knight, twice in the paragraph beginning at the bottom of p. 51 contradicting Kaldor, Austin Robinson, and Joan Robinson. It shows too in the overuse of "not only . . . but" (an ornament of Latin origin, though Coase disclaims Latin: "*non solum . . . sed etiam*"), as twice in the first paragraph.

Another lawyerly habit is Coase's frequent appeals to political relevance, against the academic rhetoric by then typical of economics. In this he was not unusual. The waste of the 1930s had made many economists, and even many poets, politically alert. The alternative of socialism was always on their minds: the puzzle of planning can "be summed up in one word, Russia" (1988b, p. 8). Thus, "Those who object to economic planning on the grounds that the problem is solved by price movements can be answered by pointing out that there is planning within our economic system which is quite different from the individual planning mentioned above [by which he means 'individuals . . . exercise foresight and choose between alternatives' (p. 34)], and which is akin to what is normally called economic planning" (Coase 1937, p. 35).

Coase is an attorney of economics in the arrangement, too. He follows the model of forensic speech, the six parts of a classical oration (for which see Lanham 1991, p. 171). The *exordium* catches the reader's attention and is accomplished in his paper in the unnumbered paragraph preceding Section I. The *narratio* sets forth the facts and is followed by a *partitio* dividing controversial from uncontroverial propositions in explanation of the facts. Coase does both in Section I. The fact is the existence of the firm, which can be "explained" uncontroversially by positing an "entrepreneur" who organizes it (Coase 1937, p. 35). We must, however, narrow down the point of controversy to the "islands of conscious power in this ocean of unconscious co-operation like lumps of butter," in a memorable phrase of Dennis Robertson's, memorable mainly because Coase quoted it so aptly (p. 35). "The distinguishing mark of the firm is the supersession of the price mechanism" (p. 36). All right: Why supercede it? The answer is the *probatio*, the proof, given in the long Section II, ten pages out of twenty-two. The proposition is that "the main reason why it is profitable to establish a firm would seem to be that there is a cost of using the price mechanism" (p. 38). The proof imitates the rhetoric of law rather than that of mathematics except at the end, a peroration in the middle of an oration, which is expressed in the language of Scientific Law. In classical form, Sections III and IV constitute a *refutatio*, telling "why the reasons given above . . . are to be preferred to the other explanations," such as Knight's notion of "uncertainty" or the rising cost curve (p. 47, at the beginning of Section III). Section V is a *peroratio*, appealing briefly to the rhetoric of scientific test, and then claiming that the new way of looking at the firm is scientifically "manageable."

The peroration is in fact curiously muted, a British touch (thus the last paragraph of the two-page announcement of the discovery of DNA was devoted to thanking the sources of funding). The final sentence in the essay deprecates what has gone before: "But an elaboration of this point would take us far from our comparatively simple task of definition and clarification," the comparatively simple task of reorienting economics. A barrister might end her case so before the court of Queen's Bench; a French *avocat* or an American lawyer would not be able to resist the temptation to bluster.

The Lawyerly Rhetoric Appeals to the Facts

Another lawyerly (and British) feature of Coase's rhetoric is that facts or alleged facts of the world are repeatedly brought in to settle matters. You might imagine that economics would appeal to facts anyway, as a science. But economists are social philosophers as much as social historians, and have developed various rhetorical excuses to stay on the blackboard as long as possible. The mathematical economist Tjalling Koopmans argued in his influential tract *Three Essays on the State of Economic Science* (1957) for a program of research in economics of accumulating blackboard results strictly separated from facts, "for the protection of both. It recommends the postulational method [Descartes again] as the principal instrument by which this separation is secured" (p. viii). Economists will routinely claim that they have fewer facts to conjure with than do, say, physicists (the claim is false), and must therefore rely on postulation methods. Another mathematical economist, Gerhard Debreu, argued so in his presidential address to the American Economic Association. The physicists who economists imagine they are emulating do not care about postulational consistency, Debreu admitted, but economics is "denied a sufficiently secure experimental base," and therefore, "economic theory has had to adhere to the rules of logical discourse and must renounce the facility of internal inconsistency" and stay on the blackboard (Debreu 1991, p. 2).

Not Coase, who has inveighed often against "blackboard economics" (Coase 1988a, pp. 19, 28). Coase has been from the beginning of his career a keen visitor of economic sites, an astronomer of the business world, engaging for example in economic sociology in his trip to America in 1932 while he was wrestling with the theory of the firm: "I still remember one most instructive day spent in the office of a purchasing agent, I think Union Carbide, listening to his telephone conversation" (1988b, pp. 8–9). He quotes a letter he wrote to a friend at the time boasting that "I am quite a lawyer in my craftiness of putting questions. I can get admissions regarding costs out of [businesspeople] without them realizing that they have done so. . . . I can always get almost whatever I want" (1988b, p. 14). Coase, contrary to the method economists espouse, actually talked to businesspeople. Shocking, really. In 1932, "I confirmed that the risk [of exploitation of suppliers who had invested to supply one demander] was real by discussion with businessmen. . . . [But] I found that the problem worried me more than the businessmen who had to deal with it" (Coase 1988d, p. 44).

And again the mere diction in "The Nature of the Firm" shows the empirical lean. Coase for example favors the ugly phrase "the fact that," though in fact employing it usually to introduce a logical consideration, not a fact (Coase 1937, pp. 35, 37, 52). A Cartesian rhetoric would focus on consistencies and inconsistencies of logic in a strict sense, as economics has under Samuelson-Koopmans-Debreu. The frequency of Coase's appeal to facts is more lawyerly than it is late-twentieth-century economistic. The sentence, "In fact, nothing could be more diverse than the actual transactions which take place in our modern world" (Coase 1937, p. 45), is one that Paul Samuelson could not have written.

And a Scientific rhetoric would confine the facts, if any, to the end of the paper, as a Test of the Hypothesis. Coase's paper seems to have been influenced in this regard by a Scientific model, propounded by Lionel Robbins at the London School of Economics. As I have noted, Section V, the *peroratio*, announces itself as asking how the theory "fits in with . . . the real world" (Coase 1937, p. 53). The received arrangement of modern articles in economics is, first, many pages of Theory and then, after a long time, the Test, in imitation of what the economists conceive to be Scientific Method. Coase's turn here seems parallel. But the effect of the "fit" in Section V is odd, since the paper is filled from beginning to end in a lawyerly way with appeals to the world's facts. Again and again the appeal is to the "relevance" of arguments (p. 53: "The factors mentioned above would seem to be the relevant ones"). Coase does not here, or ever in his career, launch out into model space far from the gravity of the world's facts. (Half of the articles in the more prestigious journals in economics nowadays achieve escape velocity [Leontief 1982]; it is notable that in 1932 Coase visited Leontief, who had just emigrated from Russia, and discussed the problem of the firm with him [Coase 1988b, p. 12]). And his end-game "fitting" with the world takes the form of a long quotation from a law book, which would hardly seem a clincher in the quantitative rhetoric of economics now. The recognition that laws are evidence is one of the fruits of the law and economics movement. Such evidence has never fit well with the 3-by-5 card version of Scientific Method that economists carry about, according to which a mere word is a nullity and numbers alone constitute Tests.

Thus Coase rejects the notion that people might set up firms for the sheer pleasure of bossing by noting that bosses normally make more than their subordinates (that is, the bosses do not seem to be paying for their pleasures, as the hypothesis of sheer pleasure would lead one to expect) and that firms exist in places where the pleasures of bossing must be small (Coase 1937, p. 38 and p. 38n. 16; cf. p. 43n. 26). The argument is not logically or empirically decisive. It is no theorem, certainly, in a Samuelsonian sense. And it is not a knock-down Scientific Test. Businesspeople speak often of their pleasure in being the boss, saying that they collect the salary merely to keep score. Yet as one argument in a legal case for a transaction-cost theory of the firm, Coase's little argument is fine. As Aristotle put it, such arguments are "enthymemes," that is, incomplete syllogisms of the sort that all science and law depend on.

And Yet Coase Is Indubitably an Economist

The third part of classical rhetoric, after Style and Arrangement, is Invention, the finding of arguments. By contrast with his style and arrangement, Coase's art of invention is not lawyerly. It is thoroughly and unblinkingly economistic. If his style and arrangement puzzle economists, his invention puzzles lawyers. Puzzling people is not a good way to get readers. Coase was creating—with a lag, he notes, of "thirty or forty years" (Coase 1988d, p. 33)—a new audience that could appreciate a lawyerly style of respect for facts and disputation combined with an economistic choice of postulates. Like Fogel, he was, in the French word popular with literary critics, an *auteur*, a maker of new forms. Coase's implied audience of lawyerly economists or economistic lawyers did not exist in 1937.

What is so deeply economistic and unlawyerly about Coase's reasoning is its apparent turning away from the matter at hand in order to settle it by looking at the alternatives. It would be as though a lawyer defending a thief were to argue that after all the man could have been a murderer, too, and should therefore be given credit for his restraint. An economist looks always at the other possibilities in a world of imagination, the opportunity cost, the alternatives forgone by the action in question. If the young man writing a lecture on the firm in 1932 "knew virtually no economics" he knew this lesson better than many professors of the subject do. In his paper discussing the meaning of the article Coase admires some notes of his around 1934 where he examined the prevention of fraud as a reason for making a firm. He argues from alternatives forgone: "a wholesaler may specialize on [*sic*] discovering who are reliable . . . and thus by using him, a consuming firm may eliminate the effects of fraud. But it is a cost and may be eliminated . . . by integration," that is, by making the consuming firm and the supplying firm into one big firm (Coase 1988c, p. 30). This sort of reasoning is at the heart of "The Nature of the Firm."

The reasoning is counterfactual, in a way that lawyers and historians find unsettling but economists like Coase (and Fogel and Muth and the rest) think is the only way of thinking. A lawyer thinking about someone violating a contract looks for what Aristotle called "efficient" causes, the immediate gain to be had, for example. An economist will look for "final" causes, the ultimate purpose served by taking one road rather than another diverging in a yellow wood.

Coase's rhetoric, in short, is mixed and therefore disorienting, which explains the long lag between the publication of the article and its influence. Although in some ways a typical piece of 1930s economics, its rhetoric is quite lawyerly. Yet it was equally fervent in its devotion to economic reasoning (Coase attributes it to his teacher Arnold Plant: "I was the beneficiary of an extraordinary piece of luck" [Coase 1988b, p. 6], Plant's appointment to the London School of Economics in 1930). So Coase did not in 1937 have an audience of lawyers, either.

His Article Was about the Rhetoric in the Economy

There is another sense of the "rhetoric" of "The Nature of the Firm." Coase's work extends economics out into the world in which people speak to each other, that is, in which they practice rhetoric. Adam Smith, as usual, put the issue well two centuries ago. The division of labor, he wrote, is the "consequence of a certain propensity . . . to truck, barter, and exchange. . . . [I will not further consider] whether this propensity be one of those original principles in human nature . . . or whether, as seems more probable, it be the necessary consequence of the *faculties of reason and speech*" (1776, p. 17). *The Wealth of Nations* does not again mention the faculty of speech in a foundational role, though Smith, who began as a professor of rhetoric, did remark frequently on how business people and politicians talked. Half of his foundational formula, the faculty of reason, became in time the characteristic obsession of economists, though again Smith did not much pursue it. Economic Man is not a Smithian character. It was later economists, especially Paul Samuelson, who reduced economics to the reasoning of a constrained maximizer, Seeking Man. *Speaking* Man never figured much, by contrast, even among institutionalist economists. A man acted silently, by and for himself. That is what utility functions or institutions or social classes or property rights are about, said the economists before Coase. As Coase summarized it, "The consumer [in conventional economic theory] is not a human being but a consistent set of preferences. . . . We have consumers without humanity, firms without organization, and even exchange without markets" (1988a, p. 3). No need to speak.

Smith would not have agreed. In his other book he dug behind the faculty of speech (which led to the propensity to exchange, which led to the division of labor, which led to the wealth of nations). He connected it to persuasion, which is to say, speech meant to influence others: "The desire of being believed, the desire of persuading, of leading and directing other people, seems to be one of the strongest of all our natural desires. It is, perhaps, the instinct on which is founded the faculty of speech, the characteristic faculty of human nature" (1790, VII.iv.25, p. 336); Smith was the sort of writer who would have been well aware that he was using the same phrase here in *The Theory of Moral Sentiments* as he used in *The Wealth of Nations*.

The faculty of speech, so much the stock-in-trade of lawyers, is a mystery to economists. But it is a startlingly large part of economic activity and cannot continue to be ignored. Take the categories of employment and make an educated guess as to the percentage of time spent on persuasion in each category. The preliminary result (see Klamer and McCloskey 1995) is that 28.2 million out of 115 million civilian employees, or about a quarter of the labor force, is devoted to persuasion.

The result can be confirmed in other measures. Wallis and North measure 50 percent of national income as Coasean transaction costs, negotiation costs being part of these. Similarly, over half of American workers are white-collar. Some do not talk for a living, but in an extended sense many do, as for that matter do many blue-collar and especially pink-collar workers. And of the talkers a good percentage are persuaders. The secretary shepherding a document through the company bureaucracy is often called on to exercise sweet talk and veiled threats. Or notice the persuasion exercised the next time you buy a suit. Specialty clothing stores charge more than discount stores not staffed with rhetoricians. The differential pays for the persuasion: "It's you, my dear" or "The fish tie makes a statement." As Smith says (1762–1763, p. 352, spelling modernized), "everyone is practising oratory . . . [and therefore] they acquire a certain dexterity and address in managing their affairs, or in other words in managing of men; and this is altogether the practise of every man in most ordinary affairs . . . , the constant employment or trade of every man" and woman. Not constant, perhaps, but in Smith's time a substantial percentage and in modern times fully 25 percent.

Coase in other words is returning to the Smithian rhetorical program. He is extending the wholly silent economics of Marshall (which Axel Leijonhufvud has characterized, not without sympathy, as an economics of wind-up toys) to the faculty of speech. Coase's transactions costs are in fact the costs of talking. What makes for low transaction costs is exactly what makes for smooth conversation, the common tongue, the "precise definition" of the mathematician. What lies behind the phrase "transaction costs" are precisely the talk of businesspeople. "I will buy with you, sell with you, talk with you, and so following. . . . What news on the Rialto?" Talk establishes the relationships for doing business. You might say that it establishes a repeated game—or at least the atmosphere of a repeated game, reassuring people that they have implicitly promised to act as though they were friends with the other. Imagine a blackjack table without banter. The economic purpose of the table is to separate the sucker from his money in a pleasant way. If the dealer were merely coldly efficient then the machines that simulate blackjack would be just as popular as the live tables. They are not.

Coase's bridge between institutions and neoclassical economics is of course what has come to be called "transaction costs" (he called them "marketing costs"; Coase 1937, pp. 40, 42, 43, 43 n.24). These are the costs of "discovering what the relevant prices are" (p. 38), "negotiating and concluding a separate contract for each transaction" (pp. 38–39), "forecasting" (p. 39), "uncertainty" (p. 40), and sales taxes and price controls (p. 41). By his own account, "The solution [to the problem of why firms were necessary, considering that markets made decisions automatically] was to realize that there were costs of making transactions in a market economy and that it was necessary to incorporate them into the analysis" (1988b, p. 17).

But Coase's extension of economics into the world of lawyerly talk is cautious, keeping the faculty of reason constantly in view. Coase asks what a reasoning manager would do when faced by an offer from the market to produce crank shafts at a lower price than his own plant. The analysis looks into the firm, but the viewpoint is still that of the bourse. For example, the desires for independence or mastery do not function alone. Coase puts them in a market, noting as an economist reflexively would that workers enjoying subordination "would accept less work under someone" and that bosses enjoying bossing "might be willing to give up something in order to direct others" (1937, p. 38).

The older institutionalists in Germany and the United States had noted before the First World War that neoclassical economics ignores institutions. But they made a mistake that the slow development of a Coasean institutionalism has avoided. The leap to the direct study of institutions, though obvious and understandable, proved to be a mistake because it unnecessarily abandoned the Faculty of Reason in order to better pursue the Faculty of Speech. It was lawyerly without being also economistic. Most of the law professors critical of the law and economics movement have this problem, that they have not mastered as Coase had at age twenty-one the reasoning of opportunity cost. A modern embodiment of the mistake, for example, is the work of the business historian Alfred Chandler, who knows as much about economic reasoning as a Samuelsonian economist knows about business speech. Both are glad of their ignorance. A Coasean economics, by contrast, learns both.

Coasean Economics Is Anti-Modernist, "Gothic," Postmodern in Its Rhetoric

I have said that Coasean economics as exhibited even in the article of 1937 is British, lawyerly, empirical; not French, Samuelsonian, and mathematical. John Ruskin, the nineteenth-century critic of architecture (I do not recommend his views on economics), noted that the search for a crystalline Ideal has been an incubus on classical and Renaissance, and now we may say modernist, architecture. He attacked the tyranny of the lonely genius, seeking by contemplation in his warm room a system to impose upon us all. Of the Renaissance he wrote,

> Its main mistake . . . was the unwholesome demand for perfection at any cost. . . . Men like Verrocchio and Ghiberti [consider Marx or Samuelson] were not to be had every day. . . . Their strength was great enough to enable them to join science with invention, method with emotion, finish with fire. . . . Europe saw in them only the method and the finish. This was new to the minds of men, and they pursued it to the neglect of everything else. "This," they cried, "we must have in our work henceforward"; and they were obeyed. The lower workman secured method and finish, and lost, in exchange for them, his soul. (Ruskin 1851–1853, pp. 228–29)

Ruskin's argument fits positivism in economics and elsewhere, which seeks an all-embracing, testable Theory apart from the practical skills of the statesman, the craftsman, or the economic scientist. An "interpretive economics," as Arjo Klamer, Metin Cosgel, and Don Lavoie began to call it at the end of the 1980s, would turn the other way, as economists do in practical work (see Lavoie 1990, Cosgel and Klamer 1990). It is in Ruskin's terms "Gothic economics," an end to searching for a grail of a unified field theory, an awakening from Descartes' Dream. As Ruskin said again, "It requires a strong effort of common sense to shake ourselves quit of all that we have been taught for the last two centuries, and wake to the perception of a truth . . . : that great art . . . does *not* say the same thing over and over again. . . . [T]he Gothic spirit . . . not only dared, but delighted in, the infringement of every servile principle" (Ruskin 1851–1853, pp. 166–67).

And that is the point of Coase's rhetoric, evident even in his maiden effort. He inverts the hierarchy of theory and practice. Most people have a simple theory of theory, in which mere dolts apply to practice the "method and finish" of theorists. But it is a servile theory. The Gothic spirit is seen in the best works of applied economics, from the economic historian Robert Fogel, say, or the agricultural economist Theodore Schultz; from the financial economist Robert Shiller or the statistical economist Edward Leamer; and above all in the legal economics of Ronald Coase. It is not seen in the routine science of the field, servile to the undoubted genius of Paul Samuelson, Kenneth Arrow, and Lawrence Klein.

George Stigler and other methodologists who huddled around the corpse of logical positivism in the 1950s and 1960s succeeded in overcoming such common sense. Positive economics was useful for a time, up to about 1965, in forcing economists into a narrow program worth attempting. But it was and is a sort of voluntary imbecility, as the crystallographer and philosopher Michael Polanyi described the 3-by-5 card theory of Scientific Method. It was the bad rhetoric that only a narrow range of reasoning is needed because only the narrow reasoning is properly Scientific. Under such a methodology it does not matter whether an argument is rich or relevant or persuasive. We are to be nourished on certain scraps of utilitarian ethics, certain demonstrably irrelevant statistical tests, and certain rules of evidence enshrined in the oldest handbooks of positivism and behaviorism. The rhetoric has had a disastrous effect on scholarly standards in Chicago School economics, and if it had been even more strenuously enforced would have made Ronald Coase's career impossible.

Coase's "Gothic" economics, on the contrary—to revive another word much maligned that embodies common sense and common morality—is "casuistic" rather than universalist, common law rather than jurisprudential. It is a case-by-case approach: if you think on the blackboard the lighthouses are perfect examples of pure public goods, pull down the books, take depositions, and examine the actual case (thus Coase 1974). If you think that beekeepers and orchardmen are perfect examples of the impossibility of solving externalities by contract, do the same (Cheung 1973). Albert Jonsen and Stephen Toulmin have rescued the word "casuistic" from the contempt into which it has fallen (compare "rhetoric," "pragmatism," "anarchism"). They take it as a throughly modern approach to ethics, in the context of the revival of the Aristotelian studies of the particular virtues (Jonsen and Toulmin 1988). Coase's approach to economics is in this sense precisely casuistic, looking for the stories and metaphors and facts and logics that fit the case at hand, and avoiding the unreasonable obsession with one of them alone. A style of ethical storytelling that insists that cases matter as much as principles is foreign to most of modern economics. As Coase has argued since 1937, largely unheeded, economics and law need a rhetoric that is lawyerly and economistic at the same time.

7 THE UNEXAMINED RHETORIC

OF ECONOMIC QUANTIFICATION

Even in the most narrowly technical matters economists have shared convictions about what makes an argument strong, convictions which they have not examined, which they can communicate to graduate students only tacitly, and which contain embarrassments to the official rhetoric.

Rhetorical Standards, for Example, Are Necessary to Measure the Integration of Markets

Do numbers tell? According to the official rhetoric, yes: only numbers. Most economists believe that once you have reduced a question to numbers you have taken it out of human hands. That's where the rhetoric of quantification goes crazily wrong.

The best quantitative economists know it. The rhetorical point is idiotically simple. It is that in a human conversation a number is high or low relative only to some standard, and the only relevant standard is provided by the humans involved. Ten degrees below zero is paralyzing cold by the standard of Virginia, a normal day by the standard of Saskatoon in January, and a heat wave by the standard of most interstellar gas. Everyone knows this. A *New Yorker* cartoon shows faucets labeled "Hot: A Relative Concept" and "Cold: A Relative Concept." A thing is not large in itself. It is large (or yellow, rich, cold, stable, well-integrated, selfish, free, rising, monopolistic) relative to something else, and this something has to be specified. The question "But how large is large?" applies to any quantitative argument. It gets some of its excellence from its father in thought, the terrifying, mind-stunning "So what?" and from its Jewish mother, "So what else is new?" Few better questions can be asked, because most inadequate scholarship errs more in relevance than in execution.

What is remarkable about this obvious question is how often it is not

100

asked. On the issue of how much better black children do in nonsegregated schools, for example, Robert Crain of the Johns Hopkins Center for Social Organization of Schools remarks that "there is a great deal of debate about when improvement is a big deal and when it isn't a big deal." Complaining that social scientists have been trained to think in terms of merely statistical significance, he notes that they "have never arrived at a consensus on how big a number is big" (1984, p. 12). The same point can be made about the collateral controversy over race and I.Q. revived again in the debate over *The Bell Curve*. The technical issue is whether or not the averages of white and and black I.Q.s are different statistically. I.Q. is a questionable notion to begin with and hard to measure free of cultural bias. The point I am making here, however, observes that the distributions of black and white I.Q.s largely overlap. An alleged difference in averages, however certified by the standard of merely statistical significance, might *not* therefore be a Big Deal. It has no practical use. On the basis of a statistically significant difference between the races in average I.Q., for instance, you would hardly propose to use race as a criterion for excluding certain children from certain schools. Under such a policy, even accepting its repulsive moral base, most of the students would be placed in the wrong school. Statistically significant or not, the difference is too small to matter.

The point comes up repeatedly in statistical thinking. The rhetorically savvy scientist asks every time, "So what?" "How large is large?" "What does it matter for the intellectual or political or moral issue at hand?" Much of economics turns on quarrels of characterization: Is America monopolistic? Were medieval peasants selfish? Is the market for goods worldwide? Is capitalism stable? These are quantitative questions, all depending on answers to the question "How large is large?" That the quarrels of characterization go on and on, passing from one century to the next unanswered, suggests that the rhetoric has failed. No one answers the question "How large is large?" Everyone knows it has to be asked, but no one answers it.

The last step of most calculations in economics or history therefore is sleight of hand, the more convincing because the magician performs it so absent-mindedly: "The coefficient in a regression of domestic prices on foreign prices is statistically insignificantly different from 1.00, and *therefore* purchasing power parity is true." "The number of formal whippings of slaves was less than 0.7 [or perhaps 1.2] a year, and *therefore* the lash was insignificant [or perhaps significant]."

A typical case is the economics of market integration. For decades certain economists have been measuring the correlation between two parts of a market and concluding triumphantly that the market was indeed integrated. The trouble is that other economists, often using the same statistics, have concluded gloatingly that it was not.

Historical economists have more often seen the need for a standard, if only the standard that, yes, the integration of markets did increase as better ships were built for sea lanes cleared of pirates and as postroads, semaphores, and finally telegraph poles tied prices together. Knowing that from 1400 to 1760 the spread of prices of grain in Europe fell steadily (as you can see in the grand diagrams accompanying Braudel and Spooner's contribution to the _Cambridge Economic History of Europe,_ vol. IV, p. 470) is at least better than knowing merely that around 1600 the ratio of the wheat price in Venice to the price in Warsaw was five to one.

From the bare, lone five to one you can infer nothing, because _no standard comes with the numbers themselves._ You say a market is "integrated" when judging the differential to be small, but the word means only what we together have agreed for the moment to let it mean, namely, a "small" differential. In a particular conversation about the wheat market we implicitly take the words "a small differential" to mean whatever the character of wheat trading was in some standard time and place, say Europe in 1900. Like Humpty Dumpty, in _Through the Looking Glass_ we choose the words of characterization to do our bidding—the market is "integrated" or "competitive" or "black"—and feel free to order them about. But to talk as though the lone number for 1600 shorn of rhetorical context says anything about market integration in 1600 is to play a less reasonable game in Humpty's repertoire. "Why," he asked, "is a mouse when it spins?" And answered, "The higher the fewer."

Suppose, for example, that the average correlation of prices of wheat in cities a hundred miles apart in Europe was +.95 in 1900 (expressing prices in the same currency, taking the correlations over decades, using weekly data, and so forth). Suppose, too, that we agree "for purposes of argument" (as the sensible phrase goes) that the European wheat market in 1900 is what we mean by well-integrated. We have then a standard by which to judge the degree of integration of the wheat market in Europe in 1600, or of China in 1900, or of the Western Mediterranean in the fifth century B.C. The particular standard is not very helpful, of course, because by the standard of 1900 none of these markets were "well-integrated." But at least we know that. (It is "we" who know it: rhetoric is social.) To know merely that the correlation of grain prices between Shanghai and Peking in A.D. 1900 was +.85 or between Athens and Syracuse in 430 B.C. was +.70 is by itself to know nothing at all.

One needs a standard. You persuade your audience that something is big by laying it down on a ruler that the audience considers relevant. It is obvious that a certain platinum-iridium bar at the International Bureau of Standards outside Paris is "the meter." No one would propose to call a race a "10,000" with the units left off, leaving it to the internal scales of the runners to decide whether it was 10,000 meters or 10,000 inches (or tons or Greek mercenaries, for that matter: the higher the fewer). The official meter bar, a socially agreed-upon way of speaking for the sake of argument, gives the 10,000 its meaning, or, as we say, its units. And the rest of the way that people feel about 10,000 meter races gives the rest of the context, that it is a long way for an out-of-shape fraternity boy to run, for example. Race numbers or correlations get their units and their significance from people, not from God. The numbers are essential for scientific work; but scientific judgment takes the last step.

The so-called Genberg-Zecher criterion is one, the standard of sameness in markets *within* the two countries (after its inventors Genberg 1976; McCloskey and Zecher 1976). We speak of Britain's money supply as something needing special consideration in our theories, as Midlothian's money supply or Cornwall's does not. We speak of America's money supply as though "America" were a significant aggregate for some purpose, but we do not speak of California's money supply or Vermont's. Behind the speaking, then, must lie an implicit standard. The standard is that a market area in bricks, saws, and sweaters defined to contain without comment both California and Vermont is apparently not disparate enough to require a separate money supply. The degree to which the prices of bricks, saws, and sweaters move parallel in California and Vermont, therefore, provides a criterion (the Genberg-Zecher one) for measuring the degree of integration between America as a whole and Britain. If the degree of parallelism is no larger between America and Britain than it is between California and Vermont, then— for purposes of argument—one might as well include Britain as California in America's money supply. The borders of countries will in this conversation lack point.

The reasoning applies to other cases of market integration. A battle of books has long been waged among American colonial historians over whether or not Americans in the eighteenth century participated in a market economy. Another heats up from time to time over whether and when the British labor market became integrated in the nineteenth century. And still another has raged since World War I, fought out by each generation of economists since Taussig and Wicksell, over whether nations participate fully in a world market for goods in the twentieth century. The outcomes matter. The smaller stakes are whether or not simple

economic models of supply and demand can be applied to whole nations or whole worlds. It would be nice to avoid having separate models for each isolated New England farm or modern nation. But there are
stakes beyond neatness. The very use of economic models in classical
economic history, the dating of capitalism in America's infancy, the
causes of British growth during the nineteenth century, the rationality
(if any) of the efforts since Keynes to understand and govern economies
at the merely national level all depend on the largeness of some measure of integration. Yet none of the discussions face up to the question
of "How large is large?" That's why they are never resolved.

Attempts to measure the largeness of birthrates in the eighteenth
century, of social and geographical mobility in the nineteenth century,
of entrepreneurial failure in Britain, and of the influence of Federal Reserve policy in America must all answer "How large is large?" They
usually don't. The answer to the question has to be framed comparatively, speaking of some other time or place in which we agree the
birthrate was low, mobility high, entrepreneurship trivial, or monetary
policy strong.

In Like Fashion, Rhetorical Standards Are Necessary in Linguistics to Measure the Similarity of Languages

The question whether Danish or Norwegian are to
count as separate languages is parallel to the question whether Copenhagen and Oslo are to be counted as separate markets for labor. The two
influence each other. Wider politics affect both, since it matters whether
one language or wage level is treated as standard relative to the other. If
Danish were the tongue of influence in a Dano-Norwegian kingdom (as
it once was, producing the *Riksmaal*, or realm-speech), Norwegian would
be treated as a provincial dialect (*Landsmaal*, or country-talk), the way
Lowland Scots is treated as a provincial dialect relative to Southeastern
English. If wages in Copenhagen were taken as the standard in the kingdom for subsidy payments or for setting the salaries of government
workers, then the labor markets of far Oslo would be treated as a provincial branch of the central market in Denmark. The distinctions between
languages are made by human rhetoric, not written in the heavens.

The point is that linguists face the same puzzle that economists face:
How large is large? How large do the differences between dialects of
Dano-Norwegian have to be before you count Danish and Norwegian
as separate languages? You can watch the linguists missing the point

just as the economists do. The linguists sometimes use "mutual intelligibility" as a standard for defining a language, but like the correlation of prices, it immediately demands a higher-order standard. If you say that a correlation of +.80 between prices of grain in Glasgow and London is "high" you are assuming a rhetorical context that provides a scale along which the number is in fact high. If you say that the phrase "days of auld lang syne" is mutually intelligible to a Glaswegian and a Cockney you must have some standard. How intelligible? When speaking slowly with an attempt to approach the standard dialect? In the newspaper? At a pub sing-song? How large is large?

L. R. Palmer worried in the early pages of his standard treatment of *The Latin Language* (1954) about whether Oscan, Umbrian, Sabellian, and Volscian should be taken as languages separate from Latin or together with Latin as mere dialects of a common "Italic." He remarks that "this is largely a dispute about terms that have no precise scientific definition" (p. 6), by which he seems to mean, as people do when they talk this way, no definition that would end argument forever. His definition of language ("a system of vocal signals used by a given community") reduces to mutual intelligibility. His standard of intelligibility, to which he appends a condition of social "solidarity" in order to allow for such cases as the political divisions of Scandinavia, is whether native speakers feel they are speaking the same language. He uses, too, a definition by questionnaire—asking the native speakers. This is of course reasonable, though for a dead language with very limited early remains he is in practice driven back to more objective but less persuasive standards: for the case of Umbrian, "it has been calculated that 60–70 percent of the words contained in the Iguvinian Tables are different from Latin, whereas for Greek only 10–15 percent of the words occurring in the Cretan Gortynian Laws are not found in Attic" (p. 7). Note in this the explicitly comparative standard. When Palmer wants to persuade a reader that Latin and Umbrian are to be accounted different languages, he places the two on a scale defined by dialects of Greek.

The study of languages and the study of markets have a diachronic as well as a synchronic aspect. Since linguists are interested in how languages came to be what they are as well as how they work at a particular time, they have available another, developmental definition to set beside the puzzles of such static definitions, namely, genealogy. If Italic begat both Osco-Umbrian and Latin, then the latter are sister tongues and that is that. In the simple case of one language developing without external influences the genealogical definition supplies its own standards. Latin developed into Italian and Rumanian. But the case of "Italic" developing into Latin and Osco-Umbrian, it happens, is more cloudy.

The Unexamined Rhetoric of Economic Quantification

One might well apply the genealogical definition to the problem of markets. If two allegedly distinct markets had common ancestors—or, what would be more useful, common descendants—then you might agree to call them one. Such a definition would not be very persuasive, though perhaps interesting for some other purpose. Institutionalists in economics—who include anthropologists and geographers interested in economic affairs but not trained in modern, static, synchronic, neo-classical economics—take an interest in the diachronic story. They want to know who the grandfathers of the present traders were, where the market "came from," "how it was financed," how it is "reproduced" from generation to generation, none of which is of any use to a static study of markets. The static study demands a definition free of historical context. (You might say so much the worse for the static study.) It demands not a story but a rule.

Linguists draw maps of "isoglosses," similar to isoquants in production theory or isobars in meteorology, which show where dialect words are the same. The words "purse" and "pocketbook," "brook" and "rill," can be plotted on a map and their boundaries discerned. (Somewhere between Chicago and Iowa City a "bag" in a grocery store changes to a "sack.") If the isoglosses seem to pile up on top of each other, then you are looking at a line between distinct dialects or languages. You could do the same with correlations of prices, mapping the rings of isocorrelation around marketing centers, for instance, or plotting the frequency distribution of correlations for products ranging from the traceable to the strictly local. Geographers do. But anyway you need a standard, and the standard depends on what it takes to persuade other scholars.

Linguists, like economists, come often to the verge of standards without crossing over into articulating them. Saussure remarks that "a dialect is defined, roughly speaking, by a sufficient accumulation of such concordances [of isoglosses]" (1915, p. 203). But how sufficient? In his *Descriptive and Comparative Linguistics: A Critical Introduction* (1972), Palmer treats dialectology most lucidly, but stops the search for standards on page 278: dialectical boundaries are places where "within such a bundle of isoglosses there is a palpable degree of uniformity." But palpability lies in the fingers of the toucher. In *Defining a Linguistic Area: South Asia*, Colin Masica, speaking of the clustering of isoglosses, says, "Opinions may, of course, differ on what constitutes a significant degree of clustering, even though mathematical procedures would appear to offer a way of deciding" (1976, p. 6). Would that it were so. Quantification raises in a usefully clear form the question of how large is large; but quantification without a rhetoric of the scholarly conversation does not answer it.

That Is, the Speech Acts of Scientists Are Conversations, Good or Bad

You can always ask "So what?" And the answer will always depend on one's audience and the human purposes involved. Assertions are made for purposes of persuading some audience. This is not a shameful fact: it is charming that human beings are cuddly, preferring to cling together against the indifferent cold. Their sociability leads them to make remarks they hope others will believe and use.

Even scholars are human beings. When they come to interpret a "plain fact," such as the extent of the American market or the degree of similarity among Italic languages, the economic and historical and linguistic scholars must be appealing to other human beings. The assertion of a plain fact derives its force—which J. L. Austin called its "performative" character and "perloctionary" force, as contrasted with its "constative" or merely declarative character—from the conventions of conversation in which it takes place: "We must consider the total situation in which the utterance is issued—the total speech-act" (Austin 1955, p. 52). The functioning of the American capital market, it is said, became significantly better in the closing years of the nineteenth century (Davis 1965). A rise in the American money supply, it is said, will cause a significant amount of inflation, albeit with a long and variable lag. The "significance" here must be relative to some experience in conversation that American economic historians and economists have had. Otherwise the assertions do not do their work. Especially the assertions are not just true or false in themselves. In his *How to Do Things with Words*, Austin wrote,

> Suppose that we confront "France is hexagonical" with the facts, in this case, I suppose, with France, is it true or false? Well, if you like up to a point, it is true for certain intents and purposes. It is good enough for a general, perhaps, but not for a geographer. But then someone says . . . "it has to be true or false—it's a statement, isn't it?" How can one answer? . . . It is just rough, and that is the right and final answer. It is a rough description; it is not a true or false one. "True" and "false" . . . do not stand for anything simple at all; but only for a general dimension of being a right or proper thing to say . . . in these circumstances, to this audience, for these purposes and with these intentions. (Austin 1955, pp. 143, 145)

In commenting on this passage the literary critic Stanley Fish makes exactly the point here about quantitative thinking in economics:

> All utterances are . . . produced and understood within the assumption of some socially conceived and understood dimension of assessment. . . . The one thing you can never say about France is what it is *really* like, if by "really" you mean France as it exists independently of any dimension of assessment whatever. The France you are talking about will always be the product of the talk about it, and will never be independently available. What the example of France shows is that all facts are discourse specific . . . and that therefore no one can claim for any language a special relationship to the facts as they "simply are," unmediated by social or conventional assumptions. (1980, pp. 198–99)

It may help in swallowing such a relativistic pill to note that not only ordinary-language philosophers and modern literary critics talk this way. Modern physicists say similar things about the realest of realities. And Beltrami's proof in 1868 (a proof that Lobachevskian geometry can have no possible self-contradictions *if* Euclidean geometry has none) has been taken as the model of how to go about such tasks in mathematics. There are no proofs of consistency available for every mathematical system (as was later proved by Gödel with perfect generality), only proofs for some that attach one part of mathematical discourse to another.

The social and persuasive character of the act of assertion is, after all, routinely sensible, something on which we act daily. We look naturally for external standards with which to make judgments, quantitative or not. Does your son have big feet? Well, how many fourteen-year-olds *do* have size thirteen shoes? Reporting "size thirteen" without some conversational context would not advance the discussion. Is "Ode on a Grecian Urn" a good poem? Well, compare and contrast it with one hundred randomly selected poems. Decisions such as these cannot be made independent of the conversations of humankind. *We* decide what are big feet, good poems, and large statistics of market integration. The criteria are social, not solipsistic. They are written in the literary conversations of scholars, not in the stars or in statistical tables of the levels of significance of Student's-*t*.

The social character of scientific knowledge does not make it arbitrary, touchie-feelie, mob-governed, or anything else likely to bring it into disrepute. It is still, for instance, "objective," if that is a worry. In vulgar usage the objective/subjective distinction beloved of Western philosophy since Descartes means discussable/undiscussable. But even in a sophisticated sense "objectivity" has a necessarily social definition: we know that the yield of corn in the Middle Ages was objectively low because we converse with people who agree with our evidence and our calculations and our standard of comparison validating the word "low."

Nor are such human standards peculiar to the human sciences. The mathematician Armand Borel notes that "something becomes objective . . . as soon as we are persuaded that it exists in the minds of others in the same form that it does in ours, and that we can think about it and discuss it together" (1983, p. 13). A scale of particle durations, star sizes, or electrical activity of the brain depends on being able to "discuss it together." The scale, to repeat, is of humans, not of God.

The standards for quantitative statements, then, have to be rhetorical. It is only because a conversation about nuclear particles or market integration has arrived at a certain point that calculations of rates of decay or of correlations of prices are to the point. The rhetoric of conversation, not the logic of inquiry, provides the standards for science.

The Conversation on Purchasing Power Parity, for Example, Is Rhetorically Muddled

But a rhetorical, conversational standard for science does not mean that anything goes. On the contrary, only if you know the rhetoric can you see the arguments and apply argumentative standards.

A good example of low standards in official rhetoric is the literature on purchasing power parity. The economic question at stake in the conversation is again the question of whether markets are integrated. Is the world's economy like the economy of the Midwest, in which Iowa City and Madison and Champaign all face given prices for goods? Or is it more like the solar system, in which each planet's economy is properly thought of in isolation? If the Iowa City view is correct, then the prices of all goods will move together everywhere, allowing for exchange rates between currencies. If the Martian view is correct, they will move differently. If the Iowa City view is correct, then all economic models closed to the rest of the world, whether Keynesian or monetarist or rationally expecting, are wrong; if the Martian view is correct, then economists can (as they do) go on testing macroeconomic faiths against merely American experience since the 1940s.

The question of whether prices are closely connected internationally, then, is important. The official rhetoric does not leave much doubt as to what is required to answer it: collect facts on prices in, say, the United States and Canada and then . . . well . . . *test* the hypothesis. A large number of economists have done this. Half of them conclude that purchasing power parity works; the other half conclude that it fails. The conclusions diverge not because the economists are stupid or because economics is arbitrary but because the disputants have not considered their statistical rhetoric.

A paper by Irving Kravis and Robert Lipsey on the subject, for instance, concludes that purchasing power parity fails: "We think it *unlikely* that the *high* degree of national and international commodity arbitrage that many versions of the monetarist theory of the balance of payments contemplate is *typical* of the real world. This is not to deny that the price structures of the advanced industrial countries *are linked* together, but it is to suggest that the links are *loose* rather than *rigid*" (1978, p. 243; italics supplied). Every italicized word involves a comparison against some standard of what constitutes unlikelihood or highness or typicality or being linked or looseness or rigidity. Yet here and elsewhere in the tortured literature of purchasing power parity no standard is proposed.

The narrowest test of purchasing power parity, and the one that dominates the official rhetoric, is to plot the price in the United States (of steel or of goods in general, in levels or in differences) against the corresponding price abroad, allowing for the exchange rate. If the slope of the line thus fitted is 1.00 the hypothesis of purchasing power parity is said to be confirmed; if not, not.

Kravis and Lipsey perform such a test. Being good economists they are evidently made a little uncomfortable by the rhetoric involved. They admit that "each analyst will have to decide in the light of his purposes whether the purchasing power parity relationships fall close enough to 1.00 to satisfy the theories" (p. 214). Precisely. In the next sentence, though, they lose sight of the need for an explicit standard if their argument is to be cogent: "As a matter of general judgment we express our opinion that the results do not support the notion of a tightly integrated international price structure." They do not say what a "general judgment" is or how you might recognize it. The purpose of an explicit economic rhetoric would be to provide guidance.

The guidance Kravis and Lipsey provide for evaluating their general judgment is a footnote (p. 214) reporting the general judgments of Houthakker, Haberler, and Johnson that deviations from parity of anything under 10 or 20 percent are acceptable to the hypothesis. (It happens, incidentally, that the bulk of the evidence offered by Kravis and Lipsey passes rather than fails such a test, belying their conclusions.) But accepting or rejecting one unargued standard by comparing it with another unargued standard does not much advance the art of argument in economics.

Kravis and Lipsey, to be quite fair, are unusually sensitive to the desirability of having some standard, more sensitive than are most economists working the field. They return repeatedly to the question of a standard, though without resolving it. It reminds you of the linguists grasping for a standard for "a language." They reject in one unpersuasive sentence on page 204 the only standard proposed in the literature so far, the Genberg-Zecher criterion described earlier.

They are left, like most economists, with a senseless rhetoric of quantification: the "statistical test of significance." It is the consequence of not asking "How Large is Large?" Something has gone very wrong with the quantitative rhetoric of economics.

THE RHETORIC OF

SIGNIFICANCE TESTS

Statistical Significance Has Ruined
Empirical Work in Economics

Econometrics in particular has made a tragic mistake by not facing its rhetoric of importance. The tragic mistake is to *turn back to statistics itself* to answer the question whether the deviations from purchasing power parity are important. It makes the statistical machinery into something that takes care of the *whole* scientific job, from start to finish, soup to nuts. But you can see that something is wrong. We care about the statistics of purchasing power parity because we are humans with some purpose in mind, not because some number is absolutely high or low.

At some point, in other words, you have to turn *away* from your statistical machinery and ask the common-sense question, "All right, people: What does it matter?" Is the gravitational effect of one galaxy on another worth taking account of? Is the effect of the meteor big enough to account for the extinction of the dinosaurs? Are the prices in the United States importantly connected to those in the rest of the world? The numbers are necessary material. *But they are not sufficient to bring the matter to a scientific conclusion.* Only the scientists can do that, because "conclusion" is a human idea, not Nature's. It is a property of human minds, not of the statistics.

The tragic turn was taken in the 1940s by Lawrence Klein and other inventors of modern econometrics. What Klein and everyone in modern science is looking for is a mechanical, uncontroversial way of deciding whether some effect is large or small. No human judgments, please: we're scientists. Unfortunately for economic science, and some other sciences like medicine, right at Klein's elbow in the 1940s was a machine that seemed to promise an uncontroversial way of deciding whether a number is large or small, inside statistics, without messing with human judgment. Horribly for the outcome in economics the machine was already called "statistical *significance*," and had been so called for seventy years. This was unspeakably sad. Klein picked up the machine and started using it to claim he had gotten "significant" results. No need to assess whether a number was large or small. *Klein believed that the very statistics used to estimate, say, the effects of the foreign prices on American prices could be used to decide on their own whether they really mattered,* whether a slope of 1.20, or 0.80, or .08, for that matter, was worth getting excited about.

In Klein's very first scientific paper, published in 1943 when he had just gotten his Ph.D. in Economics from MIT (Paul Samuelson supervised his dissertation), he says at one point, in words that were to become formulaic in people who followed him, "The role of Y in the regression is not statistically significant. The ratio of the regression coefficient to its standard error is only 1.812. This low value of the ratio means that we *cannot* reject the hypothesis that the true value of the regression coefficient is zero" (1985, p. 35). Others imitated him, with much less discernment. The practice grew and grew, especially in the 1970s when the computer chip came to maturity. Pretty soon everyone in economics thought that statistical significance was the same things as scientific significance, that you could skip that last step of scientific work, the human assessment of largeness or smallness.

I said Kravis and Lipsey (1978) were good economists. They draw a distinction on pages 204–205, on page 235, and again on page 242 of their paper between the statistical and the economic significance of their results. They make the point so often that it has to be counted as one of the major points in the paper. Even small differences between domestic and export prices, they say, can make a big difference to the incentive to export: "This is a case in which statistical significance [that is, a correlation of the two prices near 1.0, which one might mistakenly suppose to imply that they were insignificantly different] does not necessarily connote economic significance" (1978, p. 205). Yet they don't follow through. No wonder: without a rhetoric of *economic* significance, and in the face of a rhetoric of statistical significance with the prestige of alleged science behind it, they are not aware they need to: the statistics take care of themselves.

The abuse of the word "significant" in connection with statistical arguments in economics is universal. Statistical significance seems to give a criterion by which to judge whether a hypothesis is true or false. The criterion seems to be independent of any tiresome consideration of how true a hypothesis must be to be true enough. But the world does not serve up free intellectual lunches. Tables of Student's-*t* cannot properly nourish a science.

The standard used is the irrelevant one of statistical significance, that is, how likely it is that the result might arise from the chances of the sample, in view of how large the so-called sample is, and *without* a view of what magnitude for the variable is scientifically important. By such a rhetorical device a sample size of a million yielding a tight estimate that the slope was 0.9999—if "significantly" different from 1.00000—could be produced as evidence that purchasing power parity had "failed," at least if the logic of the usual method were to be followed consistently. Common sense, presumably, would rescue the scholar from asserting that an estimate of 0.9999 with a standard error of 0.0000001 was significantly different from unity in a significant meaning of significance. Such common sense should be applied to findings of slopes of .90 or 1.20. It is not.

An example is J. D. Richardson's paper "Some Empirical Evidence on Commodity Arbitrage and the Law of One Price" (1978). He regresses Canadian prices on American prices multiplied by the exchange rate for a number of industries and concludes, "It is notable that the 'law of one price' fails uniformly. The hypothesis of *perfect* commodity arbitrage is rejected with 95 percent confidence for every commodity group" (p. 347; italics supplied). The question is, Why in an imperfect world would it matter that *perfect* arbitrage is rejected?

The irrelevance of the merely statistical criterion undermines the literature, whether favorable or unfavorable toward purchasing power parity. For instance, toward the end of an article favorable to purchasing power parity, Paul Krugman writes, "There are several ways in which we might try to evaluate purchasing power parity as a theory. We can ask how much it explains [that is, R-square, a variant of statistical significance]; we can ask how large the deviations from purchasing power parity are in some absolute sense; and we can ask whether the deviations from purchasing power parity are in some sense systematic" (1978, p. 405). The defensive usage "in some absolute sense" and "in some sense" betrays his unease, which is in the event justified. There is no "absolute sense" in which a description is good or bad. The sense must be comparative to a standard, and the standard must be argued.

Similarly, Jacob Frenkel, once an enthusiast for purchasing power parity as such things go among economists but momentarily bewitched by the ceremony of statistical line-fitting, said that "if the market is efficient and if the forward exchange rate is an unbiased forecast of the future spot exchange rate, the constant [in a fit of the spot rate today on the future rate for today quoted yesterday] . . . should not differ *significantly* from unity" (1978, p. 175; italics supplied). In a footnote on the next page, speaking of the standard errors of the estimates for such an equation in the 1920s, he argues that "while these results indicate that markets were efficient and that on average forward rates were unbiased forecasts of future spot rates, the 2–8 percent errors were *significant*" (p. 176n; italics supplied). He evidently has forgotten his usage of "significant" in another signification. What he seems to mean is that he judges errors of 2–8 percent to be large in some unspecified economic sense, perhaps as offering significant profits for lucky guessers of the correct spot rate. In any event, it is unclear what his results imply about their subject, purchasing power parity, because significance in statistics, however useful it sometimes might be, is not the same thing as economic significance.

The argument is not that levels of significance are arbitrary. Of course they are. The argument is that it is not known whether the range picked out by the level of significance affirms or denies the hypothesis. Nor is it that economists often should use intervals rather than points for their null hypotheses. True as it is, the interval would still have to be chosen, *by discussing the rhetoric of the economic issue.* Tables of Student's-*t* do not make the choice. They are relevant only if you have *already chosen, on scientific grounds, what constitutes Big and Small* (and, by the way, if you have in fact a problem of inferring from a sample to a universe). Nor certainly is the argument that econometrics should be disdained. Quite the contrary. The argument is that the econometrics has not followed its own rhetoric of hypothesis testing. Nowhere in the literature of tests of purchasing power parity does there appear a loss function. We do not know how much it will cost in policy wrecked or analysis misapplied or reputation ruined if purchasing power parity is said to be true when, by the measure of the slope coefficient, it is only, say, 85 percent true.

The Genberg-Zecher criterion is not the only conceivable standard. The degree of market integration in some golden age (1880–1913 perhaps, or 1950–1970) might be one; the profits from arbitrage above normal profits might be another; the extent to which an X percentage deviation from purchasing power parity does or does not disturb some assertion about the causes of inflation might be still another. The point is to have standards of argument, to go beyond the inconclusive rhetoric provided by the pseudoscientific ceremony in most of modern economics of hypothesize, fit, significance-test, publish.

Econometrics Confuses Statistical and Scientific Significance

William Kruskal, past president of the American Statistical Association, exclaimed once that "surely such fundamental points as the distinction between statistical and substantive significance must be elementary to econometricians who readily handle five-stage maximum likelihood estimation and utility functions with values in Banach spaces" (letter to the author, April 26, 1982). Unfortunately not. The warnings in his article on significance tests in the *International Encyclopedia of Statistics* (1968) are commonplaces among statisticians, but unknown by most economists. The rhetoric of statistical significance is sleepwalking.

Only a few economists appreciate the narrowness of what tests of significance can do. Edward Leamer argued in "Let's Take the Con Out of Econometrics" (1983) that the specification error from omitting an important variable—and what student of society imagines she has kept in mind every important variable?—leaves a term in the expression for the sample covariance that does *not* go to zero as the sample size increases. The term does not change at all, because it is not caused by sampling error; it is caused (as I just said) by specification error. The precision of the statistical estimates therefore does *not* increase much with a larger sample. The methods of statistics deal, quite properly, with sampling errors alone, and cannot be expected to help with others. When these others are serious, as we all believe they usually are, there is no point in continuing to talk relatively much about the (relatively small) sampling error. To do so, as economists and other quantifiers do nowadays on a massive scale, is to imitate the drunk who looks for his keys under the lamp post because the light is better there. Leamer's solution to the problem will please historians, anthropologists, geologists, and other scholars who have more patience with facts than economists have. Go back into the dark and look for other kinds of evidence, not more evidence of the same kind (the sampling problem oversolved again), but evidence of different kinds, whose biases are distributed independently of the biases in the first kind. Including these will cut the error in half. Including a third kind will cut it to a third.

Almost none of the textbooks in econometrics mention that there is a difference between statistical and substantive significance. When Arthur Goldberger did mention it in his recent *A Course in Econometrics* (1991, pp. 240–41) it caught the attention of another eminent econometrician reviewing the four leading textbooks: "When the link is made [in Goldberger between economics and technical statistics] some important insights arise, as for example the section discussing statistical and economic significance, *a topic not mentioned in the other books*" (Granger 1994, p. 118; italics supplied). Not mentioned. The ministers devote sermon after sermon to explaining how to steal, but do not mention that it is a mortal sin.

The three massive volumes of the *Handbook of Econometrics* (Griliches and Intriligator 1983, 1984, 1986), written by many hands, contain exactly one mention of the difference between statistical and scientific significance (by Edward Leamer). In the 762 pages of the recent companion volume, volume 11 of the *Handbook of Statistics* (Maddala et al. 1993), there is a lone sentence, which notes that at large enough sample sizes all coefficients are "significant." It's worse: it's as though St. Thomas Aquinas had written his *Summa* but had neglected to mention sin at all.

In the second edition of his pioneering textbook in econometrics (I learned econometrics from his first edition), J. Johnston (1972) gives an example extending over twenty-six pages of how to run a regression, of road casualties on vehicle registration in the U.K., 1947–1957. He illustrates the use of statistical significance (which he nowhere in his book distinguishes from substantive significance) by imagining a small reduction in road casualties at the end of the period, perhaps after sterner penalties are introduced. Is the imagined reduction real or random? Important or not? (The two are not the same question, but as I say, Johnston never says so.) He concludes, "the computed value is *suggestive of* a reduction, being [statistically] significant at the 5 percent, *but not at the one percent,* level" This means that if you are going to be very rigorous about it (the 1 percent level), you might conclude that after all there was *no* effect, and we might as well not have had the sterner penalties. But he is imagining, remember, a fall in road casualties in the thousands. Having confused statistical and substantive significance, and thinking that statistical significance is all that matters for making judgments, he falls headlong into the fallacy. He turns away from the human significance of what he has imagined and concludes from his table of Student's-*t* that thousands of casualties avoided after all might not be "significant" if you, the researcher, sitting in your warm room with a nice cup of tea, wish strongly enough not to *over*estimate the effect, considering the small sample.

You hear a woman screaming for help over your shortwave radio, but the signal is somewhat weak, obscured some by static, so you are not too sure and you do nothing. She might be saying, "My house is being invaded by robbers. Call the cops!" Or she might possibly be saying "My house is being painted by jobbers. Walls and tops!" So you do nothing, merely because the signal is noisy. It will strike outsiders to the sandbox game of statistical significance as incredible that Johnston should leave such an impression, that thousands of casualties are as nothing beside the embarrassment of a researcher who might overestimate the effect of sterner penalties. But that is how the procedures lead the econometrician to act.

It is not true, as most economists think, that nonetheless statistical significance is a preliminary screen, a necessary condition, through which empirical estimates should be put. Economists will say, "Well, I want to know at least if the coefficient *exists,* don't I?" Yes, but statistical significance can't tell you. Only the magnitude of the coefficient, on the scale of what counts in practical, engineering terms as non-zero, tells you. *It is not the case that statistically insignificant coefficients are in effect zero.* The experiments on aspirin and heart disease were halted short of statistical significance (at the level the medical researchers wanted to have) because the effect was so large in life-saving terms that it was immoral to go on with the double-blind experiment in which some people did not get their daily dose of aspirin. You can't run a science without a loss function.

I am *not* saying that only the average value of a fitted coefficient is important. That is, I am not saying that only the first moment matters. The second and higher moments might well have scientific interest. But if they did, what we would want to know is the second moment of the *population,* σ^2 (or the square root of the second moment, σ, pretty well estimated by just the square root of the sampling variance, s^2). But the second moment of the population, σ, is not the same as the number you examine for statistical significance, the second moment of the *estimate,* viewing the estimate itself as a random variate. By the Master Formula of Testing for Sampling Error the second moment of the estimate is σ *divided by the square root of N.* The two numbers are not the same: they just aren't; dividing by the square root of N changes a number. I'm saying that for most scientific problems the standard error of the estimate does not answer the question, How Big is Big.

An example: suppose you are interested in the height of Dutch women. You will get in a sample size of N = 30, say, some sampling variation around the average height. The variation *of the population from which the sample is drawn* might well be itself interesting to you, as a scientist or as a clothing manufacturer. For numerous scientific or practical questions you would like to know the variation, σ, in the population, estimated by s. You would then have to form a judgment—having nothing whatever to do with the sample size or its square root—about whether the variation is large or small, and how it affects your purposes. What proportion of your skirts as a clothing manufacturer should be sized for tall women?

But the variation *around the estimate of the average* ($\sigma/\sqrt{N}$) is not the same thing as the variation you are in fact interested in for business or scientific purposes, just σ. The estimate itself does have a distribution, which converges to a zero variance around the average as N gets large, because of the Master Formula. That's true and nice in the very rare cases where it *is* The Scientific Problem. But unless you really do have a loss function associated with the variation of the *estimate* you have no proper interest in $\sigma/\sqrt{N}$. Even if you do have such a loss function, you have still not confronted the loss function that speaks of *substantive* significance. And you would be kidding yourself in most economic applications to imagine that this one source of variation that you can control, variation of a proper random sample from a distribution with classical properties, is an important part of the total variation due to other errors, such as bias from misspecification, simultaneous equations, truncated samples, errors in variables, or sheer mismeasurement. The variation of the *estimate,* as contrasted with the variation of the population, is not the answer to most questions. For some it is interesting, for most it is irrelevant. That the light shines brightly under the lamp post is not a case for pretending that a question about substantive magnitudes (first, second, third, etc., moments about the average) is the same as a question about how unfortunate it is that having too small a sample creates a certain fuzziness in the estimate.

A defender of contemporary usage might argue that Johnston and the other econometricians who ignore the difference between statistical and scientific significance presume the reader already understands the difference between economic and statistical significance, having acquired it in elementary courses on statistics. The argument is testable. In his preface Johnston directs the reader who has difficulty with his first chapter to examine a "good introductory" book on statistics, mentioning Paul G. Hoel's *Introduction to Mathematical Statistics* (1954), Alexander M. Mood's *Introduction to the Theory of Statistics* (1950), and D. A. S. Fraser's *Statistics: An Introduction* (1958) (Johnston 1972, p. ix). These are fine books: Mood, for example, gives a good treatment of power functions, pointing to their relevance in applied work. But none of them makes a distinction between substantive and statistical significance. Hoel writes, "There are several words and phrases used in connection with testing hypotheses that should be brought to the attention of students. When a test of a hypothesis produces a sample value falling in the critical region of the test, the result is said to be *significant*; otherwise one says that the result is *not significant*" (p. 176, his italics). The student from the outset of her statistical education, therefore, is led to believe that economic (or substantive) significance and statistical significance are the same thing. Hoel explains, "This word ['not significant'] arises from the fact that such a sample value is not compatible with the hypothesis and therefore signifies that some other hypothesis is necessary" (p. 176). It won't do.

The Rhetorical History of Statistics
Is the Source of the Difficulty

If you dig back into the rhetorical history of significance tests you see how the economists (and medical scientists and sociometricians and psychometricians and political scientists and educationists and so forth) lost their way. The misuse of statistical significance arises partly from the rhetoric in its name. Surely we serious scientists, it insinuates, should be interested first of all in "significant" coefficients: we the great and good would not wish to waste our time on trivialities. The British statistical tradition was dominated in its childhood by Karl Pearson and in its adolescence by R. A. Fisher. Both, and especially Fisher, had a gift for naming their ideas. As William Kruskal has argued,

> Suppose that Sir R. A. Fisher—a master of public relations—had not taken over from ordinary English such evocative words as "sufficient," "efficient," and "consistent" and made them into precisely defined terms of statistical theory. He might, after all, have used utterly dull terms for those properties of estimators, calling them characteristics A, B, and C. Would his work have had the same smashing influence that it did? I think not, or at least not as rapidly. Or turn to Fisher's wonderful phrase "analysis of variance." Is it too cynical to think that the lovely term—half-mystery, half-promise—and the orderly tables helped to win acceptance, quite aside from the underlying theory? (Kruskal 1978, p. 98)

"Significance" is a still older coinage. The idea of statistical significance is old and good, though subject to misuse. In Cicero's *De Divinatione*, Quintus argues for belief in signs from the gods: "'Mere accidents,' you say. Now, really, is that so? Can anything be an 'accident' which bears on itself every mark of truth? Four dice are cast and a Venus throw [four different numbers] results—that is chance; but do you think it would be chance, too, if in one hundred casts you made one hundred Venus throws?" (*Div.*, I, 23). In the early eighteenth century John Arbuthnot observed that more girls than boys had been born in London in every one of the previous eighty-two years, and deduced from the low probability of such an event under a null of $p = .50$ that God had preference for . . . males (Denton 1988, p. 164). The first important scientific use of the idea is Laplace's memoir of 1773 on the distribution of the orbits of twelve comets: he was able to reject the hypothesis that they were in the same plane as the planets and was able therefore to affirm that they originated outside the solar system (Scott 1953, p. 202).

Lancelot Hogben thought the first statistical use of the word was John Venn's, in 1888, speaking of differences expressed in units of probable error: "They inform us which of the differences in the above tables are permanent and significant, in the sense that we may be tolerably confident that if we took another similar batch we should find a similar difference; and which are merely transient and insignificant, in the sense that another similar batch is about as likely as not to reverse the conclusion we have obtained" (quoted in Hogben 1968, p. 325). Stephen Stigler has shown it was F. Y. Edgeworth in 1885, not Venn in 1888, who first used the very word: "The fluctuations being ascertained, we can assert confidently that the difference between two statistical figures is either not even *prima facie* significant, or corresponds to a real difference in fact" (from an 1885 syllabus for a King's College lecture, quoted in Stigler 1986, p. 364). Anyway the 1880s in English. The argument is reasonable: when properly applied to a literal sample, significance *does* entail permanence in the statistical sense Venn described, or in some sense a "real difference in fact" as Edgeworth puts it (less satisfactorily, though, and more likely to be misunderstood as scientific significance). Yet a difference—for instance between 0.999 and 1.000 in a regression of American on foreign prices—could be permanent (not likely to be an accident of the sample) without being "significant" in any other meaning.

This is the mischief. By the 1910s and 1920s the usage was becoming common among sophisticated research workers (Pearson 1911; Yule and Greenwood 1915; Fisher 1925, p. 43). As it spread to the less sophisticated the losing battle to undo the rhetorical damage began. The first of many works making the same point I am making here was written as early as 1919 (Boring 1919). Argument against the mechanical use of significance became early on a commonplace in statistical education. By 1939, for example, a *Statistical Dictionary of Terms and Symbols* of no great intellectual pretensions was putting the point plainly: "A significant difference is not necessarily large, since, in large samples, even a small difference may prove to be a significant difference. Further, the existence of a significant difference may or may not be of practical significance" (Kurtz and Edgerton 1939, s.v. "Significant Difference"). Kendall and Stuart's *Advanced Theory of Statistics* explicitly recognized the mischief in the rhetoric, recommending the colorless phrase "size of the test" in preference to "significance level" (Kendall and Stuart 1951, p. 163n; compare Morrison and Henkel 1969, who proposed the even less colorful phrase "sample error decision procedure" to replace "significance test" [p. 198]).

The Rhetoric of Significance Tests

The notion that statistical significance is a machine for important scientific inferences was first articulated in the 1920s by R. A. Fisher. His opposition to more rhetorically sensible procedures was robust and sufficient. The inner history of modern statistics is that Fisher won, against reason. In the 1930s Jerzy Neyman and E. S. Pearson (son of Karl), and then more explicitly Abraham Wald, argued that actual statistical decisions should depend on substantive, not merely statistical, significance. In 1933 Neyman and Pearson wrote (of type I and type II errors),

> Is it more serious to convict an innocent man or to acquit a
> guilty? That will depend on the consequences of the error; is the
> punishment death or fine; what is the danger to the community
> of released criminals; what are the current ethical views on
> punishment? From the point of view of mathematical theory
> all that we can do is to show how the risk of the errors may be
> controlled and minimised. The use of these statistical tools in any
> given case, in determining just how the balance should be struck,
> *must be left to the investigator.* (1933, p. 296; italics supplied)

Wald went further: "The question as to how the form of the weight [i.e., loss] function W should be determined, is not a mathematical or statistical one. The statistician who wants to test certain hypotheses must first determine the relative importance of all possible errors, *which will entirely depend on the special purposes of his investigation*" (Wald 1939, p. 302; italics supplied). Such notions of bringing cost and benefit into the scientific decision are attractive to economists (and no wonder, for Wald was one, having studied with Karl Menger in Vienna in the 1920s). But his suggestions have been ignored by economists, in favor of conventions about publishable levels of significance advocated by Fisher so long ago.

Statisticians are more aware of the intellectual foundations of their discipline, but many of them are confused. A practical difficulty in the way of using the Wald theory in pure form, A. F. Mood and F. A. Graybill complain, is that "the loss function is not known at all or else it is not known accurately enough to warrant its use. If the loss function is not known, it seems that a decision function that in some sense minimizes the error probabilities will be a reasonable procedure" (1963, p. 278). The phrase "in some sense" seems to be a marker of unexplored rhetoric among the intellectually honest. In any event, the procedure they suggest might be reasonable for a general statistician, who makes no claim to know what is a good or bad approximation to truth in fields outside statistics. It is not reasonable for a specialist in international trade or macroeconomics. If the loss function is not known, it should be discovered. And that will entail a study of the question's rhetoric, productive of standards.

When after the Second World War the various X-ometrics associated with positivism in philosophy and social engineering in politics became normal in social science, the test of significance became a universal reflex. A few sociologists and psychologists in the late 1950s and 1960s protested. Their protest is known as the Significance Test Controversy, in a reader edited by Denton E. Morrison and Ramon E. Henkel (1970; see also Lieberman 1971, and works on the same point by Frank Schmidt at the University of Iowa, Gerd Gigerenzer at the University of Munich, and Louis Guttman of Hebrew University). Economists are accustomed to supposing that they are ahead of other social scientists in statistical sophistication. In this matter, with a few exceptions (Arrow 1959; Griliches 1976), they are not.

The old classic by W. Allen Wallis and Harry V. Roberts, *Statistics: A New Approach*, first published in 1956, made the point clear: "It is essential not to confuse the statistical usage of 'significant' with the everyday usage. In everyday usage, 'significant' means 'of practical importance,' or simply 'important.' In statistical usage, 'significant' means 'signifying a characteristic of the population from which the sample is drawn,' regardless of whether the characteristic is important (1956, p. 385). The point has been revived in elementary statistics books, though only a few emphasize it. In their leading elementary book the statisticians David Freedman, Robert Pisani, and Roger Purves (1978) could not be plainer. In one of numerous places where they make the point they write, "This chapter . . . explains the limitations of significance tests. The first one is that 'significance' is a technical word. A test can only deal with the question of whether a difference is real [permanent in Venn's sense], or just a chance variation. *It is not designed to see whether the difference is important*" (p. 487, italics supplied; the distinction is also made sharply in David S. Moore and George P. McCabe [1993, p. 474]).

Morris DeGroot, a statistician with sophistication in economics, was emphatic on the point:

> It is extremely important . . . to distinguish between an observed value of U that is statistically significant and an actual value of the parameter. . . . In a given problem, the tail area corresponding to the observed value of U might be very small; and yet the actual value . . . might be so close to [the null] that, for practical purposes, the experimenter would not regard [it] as being

> [substantively] different from [the null]. . . . [I]t is very likely that
> the *t*-test based on the sample of 20,000 will lead to a statistically
> significant value of *U*. . . . [The experimenter] knows in advance
> that there is a high probability of rejecting [the null] even when
> the true value . . . differs [arithmetically] only slightly from [the
> null]. (1975, pp. 469–97)

But few other econometricians distinguish economic significance
from statistical significance: Frank Denton does (1988); Goldberger, as
I've noted; a few others. And fewer emphasize economic significance.
In the econometrics texts widely used in the 1970s and 1980s, when the
practice was becoming standard, such as Jan Kmenta's *Elements of
Econometrics* (1971) and Johnston's *Econometric Methods* (1984, first
published in 1963), there is no mention of economic as against statistical significance. Peter Kennedy, in his *A Guide to Econometrics* (1985),
briefly mentions that a large enough sample always gives statistically
significant differences. This is part of the argument but not all of it, and
Kennedy in any case relegates the partial argument to an endnote
(p. 62).

In their elementary book, *Statistics: Discovering Its Power*, Ronald J.
Wonnacott (an economist) and Thomas H. Wonnacott put the point in
a nutshell:

> There is a problem with the term "statistical significance." It is a
> technical phrase that simply means that enough data has been
> collected to establish that a difference does exist. [This is wrong,
> Aunt Deirdre protests, an intrusion of Math Department values
> of existence into what is a practical, Engineering Department
> question of How Big; but the next sentence is correct.] It does *not*
> mean that the difference is necessarily important. For example, if
> we had taken huge samples from nearly identical populations . . .
> the difference [might be] so minuscule that we could dismiss it as
> being of no *real* significance, even though it is just as *statistically*
> significant. In other words, *statistical* significance is a technical
> term, with a far different meaning than *ordinary* significance. . . .
> Unfortunately, but understandably, many people tend to confuse
> statistical significance with ordinary significance. (1982, p. 160;
> their italics)

My only complaint is that the Wonnacotts don't go far enough. It is false
that statistical significance shows that "enough data has been collected
to establish that a difference does exist." That way of putting it makes
the use of significance as a screening device seem all right. No.

A Lot Can Go Wrong When Using Statistical Significance

It is not easy, then, to justify the use of probabilistic models to answer nonprobabilistic questions. You might retort that economists, or at least good ones, do not make such mistakes. But they do, as may be seen from their best practice, in the *American Economic Review*. Stephen Ziliak and I took every full-length empirical paper published in the *Review* during the 1980s and subjected it to a nineteen-item questionnaire (McCloskey and Ziliak 1996). The survey questions are as follows:

1. *Does the paper use a small number of observations, such that statistically significant differences are not found at the conventional levels merely by choosing a large number of observations?* The power of a test is high if the significance level at N = 30,000 is carried over from situations in which the sample is 30 or 300. For example in Glen C. Blomquist, Mark C. Berger, and John P. Hoehn, N = 34,414 housing units and 46,004 individuals (March 1988, p. 93). At such large sample sizes the authors need to pay attention to the trade-off between power and the size of the test, and to the economic significance of the power against alternatives.

2. *Are the units and descriptive statistics for all regression variables included?* Empirical work in economics is measurement. It is elementary to include units of the variables, and then also to give means.

3. *Are coefficients reported in elasticity form, or in some interpretable form relevant for the problem at hand and consistent with economic theory, so that readers can discern the economic impact of regressors?* Wallis and Roberts long ago complained that "sometimes authors are so intrigued by tests of significance that they fail even to state the actual *amount* of the effect, much less to appraise its practical importance" (1956, p. 409). In some fields (not much in economics, though we did find one example) the investigator will publish tables that consist only of asterisks indicating levels of significance.

4. *Are the proper null hypotheses specified?* The most common problem would be to test against a null of zero when some other null is to the point. Such an error would be the result of allowing a canned program to make scientific decisions. If a null hypothesis is $\beta_1 + \beta_2 = 1$, there is not much to be gained from testing the hypothesis that each coefficient is statistically significantly different from zero. The most fruitful application of the Neyman-Pearson test specifies the null hypothesis as something the researcher believes to be

true. The only result that leads to a definitive conclusion is a rejection of the null hypothesis. Failing to reject does not of course imply that the null is therefore true. And rejecting the null does not imply that the alternative hypothesis is true: there may be other alternatives (a range that investigators agree is relevant, for example) which would cause rejection of the null. The rhetoric of rejection promotes a lexicographic procedure of "regress height, income, country, age"; inspect t-values; discard as unimportant if $t < 2$; circulate as important if $t > 2$.

5. *Are coefficients carefully interpreted?* Goldberger has an illustration of this similar to many issues in economic policy (1991). Suppose the dependent variable is "weight in pounds," the large coefficient is on "height," the smaller coefficient is on "exercise," and the estimated coefficients have the same standard errors. Neither the physician nor the patient would profit from an analysis that says height is "more important" (its coefficient being more standard errors away from zero in this sample), offering the overweight patient in effect the advice that he's not too fat, merely too short for his weight. "The moral of this example is that statistical measures of 'importance' are a diversion from the proper target of research— estimation of relevant parameters—to the task of 'explaining variation' in the dependent variable" (p. 241).

6. *Does the paper eschew reporting all* t- *or F-statistics or standard errors, regardless of whether a significance test is appropriate?* Statistical computing software routinely provide t-statistics for every estimated coefficient. But the fact that programs provide them does not mean that the information is relevant for science. We suspect that referees enforce the proliferation of meaningless t- and F-statistics, out of the belief that statistical and substantive significance are the same.

7. *Is statistical significance at the first use, commonly the scientific crescendo of the paper, the only criterion of "importance"?* By "crescendo" we mean that place in the paper where the author comes to what she evidently considers the crucial test.

8. *Does the paper mention the power of the tests?* For example, Frederic S. Mishkin does, unusually, in two footnotes (June 1981, pp. 298n. 11, 305n. 27; lack of power is a persistent difficulty in capital-market studies, but is seldom faced). As DeGroot pointed out, the power of a test may be low against a nearby and substantively significant alternative. On the other hand, power may be high against a nearby and trivial alternative.

9. *If the paper mentions power, does it do anything about it?* It is true that

power can only be discussed relative to an explicit alternative hypothesis, making power analysis difficult for some of the alternatives. An example is the Durbin-Wu-Hausman tests for whether two estimators are consistent. (The survey accounts for the difficulty by coding the relevant papers "not applicable.")

10. *Does the paper eschew "asterisk econometrics," that is, ranking the coefficients according to the absolute size of* t-*statistics?*

11. *Does the paper eschew "sign econometrics," that is, remarking on the sign but not the size of the coefficients?* There is a little statistical theory in the econometrics books lying behind this customary practice (Goldberger 1991, ch. 22), though for the most part the custom outstrips the theory. But sign is not *economically* significant unless the magnitude is large enough to matter. Statistical significance does not tell whether the size is large enough to matter. It is not true, as custom seems to be arguing, that sign is a statistic independent of magnitude.

12. *Does the paper discuss the size of the coefficients?* That is, once regression results are presented, does the paper make the point that some of the coefficients and their variables are *economically* influential, while others are not? Blomquist, Berger, and Hoehn do in part, by giving their coefficients on housing and neighborhood amenities in dollar form. But they do not discuss whether the magnitudes are scientifically reasonable, or in some other way important. Contrast Christina Romer, in a nineteen-page exclusively empirical paper: "Indeed, correcting for inventory movements reduces the discrepancy . . . by approximately half. This suggests that inventory movements are [economically] important" (June 1986, p. 327). M. Boissiere, J. B. Knight, and R. H. Sabot reflect the more typical practice: "In both countries, cognitive achievement bears a highly significant relationship to educational level. . . . In Kenya, secondary education raises H by 11.75 points, or by 35 percent of the mean" (December 1985, p. 1026). They make ambiguous use of the word "significance," then draw back to the relevant question of economic significance. Later in the paragraph they return to depending on statistical significance alone: "significantly positive" and "almost significantly positive" become again their only criteria of importance.

Daniel Hamermesh, by contrast, estimates his crucial parameter K, and at the first mention says, "The estimates of K are quite large, implying that the firm varies employment only in response to very large shocks. . . . Consider what an estimate this large means" (September 1989, p. 683). The form is here close to ideal:

it gets to the scientific question of what the size of a magnitude means. Two paragraphs down he speaks of "fairly large," "very important," "small," and "important" without merging these with statistical significance. In Goldberger's terms, he focuses on "the proper target of research—estimation of relevant parameters." (Later, though, Hamermesh falls back to average practice: "The K-hat for the aggregated data in Table 2 are insignificant," though he adds wisely, "and very small; and the average values of the p-hat are much higher than in the pooled data" [p. 685].)

13. *Does the paper discuss the scientific conversation within which a coefficient would be judged "large" or "small"?* Romer, for example, remarks that "The existence of the stylized fact [that is, the scientific consensus] that the economy has stabilized implies a general consensus" (p. 322).

14. *Does the paper avoid choosing variables for inclusion solely on the basis of statistical significance?* The standard argument is that if certain variables enter the model significantly, the information should not be spurned. But such an argument merges statistical and substantive significance.

15. *After the crescendo, does the paper avoid using statistical significance as the criterion of importance?* The referees will have insisted unthinkingly on a significance test, the prudent author will have acceded to their insistence, but should, after reporting them, turn to other scientifically relevant criteria of importance.

16. *Is statistical significance decisive, the conversation stopper, conveying the sense of an ending?* Romer and Jeffrey Sachs (March 1980) both use statistical significance, and misuse it—in both cases looking to statistical significance as a criterion for how large is large. But in neither paper does statistical significance run the empirical work. The misuse in Michael Darby (June 1984) is balder: his only argument for a coefficient when he runs a regression is its statistical significance (pp. 311, 315), but on the other hand, his findings do not turn on the regression results.

17. *Does the paper ever use a simulation (as against use of the regression as an input into further argument) to determine whether the coefficients are reasonable?* To some degree Blomquist, Berger, and Hoehn do. They simulate the rankings of cities by amenity, and if the coefficients were quite wrong the rankings would be themselves unreasonable. Santa Barbara does rank high, though the differential value of amenities worst to best, at $5,146, seems low if you've been to Santa Monica and East St. Louis (March 1988, p. 96). Simulations using regression coefficients can be informative, but of

course should not use statistical significance as a screening device for input.

18. *In the "conclusions" and "implications" sections, is statistical significance kept separate from economic, policy, and scientific significance?* In Boissiere, Knight, and Sabot (December 1985) the effect of ability is isolated well, but the economic significance is not argued.

19. *Does the paper avoid using the word "significance" in ambiguous ways, meaning "statistically significant" in one sentence and "large enough to matter for policy or science" in another?* Thus Darby (June 1984): "First we wish to test whether oil prices, price controls, or both has a significant influence on productivity growth" (p. 310). The meanings are merged.

A Lot Did Go Wrong

A few of the *AER* authors, such as Romer and Hamermesh, show that they are aware of the substantive importance of the questions they ask, and of the futility of relying on a test of statistical significance for getting answers. Thus Kim B. Clark: "While the union coefficient in the sales specification is twice the size of its standard error, it is substantively small; moreover, with over 4,600 observations, the power of the evidence that the effect is different from zero is not overwhelming" (December 1984, p. 912). And Zvi Griliches:

> Here and subsequently, all statements about statistical "significance" should not be taken literally. Besides the usual issue of data mining clouding their interpretation, the "sample" analyzed comes close to covering completely the relevant population. Tests of significance are used here as a metric for discussing the relative fit of different versions of the model. In each case, the actual magnitude of the estimated coefficients is of more interest than their precise "statistical significance" (December 1986, p. 146)

Griliches understands that populations should not be treated as samples, and that statistical significance is not a substitute for economic significance. (He does not say, though, why statistical significance is a scientifically relevant "metric for discussing the relative fit of the different versions of the model.")

But most authors in the *AER* do not understand these points. The results of applying the survey to the papers of the 1980s are displayed in Table 3.

The Rhetoric of Significance Tests

Table 3. The *American Economic Review* in the 1980s Had Numerous Errors in the Use of Statistical Significance

Survey Question	Total for which the question applies	Percent Yes
Does the paper . . .		
8. Consider the power of the test?	182	4.4
6. Eschew reporting all standard errors, *t*-, *F*-statistics, when such information is irrelevant?	181	8.3
17. Do a simulation to determine whether the coefficients are reasonable?	179	13.2
9. Examine the power function?	12	16.7
13. Discuss the scientific conversation within which a coefficient would be judged large or small?	181	28.0
16. Consider more than statistical significance decisive in an empirical argument?	182	29.7
18. In the conclusions, distinguish between statistical and substantive significance?	181	30.1
2. Report descriptive statistics for regression variables?	178	32.4
15. Use other criteria of importance besides statistical significance after the crescendo?	182	40.7
19. Avoid using the word "significance" in ambiguous ways?	180	41.2
5. Carefully interpret coefficients? For example, does it pay attention to the details of the units of measurement, and to the limitations of the data?	181	44.5
11. Eschew "sign econometrics," remarking on the sign but not the size of the coefficients?	181	46.7
7. At its first use, consider statistical significance to be one among other criteria of importance?	182	47.3
3. Report coefficients in elasticities, or in some other useful form that addresses the question of "how large is large"?	173	66.5
14. Avoid choosing variables for inclusion solely on the basis of statistical significance?	180	68.1
10. Eschew "asterisk econometrics," the ranking of coefficients according to the absolute size of the test statistic?	182	74.7
12 Discuss the size of the coefficients, making points of substantive significance?	182	80.2
1. Use a small number of observations, such that statistically significant differences are not found merely by choosing a very large sample?	182	85.7
4. Test the null hypotheses that the authors said were the ones of interest?	180	97.3

Source for Tables 3–7: All full-length papers using regression analysis in the *American Economic Review*, 1980–1989, excluding the Proceedings.
Notes: "Percent Yes" is the total number of Yes responses divided by the relevant number of papers (never exceeding 182). Some questions are not generally applicable to particular papers and some questions are not applicable because they are conditional on the paper having a particular characteristic. Question 3, for example, was coded "not applicable" for papers which exclusively use nonparametric statistics. Question 19 was coded "not applicable" for papers that do not use the word "significance."

The principal findings of the survey are:

- Seventy percent of the empirical papers in the *American Economic Review* papers did not distinguish statistical significance from economic, policy, or scientific significance.
- At the first use of statistical significance, typically in the "Estimation" or "Results" section, 53 percent did not consider anything but the size of *t*- and *F*-statistics. About one third used only the size of *t*- and *F*-test statistics as a criterion for the inclusion of variables in future work.
- Seventy-two percent did not ask "How large is large?" That is, after settling on an estimate of a coefficient, 72 percent did not consider what other authors had found; they did not ask what standards other authors had used to determine "importance"; they did not provide an argument one way or another whether the estimate β = 0.999 is economically close to 1.000 and economically important even though "statistically different from one." Awareness that scientific inquiry takes place in a conversation about how large is large seemed to improve the econometric practice. Of 131 papers that did *not* mention the work of other authors as a quantitative context for their own, 78 percent let statistical significance decide questions of substantive significance. Of 50 papers that did mention the work of other authors as a context, only 20 percent let statistical significance decide.
- Fifty-nine percent used the word "significance" in ambiguous ways, at one point meaning "statistically significantly different from the null," at another "practically important" or "greatly changing our scientific opinions," with no distinction.
- Despite the advice proffered in theoretical statistics, only 4.5 percent considered the power of their tests. One percent actually inspected the power function.
- Sixty-nine percent did not report descriptive statistics—the means of the regression variables, for example—that would allow the reader to make a judgment about the economic significance of the results.
- Thirty-two percent admitted openly to using statistical significance to drop variables (question 14). One would have to have more evidence than explicit admissions to know how prevalent the practice is in fact. One-third is a lower bound.
- Multiple-author papers, as one might expect from the theory of common property resources, more often spoke of "significance" in ambiguous ways, used sign econometrics, did not discuss the size

of estimated coefficients, and found nothing more than the size of test statistics to be of importance at the first use of statistical significance (Table 4).

- Authors from "Tier 1" schools did, in some respects, a little better, but whether the difference justifies the invidious terminology of "tiers" is a scientific, not a statistical, question and must be left to the investigator (Table 5; the terminology is that of the most recent National Research Council assessment and includes Chicago, Harvard, MIT, Princeton, Stanford, and Yale).

  Though I do not here report the results, we found on the other hand that papers written by faculty at Tier 1 schools were proportionally more likely to use sampling theory on entire populations, and to treat as probability samples what are in fact samples of convenience.

The significance of such practices can be made vivid by examining a few cases in depth. I do not mention here the names of the authors, since they are merely engaging in a socially sanctioned rhetoric recommended by their teachers of econometrics. It would be cruel to hold them up for ridicule. To show I am sincere, look at the following phrases, from a (wonderful) article published in March 1984 called, "Corn at Interest: The Extent and Cost of Grain Storage in Medieval England": "The fitted *equation (standard errors in parentheses),*" "much less strongly *(though definitely),*" and "*the standard error of the coefficient . . . is one-half the value of the coefficient*" (pp. 178, 180; italics supplied).The italicized words are plain cases of misusing statistical significance to decide whether a variable is important or not. The paper appeared also in the *American Economic Review,* though not as a regular article, and so did not come into the group of papers that Ziliak and I examined. There were two authors. One of them was D. N. McCloskey.

The cases: In one paper the authors estimate benefit-cost ratios for the state of Illinois following the implementation of an unemployment insurance experiment. In one experiment a control group was given a cash bonus for getting a job quickly and keeping it for several months. In another experiment, the "Employer Experiment," *employers* were given a cash-bonus if claimants found a job quickly and retained it for some specified amount of time (September 1987, p. 517). The intent of the "Employer Experiment" was to "provide a marginal wage-bill subsidy, or training subsidy, that might reduce the duration of insured unemployment" (p. 517). Here is how the conclusion is presented:

> The fifth panel also shows that the overall benefit-cost ratio
> for the Employer Experiment is 4.29, but it is not statistically

Table 4. Multiple Authors Appear to Have Coordination Problems. Making the Abuses Worse Measured by Percent Yes

Survey Question	Multiple Authors Papers	Single Author Papers
Does the paper . . .		
7. At its first use, consider statistical significance to be one among other criteria of importance?	42.2	53.4
10. Eschew "asterisk econometrics," the ranking of coefficients according to the absolute size of the test statistic?	68.8	79.2
12. Discuss the size of the coefficients, making points of substantive significance?	76.7	84.1
1. Use a small number of observations, such that statistically significant differences are not found merely by choosing a very large sample?	77.8	84.8

Note: "Percent Yes" is the total number of Yes responses divided by the relevant number of papers.

Table 5. Authors at Tier 1 Departments Do Better than Others in Many Categories Measured by Percent Yes

Survey Question	Tier 1 Departments	Other Departments
Does the paper . . .		
1. Use a small number of observations, such that statistically significant differences are not found merely by choosing a very large sample?	91.3	83.9
12. Discuss the size of the coefficients, making points of substantive significance?	87.0	78.9
10. Eschew "asterisk econometrics," the ranking of coefficients according to the absolute size of the test statistic?	84.8	71.4
7. At its first use, consider statistical significance to be one among other criteria of importance?	65.5	41.2
5. Carefully interpret coefficients? For example, does it pay attention to the details of the units of measurement, and to the limitations of the data?	60.0	37.5
19. Avoid using the word "significance" in ambiguous ways?	52.4	37.5
18. In the conclusions, distinguish between statistical and substantive significance?	50.0	23.1

Notes: According to the most recent National Research Council assessment, the Tier 1 departments are Chicago, Harvard, MIT, Princeton, Stanford, and Yale.
"Percent Yes" is the total number of Yes responses divided by the relevant number of papers.

different from zero. The benefit-cost ratio for white women in the Employer Experiment, however, is 7.07, and is statistically different from zero. Hence, a program modeled on the Employer Experiment also might be attractive from the state's point of view if the program did not increase unemployment among nonparticipants. Since, however, the Employer Experiment affected only white women, it would be essential to understand the reasons for the uneven effects of the treatment on different groups of workers before drawing conclusions about the efficacy of such a program. (*AER* September 1987, p. 527)

Here "affected" means that the estimated coefficient is statistically significantly different from a value the authors believe to be the relevant one. The 4.29 benefit-cost ratio for the whole Employer Experiment is, according to the authors, *not useful or important for public policy.* The 7.07 ratio for white women is said to "affect"—to be important—because it passed an arbitrary significance test. That is, 7.07 *affects,* 4.29 does not. It is true that 4.29 is a realization from a noisy random variable, whereas 7.07 is from a more quiet one. Though the authors do not say so, the 4.29 benefit-cost ratio is marginally discernible from zero at about the 12 percent level (p. 527). Yet for policy purposes even a noisy benefit-cost ratio is worth talking about. The argument that the 4.29 figure does not "affect" is unsound, and could be costly in employment foregone.

Another paper offers "an alternative test of the CAPM and report[s] . . . test results that are free from the ambiguity imbedded in the past tests" (January 1980, p. 660). The authors are taking exception to Richard Roll's comment that "there is practically no possibility that such a test can be accomplished in the future" (p. 660). So they test five hypotheses: the intercept equals zero; the slope coefficients differ from zero; the adjusted coefficient of determination should be near one; there is no trend in the intercept; and there is no trend in the adjusted coefficient of determination (pp. 664–65). On several time-series they run least-squares regressions to estimate coefficients. Nowhere in the text is the size of the estimated coefficients discussed (a common mistake in the capital-market literature). Instead, the authors *rank* their results according to the number of times the absolute value of the t-statistic is greater than 2 (p. 667). Three out of four of their tables of estimation results have a column called "No. of Times $t > 2$," another column with "Average t-statistics," and one with "Adjusted R^2." They do not report coefficient estimates in the three tables, merely the t-statistics (Table 1, 2, and 3, pp. 667–68). The only "Yes" that the paper earned in our survey was for specifying the null according to what their theory suggests.

Ambiguously using the very word "significance" implies that there is no difference between economic significance and statistical significance, that nothing or little else matters. Of the 96 papers that use only the test of statistical significance as a criterion of importance at its first use, 90 percent imply—or state—that it is decisive in an empirical argument, and 70 percent use the word "significance" ambiguously. Of the other 86 papers in the survey less than half use the word ambiguously. The 96 unsound papers continue making inappropriate decisions at a higher rate than the 86 papers that acknowledge some criterion other than statistical significance. Only 7 of the 96 distinguish statistical significance from economic or policy or scientific significance in the conclusions and implications sections, while 47 of the 86 make the distinction (Table 6).

Here is an extreme case of ambiguity:

> The statistically significant [read: (1) sampling theory] inequality aversion is in addition to any unequal distribution of inputs resulting from different social welfare weights for different neighborhoods. The KP results allowing for unequal concern yield an estimate of Q of -3.4. This estimate is significantly [read: (2) some numbers are smaller than others] less than zero, indicating aggregate outcome is not maximized. At the same time, however, there is also significant [read: (3) a moral or scientific or policy matter] concern about productivity, as the inequality parameter is significantly [read: (4) a joint observation about morality and numbers] greater than the extreme concern solely with equity. (*AER* March 1987, p. 46)

In a piece on Ricardian Equivalence, statistical significance decides nearly everything:

> Notice the least significant of the variables in the constrained estimation is the second lagged value of the deficit in the government purchases equation. A natural course would be to reestimate the model for the case of two lagged values of government spending and one lagged value of the government deficit. . . . Although the elimination of [the variable] raises the confidence level at which the null hypothesis can be rejected, it remains impossible to argue that the data provides evidence against the joint proposition of Ricardian equivalence and rational expectations at conventional levels of significance. (*AER* March 1985, p. 125)

Table 6. If Only Statistical Significance Is Said to Be of Importance at Its First Use (Question 7). Then Many Other Inappropriate Decisions Are Made Measured by Percent Yes

Survey Question	If only statistical significance is important	If more than statistical significance is important
Does the paper . . .		
12. Examine the power function?	0	28.6
6. Eschew reporting all standard errors, t-, and F-statistics, when such information is irrelevant?	3.2	14.0
8. Consider the power of the test?	4.2	4.7
17. Do a simulation to determine whether the coefficients are reasonable?	6.3	17.9
18. In the conclusions, distinguish between statistical and substantive significance?	7.3	55.3
16. Consider more than statistical significance decisive in an empirical argument?	10.4	51.2
5. Carefully interpret coefficients? For example, does it pay attention to the details of the units of measurement, and to the limitations of the data?	13.7	77.9
13. Discuss the scientific conversation within which a coefficient would be judged large or small?	17.7	38.8
11. Eschew "sign econometrics," remarking on the sign but not the size of the coefficients?	21.9	74.1
2. Report descriptive statistics for regression variables?	26.3	36.1
15. Use other criteria of importance besides statistical significance after the crescendo?	30.2	52.3
19. Avoid using the word "significance" in ambiguous ways?	29.5	52.9
3. Report coefficients in elasticities, or in some other useful form that addresses the question of "how large is large?"	51.6	80.0
14. Avoid choosing variables for inclusion solely on the basis of statistical significance?	59.0	77.7
10. Eschew "asterisk econometrics," the ranking of coefficients according to the size of the test statistic?	66.7	83.7
12. Discuss the size of the coefficients, making points of substantive significance?	66.7	96.5
1. Use a small number of observations, such that statistically significant differences are not found merely by choosing a very large sample?	86.5	84.8
4. Test the null hypotheses that the authors say are the ones of interest?	94.7	100

Notes: "Percent Yes" is the total number of Yes responses divided by the relevant number of papers. Some questions are not generally applicable because they are conditional on a paper having a particular characteristic. Question 3, for example, was coded "not applicable" for papers which exclusively use nonparametirc statistics. Question 19 was coded "not applicable" for papers that do not use the word "significance."

Table 7. The Ease of Computing Statistical Significance in the Late 1970s May Have Had Bad Effects on the Use of Regression Analysis Measured by Percent Yes

	Does the paper . . .		
Date of Ph.D. Conferral	Distinguish Among Kind of Significance in the Conclusions (Question 18)	Eschew Ambiguous Usage of the Very Word (Question 19)	Consider More Than Statistical Significance Decisive in Empirical Argument (Question 16)
1940–1969	29	61	26
1970–1974	33	37	31
1975–1979	17	29	13
1980–1984	33	45	33

Note: The number of papers published by each cohort is 31, 48, 24, and 24. Multiple author papers were dated by the first name listed on the published article.

Another paper reports "significant" results on the relation between unemployment and money:

> The coefficient is significant at the 99 percent confidence level. Neither the current money shock nor all 12 coefficients as a group are significantly different from zero. The coefficient on I is negative and significant and the distributed lag on I is significant as well. In column (2) we report a regression which omits the insignificant lags on money shocks. The I distributed lag is now significant at the 1 percent confidence level. . . . We interpret these results as indicating that the primary factor determining cyclical variations in the probability of leaving unemployment is probably heterogeneity. Inventory innovations appear to play some role and surprisingly, money shocks have no significant impact. (*AER* September 1985, p. 630)

A hopeful sign is that misuses of statistical significance seem to depend in part on a vintage effect, measured by date of Ph.D. conferral. The papers authored by Ph.D.s conferred between 1975 and 1979, when inexpensively generated t-tests first reached the masses, were considerably worse than the papers of others at making a distinction between economic and statistical significance. They used the word "significance" in ambiguous ways more often than did earlier or later Ph.D.s, and were less likely to separate statistical significance from other kinds of significance in the sections on scientific and policy implications (Table 7).

If economists do not wish to leave science to chance they should rethink the rhetoric of statistical significance. Something should be done. It might be done in econometrics courses, which could teach the relevant decision theory and then actually use it for something. It would help if the standard computer packages did not generate t-statistics in such profusion. The Durbin-Watson statistic is similar, generated by the packages regardless of whether or not the data are the time series that make the statistic meaningful. Because it is there, available to demonstrate painlessly his technical competence, the young economist itches to find some use for the statistic even in a cross-section. It would be charitable to warn students off such decisive demonstrations of their incompetence by a printed question in the package: "Do you really have a time series?"

The packages might likewise ask in large type: "DO YOU REALLY HAVE A PROBABILITY SAMPLE?" "HAVE YOU CONSIDERED POWER?" and, above all, "BY WHAT SCIENTIFIC STANDARD WOULD YOU JUDGE A FITTED COEFFICIENT LARGE OR SMALL?" They might ask at the beginning, "Do you really want to look under the lamp post?" Or perhaps they could merely ask, printed in bold capitals beside each t-statistic, **"SO WHAT ELSE IS NEW?"**

9 THE POVERTY OF

ECONOMIC MODERNISM

The Mathematization of
Economics Was a Good Idea

The economic conversation has heard much eloquent talk, but its most eloquent passages have been mathematical. Especially since the 1940s economists of all schools have become enchanted by the new and scientific way of talking. Most journals of economics nowadays look like journals of applied mathematics or theoretical statistics.

The American Economic Review of the early 1930s, by contrast, contained hardly an equation; assumptions were not formalized; the graphs were plots of series, and not common; the fitting of a line to a scatter of points was rare. The consequence of the primitive machinery for conversation was an inability to speak clearly. Economists could not keep clear, for instance, the difference between the movement of an entire curve and movement along a curve. Being mathematically innocent, they were unable to talk in curvy metaphors. They might think of the Labor Problem, as Harry A. Millis did in his presidential address to the American Economic Association in December 1934, as having something to do with marginal productivity (pp. 4–5). After reading J. R. Hicks's book of 1932, *The Theory of Wages,* as Millis had without much mathematical understanding, they might recognize that marginal productivity did affect wages. But the economists before the reception of mathematics fell headlong, as Millis did, into confusions that a little mathematics would have cleared up: confusions about working conditions (which they did not see as merely another item with income in the utility function) or about bargaining strength (which they did not see as determined by aggregated marginal productivities and supply curves of labor). Mathematical metaphors were not then available to most economists.

Now they are available in bulk, especially to the bourgeois, English-speaking economists who dominate the profession, and of whom I am an example. Of the 159 full-length papers published in the *American Economic Review* during 1981, 1982, and 1983, only 6 used words alone and only 4 added to their words tabular statistics alone, the one formal device common in 1931–1933. The techniques of mathematics, statistics, diagrams, and explicit simulation, which economists viewed once as useless and arcane, had become routine. Fully two-thirds of the papers used mathematics explicitly, and most of the others were speaking in a mathematics-saturated environment in which the words "production function" and "demand curve" would call up the mathematics anyway. Nearly half of the papers used diagrams in the fashion economists have come to use them, puzzling other students of society by talking definitely about curves that do not have definite shapes. Nearly a third of the papers used regression analysis, often in quite elaborate ways. Over a tenth used explicit simulation that only academic engineers and physicists could have followed in 1934. Mathematical analysis illustrated by diagrams (and without facts, in keeping with the abstract character of economic conversation) was used in 60 of the 159. Any one of these techniques would have dazzled and dismayed an audience of economists in 1934.

But a Philosophy Got Mixed Up in the Mathematics

Yet this gain, like most gains, was achieved at a cost. Books on technical economics are no longer even superficially accessible to lay people and young economists overvalue a narrow and often silly ingenuity of technique. The main cost, though, is harder to spot. It is that along with their new mathematical way of talking the economists adopted a crusading faith, a set of *philosophical* doctrines, that makes them prone now to fanaticism and intolerance. The faith consists of scientism, behaviorism, operationalism, positive economics, and other quantifying enthusiasms of the 1930s. In the way of crusading faiths the doctrines have hardened into ceremony, and now support many monks, bishops, and cathedrals.

The connection between the mathematics and the philosophy was only psychological. A science can be mathematical without becoming positivist, behaviorist, or operationalist. But psychologically a faith of some sort was needed during the struggle for Jerusalem. No young economist in 1950 would have risked his professional life for the values merely of tolerance and methodological balance. Many of the mathematically unskilled in economics around 1950 were ignorantly obdurate: they would have none of that, and often had the institutional means to prevent it. The times warranted citadel storming.

But now, so long after the victory, you might ask whether the faith that supported it still serves a social function. You might ask whether the strident talk of Science in economics, which served well in bringing clarity and rigor to the field, has outlived its usefulness.

The Official Methodology of Economics Is "Modernist"

Economists have two attitudes toward discourse, the official and the unofficial, the explicit and the implicit. Most of what I have said so far has to do with the unofficial attitudes, exhibited in how economists actually argue. But economists put great store by their official attitudes, which they believe to be derived from the best thinking in the history and philosophy of science. The official attitude obstructs their view of how they actually argue. They cannot see how they actually argue because the scene is veiled by certain philosophies.

Their official rules of speaking well, to which economists pay homage in methodological ruminations and in teachings to the young, declare them to be Scientists in the modern mode. The credo of scientific methodology, long known to its critics as the Received View, is, roughly speaking, "positivism." It argues that knowledge is to be modeled on the early nineteenth century's understanding of certain pieces of nineteenth-century and especially seventeenth-century physics.

To emphasize its pervasiveness in modern thinking well beyond science, however, it is best called "modernism." Modernism gleams diamond-hard from many facets and the word can be fully defined only in use. But in a preliminary way it can be said to be, as the literary critic Wayne Booth has put it, the notion that we know only what we cannot doubt and cannot really know what we can merely assent to. It is the attitude that the only real knowledge is, in common parlance (sense 5b, remember), "Scientific," that is, knowledge tested by certain kinds of rigorous scepticism. Philosophically speaking, modernism is the program of Descartes, regnant in philosophy since the seventeenth century, to build knowledge on a foundation of radical doubt.

Modernism coheres, one part with the other. There are modernist philosophers, modernist architects, modernist musicians, modernist politicians, and modernist economists (Klamer 1991). That is the reason for using so many-sided a word: the thing itself is many-sided. You can detect modernism as much in Symphony Hall and the Museum of Modern Art as in the temples to social engineering in Washington or The Hague. The modernism espoused by the economist is reinforced in him from all sides.

The Poverty of Economic Modernism

As religious faith retreated among the intelligentsia in the nineteenth and twentieth centuries, a modernist faith flowed in. Its full tide shows in the way we talk. You hear on the street: "That's just your opinion"; "My biases are such and such"; "I came to this conclusion on the basis of facts"; "You're not being objective"; "That's a very subjective view"; "That's just theology"; "That's just an aesthetic judgment"; "If you can't measure it, I don't think it's objective"; "You tell me the facts, I'll decide on the values"; "You are not being scientific: why should I listen?" Sophomores talk like this. In a little more literate form their professors do the same: only falsifiable hypotheses are meaningful; the evidence is consistent with the hypothesis; *de gustibus non est disputandum,* of tastes one ought not, of course, to quarrel.

Modernism views science as axiomatic and mathematical, and takes the realm of science to be separate from the realm of form, value, beauty, goodness, and all things unmeasurable. Being functionalist and given to social engineering the modernist is antihistorical, uninterested in cultural or intellectual traditions, at least while in church. The faith can be seen in some scientists and in many who wish especially to be Scientific. At its best it produces a disinterested and efficient investigator; at its worst, a Dr. Strangelove.

The modernist comes in another, irrationalist form: at its best an artist or preacher, at worst a surfer strung out on the latest mysticism. The rationalist and the irrationalist pray to the same god. An irrationalist believes himself different from the rationalist, and in the way he cuts his hair he sometimes is. But in his theory of knowledge he is not. He is merely a protestant, irritated by the rituals of the church of science and scornful of its selling of indulgences, but sharing with it a belief in a trinity of fact, definition, and holy value. Each part of the trinity, on this view, can have its separate devotees—the scientist, the mathematician, and the litterateur. In the modernist view, whether rationalist or irrationalist, these various worshippers need not get in one another's way. Each can specialize in one kind of argument. Arguments do not cross: this year's GNP is one thing; an axiom of social choice is another; sympathy for the poor still another.

The reaction to the modernist theory of knowledge is by now broad. Its leading figures range from professional philosophers (Willard Quine, Nelson Goodman, Stephen Toulmin, Paul Feyerabend, Richard Rorty) to a miscellany of practitioners-turned-philosophers in chemistry (Michael Polanyi), law (Chaim Perelman), and literary criticism (Wayne Booth). The reach of the idea that fact is more than experiment and that argument is more than syllogism is by now long, as, for example, in the lucid treatment of it in Glenn Webster, Ada Jacox, and

Beverly Baldwin, "Nursing Theory and the Ghost of the Received View" (1981, pp. 25–35).

The reach, however, has not extended far into economics, and not into neoclassical economics at all. Austrian, institutionalist, and Marxist economists, to be sure, have for a century been attacking certain parts of modernism. But they have seized on other parts with redoubled fervor and have expressed their remaining doubts obscurely. In their own way they have been as narrow as thoroughgoing positivists: the rejection of econometrics by Austrian economists, for instance, would be reasonable only if the more naïve claims of econometrics were to be taken seriously. For the rest, economists have let philosophical scribblers of a few years back supply their official thinking about good argument.

The mark of modernism is plain in Anglo-American economics since the 1930s. Notwithstanding its gleams of steely brilliance, it has produced by now many crippled economists. Many are bored by history, disdainful of other social scientists, ignorant of their civilization, thoughtless in ethics, and unreflective in method. Even the wise and good among the congregation, who are numerous, find it hard to reconcile their faiths with the ceremonies required of them on Sunday.

Only a tired religion can be like this—at once both noble and corrupting. The Ten Commandments of modernism in economics and other sciences are

1. Prediction and control is the point of science. As Comte said, *prevoir pour pouvoir.*
2. Only the observable implications (or predictions) of a theory matter to its truth.
3. Observability entails objective, reproducible experiments; mere questionnaires interrogating human subjects are useless, because humans might lie.
4. If and only if an experimental implication of a theory proves false is the theory proved false.
5. Objectivity is to be treasured; subjective "observation" (introspection) is not scientific knowledge, because the objective and the subjective cannot be linked.
6. Kelvin's Dictum: "When you cannot express it in numbers, your knowledge is of a meagre and unsatisfactory kind" (Kelvin 1883, 1:73, quoted in Kuhn 1977, pp. 178n, 183n. An approximation to this version is inscribed on the front of the Social Science Research Building at the University of Chicago. Jacob Viner, the famous University of Chicago economist, is said to have remarked on it one day: "Yes, and when you can express it in numbers your knowl-

edge is of a meagre and unsatisfactory kind." Frank Knight, the famous University of Iowa economist, wrote, "Yes, and when you can't measure, measure anyway" [Knight 1940, p. 166n]).

7. Introspection, metaphysical belief, aesthetics, and the like may well figure in the discovery of an hypothesis but cannot figure in its justification; justifications are timeless, and the surrounding community of science irrelevant to their truth.
8. It is the business of methodology to demarcate scientific reasoning from nonscientific, positive from normative.
9. A scientific explanation of an event brings the event under a covering law.
10. Scientists—for instance, economic scientists—ought not to have anything to say as scientists about the oughts of value, whether of morality or art.

And in addition the Golden Rule, Hume's Golden Fork: "When we run over libraries persuaded of these principles, what havoc must we make? If we take in our hand any volume; of divinity or school metaphysics, for instance, let us ask, *Does it contain any abstract reasoning concerning quantity or number?* No. *Does it contain any experimental reasoning concerning matter of fact and existence?* No. Commit it then to the flames: for it can contain nothing but sophistry and illusion" (Hume 1748, last page).

It is at the level of applied, not theoretical, philosophy, among professional economists, not professional philosophers, that these commandments thrive. No more than a few philosophers now believe as many as half of the commandments. A substantial, respectable, and growing minority believes none of them. But all of them are believed by a majority of economists (and psychologists, sociologists, political scientists, medical scientists, and other nonphilosophers enchanted by modernism).

Certainly an earlier generation of economic methodologists believed them. Methodology and its search for certitude has infected each school of economics. In American economics, however, a methodology of modernism and scientism is particularly associated with the Chicago School. The main texts of economic modernism after Terence Hutchison's *The Significance and Basic Postulates of Economic Theory* (1938) are Chicago School effusions, such as Gary Becker and George Stigler's "De Gustibus Non Est Disputandum" (1977) or, above all, Milton Friedman's "The Methodology of Positive Economics (1953). The more extreme interpretations of the texts flourish among economists bearing a Chicago degree.

This is odd. It is odd that a group so annoying to other economists in most of its activities should have their assent in the matter of official method. Yet a watered-down version of Friedman's essay of 1953 is part of the intellectual equipment of most American economists, and its arguments come readily to their lips.

Premeditated writing on method is usually sweeter than methodological remarks in the course of nonmethodological business. In precept you can be sweetly vague, earning universal assent; in practice you must make enemies. To take a typical example of first-chapter methodology at the full tide of modernism, Kalman Cohen and Richard Cyert in their otherwise admirable book present an outline of modernism, asserting that it is the method "used in all scientific analyses" (1975, p. 17). The "method" they then outline, with a bibliography weighted toward logical positivism and its allies, is not much more than an appeal to be honest and thoughtful. Only when such a phrase as "at least in principle testable by experiment and observation" (p. 23) is tested by experiment and observation does it become clear what is at stake.

Friedman's essay is the central document of modernism in economics and deserves respectful review. Even though published early, before the tide of modernism had crested in the human sciences, it was more postmodernist than you might suppose from slight acquaintance with the text. Friedman did, for example, mention with approval the aesthetic criteria of simplicity and fruitfulness that an economist might use to select among a multiplicity of theories with the same predictions, though in the next sentence he attempted to reduce them to matters of prediction (1953, p. 10). He accepted that questionnaires, forbidden to the modernist in economics, are useful for suggesting hypotheses, though in the next sentence he asserted that they are "almost entirely useless as a means of *testing* the validity of economic hypotheses" (p. 31n; see Commandments 3 and 7). He emphasized the role of the community to which the scientist speaks in producing conviction—whether made up of sociologists, say, or of economists—though in the next sentence he returned to an "objective" theory of testing (see Commandment 5).

Sweetly vague precepts, of course, are sometimes good. When Friedman published his essay, the practice of economics was riven into theory without fact and fact without theory. His modernist chanting, supported by hooded choruses of philosophers, was at the time probably good for the soul. But again you must ask whether it is not time to stop the chanting.

In other words, Friedman, like Karl Popper, another transitional figure, seemed to be struggling to escape the grip of positivism and its intellectual traditions, though with only sporadic success. This *locus clas-*

sicus of economic modernism contains much antimodernism, suggesting that modernism cannot survive discussion even by its best advocates. Abraham Hirsch and Neil de Marchi (1990) have argued persuasively that the explanation for Friedman's cognitive dissonance is that in his essay he was not in fact positivist at all, not even Popperian, but Deweyan. To follow John Dewey is to be pragmatist and American, more interested in the uses of knowledge than in its foundations. The reading is satisfying, and Friedman likes it too, but the problem is then to find a reason for the misunderstanding that long associated Friedman with the more European positivism of, say, Paul Samuelson. Perhaps it was that pragmatism, along with other American toys, had already by the early 1950s acquired a musty odor; the new governess from Europe had already banished it to the attic.

However Friedman is to be taken, the unpremeditated remark in the heat of economic argument usually has a crudely modernist content, often using Friedman's words (or Fritz Machlup's words [1955], which were widely interpreted as seconding Friedman's). An important article by Richard Roll and Stephen Ross on finance, for instance, asserts that "the theory should be tested by its conclusions, not by its assumptions" and that "similarly, one should not reject the conclusions derived from firm profit maximization on the basis of sample surveys in which managers claim that they trade off profit for social good" (1980, p. 1093 and n.). The same can be found elsewhere, in nearly identical terms, dating back to Friedman's essay: William Sharpe (1970, p. 77), for instance, writing on the same matter as Roll and Ross, takes it as a rule of polite scientific behavior that "the realism of the assumptions matters little. If the implications are reasonably consistent with observed phenomena, the theory can be said to 'explain' reality." Intoned so often in harmony with others, such phrases have become incantations. Economic modernism is a revealed religion, and a ritualistic one.

Most economists, at least most English-speaking economists, would thrill to the epithet of modernist Scientist. This is one piece of evidence that economists are philosophical modernists. There is other evidence: the prevalence of methodological declarations such as those of Friedman, and especially of Friedman's followers; the feeling anyone fluent in economics has that modernism provides the grammar for discourse; and the reaction to antimodernist arguments, in which someone can be relied on to leap up and declare that "ultimately" the only "fundamental" proof of an economic assertion is "objective," quantitative "tests." It is hard to disbelieve the dominance of modernism in economics, though an objective, quantitative test would of course make it, or any assertion, more believable and would be worth doing. A proper sampling of referee reports of the *American Economic Review* would do the trick, watching out for the use of the modernist ukase ("Never ask business people what they are doing: they cannot tell the truth"; "Measure things regardless").

In any case, modernism rules: that is the main point. It will not do to say about the methodological rules of economists, as a professional philosopher might, "No one believes *that* stuff anymore." Maybe no one does in the higher reaches of sophistication in Departments of Philosophy. Most professional philosophers will claim they are not positivists, but then will come out with ugly remarks like: "If it is true that there are but two kinds of people in the world—the logical positivists and the god-damned English professors—then I suppose I am a logical positivist" (Glymour 1980, p. ix). But anyway a modernist faith of the cruder and narrower sort thrives still in the harder sciences, such as economics.

Modernism Is a Poor Method: For One Thing, It Is Obsolete in Philosophy

There are many things wrong with modernism as a methodology for science, or for economic science. The first is that the philosophical arguments for it have long been known to be unpersuasive. Even philosophical economists seem to read about as much in professional philosophy as philosophers do in professional economics. It is not surprising, therefore, that the news of the decline of modernism has not reached all ears. The logical positivists of the 1920s scorned in their time what they called "metaphysics." From the beginning, though, the scorn has refuted itself. If metaphysics is to be cast into the flames, then the methodological declarations of the modernist family from Descartes through Hume and Comte to Russell, Hempel, and Popper will be the first to go. For this and other reasons philosophers agree that strict logical positivisim is dead (see Passmore 1967). Karl Popper played a role on both the modernist and antimodernist sides. He quoted Passmore with approval for the motto of a chapter of his own entitled "Who Killed Logical Positivism?" (Popper 1976, pp. 87–90), in which he confesses to the murder. "I," said the Popper,/"with my little chopper,/I killed Logical Positivism." The length of time it has been dead raises the question whether economists are wise to carry on with their necrophilia.

In economics the metaphysical position akin to logical positivism is clumsily argued, probably because it derives more from the philosophizing of philosophical amateurs from Mach to Bridgeman than from the parallel thinking of professional philosophers themselves. Mach, Pearson, Duhem, and Ostwald—that is, scientists with an interest in the history of science—revived positivism in the 1890s, but logical positivism, the philosopher's version, was a later development.

Modernist rules in economics, therefore, are asserted but seldom argued. Consider the master rules. As often as they have been repeated, it is hard to see on the face of it, or even beneath, the appeal of "operationally meaningful statements" (Samuelson 1947, p. 3 and throughout) or "valid and meaningful predictions about phenomena not yet observed" (Friedman 1953) or "predictive value of hypothetical generalization" (Machlup 1955, p. 1) as standards against which every nonmathematical assertion is to be judged. No ordinary person follows a methodology like this in ordinary thinking, and its advocates do not make an argument for treating some kinds of thinking as extraordinary. The argument that Hutchison, Samuelson, Friedman, Machlup, and their followers gave for adopting their metaphysics was an argument from authority, at the time correct, namely, that this was what philosophers were saying. The trust in philosophy was a tactical error, for the philosophy itself was changing as they spoke (e.g., Quine 1951). As a philosopher of economics, Alexander Rosenberg, noted in 1976, "Many economists have described their views as positivist and have opened themselves to the discredit which in recent decades has accrued to this view in the philosophy of science" (1976, p. x). Some philosophers now doubt the whole enterprise of epistemology, with its claim to give foundations for knowledge. And many more, as I have already said, doubt the confident prescriptions of modernist epistemology.

And Falsification Is Not Cogent

One prescription that economic modernists have in common, for instance, is an emphasis on the crucial falsifying test, supposedly the hallmark of scientific reasoning. Scientific Method narrows reasoning to logic and narrows logic to proposition in logic, the socalled *modus tollens.* If *H* entails *O,* then not-*O* entails not-*H.*True enough, you might say, though not much (Boland 1979, p. 505). Cartesian and especially Humean scepticism would make this the only real, fundamental, ultimate test. We can never affirm (it is said, even while affirming that the class will meet today), but only falsify. Such a crude way of speaking, as the philosopher J. L. Austin once pointed out, ignores the actual richness of scientific and other ordinary speech: "The truth of a statement may be connected importantly with the truth of another without it being the case that the one entails the other in the sole sort of sense preferred by obsessional logicians" (1955, p. 54).

Philosophers have long recognized, however, that the doctrine of falsification, even in its own way of speaking, runs afoul of a criticism made by the physicist and philosopher Pierre Duhem in 1906. The criticism is apparent, without philosophical study, to any economist who has tried to use falsification. Suppose that the hypothesis H_0 ("British businessmen performed poorly relative to Americans and Germans in the late nineteenth century") implies a testing observation O ("Measures of total factor productivity in iron and steel show a large difference between British and foreign steelmaking"). The one implies the other, that is, not by itself, but only with the addition of ancillary hypotheses H_1, H_2, and so forth that make the measurement possible ("Marginal productivity theory applies to Britain from 1870 to 1913"; "British steel had no hidden inputs offsetting poor business leaderships"; and so on). Then of course not-O implies not-H_0 or not-H_1 or not-H_2 or not-H_3 or any number of failures of premises irrelevant to the main hypothesis in question. The main hypothesis is insulated from crucial test by the ancillary hypotheses necessary to bring it to any test. The test may be worth doing, as it was in the example given. It is one good argument among several against the notion that British enterprise failed. But it is not the conversation stopper that it is supposed to be in the modernist methodology. It is not a certitude, not the crucial experiment, not the Only Real Test.

This insulation from crucial test is the substance of most scientific disagreement. Economists and other scientists will complain to their fellows, "Your experiment was not properly controlled"; "You have not solved the identification problem"; "You have used an equilibrium (competitive, single-equation) model when a disequilibrium (monopolistic, five-hundred–equation) model is relevant." In sciences such as population biology or astronomy or economics, in which controlled experiment is expensive and not always convincing, the conversation can hardly begin without assuming the answers to numerous boundary questions. (And even in physics: Collins 1985.) It cannot begin, that is to say, without assuming that the scientist knows the world pretty well and is engaged in fitting new facts into the existing theories. There is no "falsification" going on.

The chemist and philosopher Michael Polanyi described a paper by Lord Rayleigh that had results too surprising to be credible: "When . . . I asked various physicists' opinions about it, they only shrugged their shoulders. They could not find fault with the experiments, yet they not only did not believe its results, but did not even think it worth while to consider what was wrong with it, let alone check up on it. [Rayleigh] should have ignored his observation, for he ought to have known there was something wrong with it" (Polanyi 1966, pp. 64f.). Compare a remark by the physicist and historian of science Thomas Kuhn that "the scientist often seems rather to be struggling with facts, trying to force them into conformity with a theory he does not doubt" (1977, p. 193). At the level of broad scientific law the scientists simply use their theories. They seldom try to falsify them.

This is why simulation—trying out scientific arguments on paper to see if they are powerful enough, in the manner of Fogel's study of the railroad—is important in economics and similar fields. Simulation is affirmative, not falsifying, asking whether you can make a case for such-and-such, not whether you can prove it wrong. It tests systems, not isolated hypotheses, and affirms a framework in which to test them. It tests the reasonableness of affirmation, not the possibility of doubt. In economics, for example, econometrics as actually practiced by people whose minds have not been emptied by statistical significance amounts to simulation. The doubting and falsifying method, enshrined in the official version of econometric method, is largely impractical.

Falsification, near enough, has been falsified.

Profitable Prediction Is Not Possible in Economics

The common claim that prediction is the defining feature of a real science, and that economics possesses the feature, is also doubtful. It is a cliché among philosophers and historians of science, for instance, that one of the most successful of all scientific theories, the theory of evolution, makes no predictions and is therefore unfalsifiable by prediction. With fruit flies and bacteria, to be sure, you can test the theory in the approved manner; but its main facts, its dinosaur bones and multicolored birds, are things to be explained, not to be predicted. Geology and evolution, or for that matter an astronomy of objects many light years away, are historical rather than predictive sciences.

It is at least suggestive of something strange in prediction as a criterion for a properly modernist economics that Darwin's theory was itself connected to the classical economics of Smith, Malthus, and Ricardo (a system, as it happens, erroneous in most of the actual predictions it made). Strangely, it was in the midst of Milton Friedman's most famous piece of predictionist metaphysics that he cites Armen Alchian's (1950) revival of the connection. Friedman says (1953, p. 19) that the evolutionary theory of trees, like a Chicago theory of companies, supposes that "the leaves are positioned *as if* each leaf deliberately sought to maximize the amount of sunlight it receives." Alchian and Friedman are well known for their support of modernist methodology. Strangely, then, the nonpredictive, historical, evolutionary argument in economics—a variant of Dr. Pangloss's belief that whatever there is, is there for a reason—is most popular among the economists who think of themselves as most rigorous about prediction.

In any event, predicting the economic future is, as Ludwig von Mises put it, "beyond the power of any mortal man" (1949, p. 867). The economics says so, as John Muth pointed out. The economist for a big bank predicts that interest rates will fall after Christmas. If before making the prediction he has not placed his net worth in margin loans on bonds, properly hedged and insured against variance, he is behaving either irrationally or self-deceivingly. He claims to know the expected value of the future, yet for some reason chooses not to take the unlimited wealth that such Faustian knowledge can bring. He is willing for some reason instead to dissipate the opportunity by the act of telling others about it. If he does not really know the future, then he does not face such an opportunity. But then he has no business talking as though he does.

Predictionism cannot be rescued by arguing that the big bank economist makes merely conditional predictions ("If the government deficit continues to grow, the interest rate will rise"). Conditional predictions are cheap: if the sea were to disappear, a rock would accelerate in falling from sea level to the sea floor at about 32.17 feet per second per second. But a serious prediction has serious boundary conditions. If it does, then it must answer the American Question: If you're so smart, why ain't you rich? As an economist would put it, in his gnomic way, at the margin (because that is where economics works) and on average (because some people are lucky) the industry of making economic predictions, which includes universities, earns merely normal returns.

Modernism Is Impossible, and Is Not Adhered To

The most damaging, though, of these lesser criticisms of modernist methodology is that if taken at its word the methodology is impossible. Consider again the steps to modernist knowledge, from predictionism through Kelvin's Dictum to Hume's Fork. If economists (or physicists) confined themselves to economic (or physical) propositions that literally conformed to such steps, they would have nothing to say. Cartesian or Humean scepticism is too corrosive a standard of belief for an actual human scientist, as Descartes and Hume both knew. To quote Polanyi again (1962, p. 88), the methodology of modernism sets up "quixotic standards of valid meaning which, if rigorously practiced, would reduce us all to voluntary imbecility."

Modernism promises knowledge free from doubt, free from metaphysics, morals, and personal conviction. It cannot deliver what it promises. Probably it should not. What it is able to deliver is what it renames as "Scientific methodology," the metaphysics, morals, and personal convictions of the scientists. I suspect, as many have recently, that scientific knowledge is not very different from other knowledge.

I am arguing that the literal application of modernist methodology cannot give a useful economics. I think it is clear from my examples of Samuelson, Solow, Muth, Fogel, Coase, and econometrics that actual arguments in economics use modernism as no more than window dressing. Other students of the rhertoric of science have found this, too. In his *Against Method* (1975), Paul Feyerabend uses an interpretation of Galileo's career to attack the claims of prescriptive methodology in physics, and the same point can be made about economics. Had the modernist criterion of persuasion been adopted by Galileo's contemporaries, Feyerabend argues, the Galilean case would have failed. A grant proposal to use the strange premise that terrestial optics applied also to the celestial sphere—to assert that the tides were the sloshing of water on a mobile earth and to suppose that the fuzzy views of Jupiter's alleged moons would prove, by a wild analogy, that the planets, too, went around the sun as did the moons around Jupiter—would not have survived the first round of peer review in a National Science Foundation of 1632. The argument applies widely to the history of physics: observational anomalies in the experiments testing Einstein's theories were ignored for many years, to be revealed as errors of measurement long after the theories had been embraced, embraced on grounds of "the reason of the matter," as Einstein was fond of saying (Feyerabend 1975, pp. 56–57).

Historians of biology have uncovered many cases of cooking the statistical results to fit modernist precepts of what counts as evidence from Pasteur and Mendel down to the present. Gerald Geison has shown that Pasteur, among other pieces of false speech, lied about the results of his experiments (Geison 1995). It has been known for a long time that Mendel's experiments were too good to be true. In "Mendel and Methodology" (1983), Robert Root-Bernstein rehabilitates Mendel in an interesting way. He argues that peas are hard to classify: some are obviously smooth, some obviously wrinkled, but some middling. Mendel got his too perfect results not by outright fraud but by doing what Kuhn and others describe as common in physics: defining the categories to suit his elegant mathematical theory. "These categories did not exist objectively or unambiguously in nature, but had to be invented by Mendel himself" (Root-Bernstein 1983, p. 289). Modernism doesn't fit any actual science. The measurement of I.Q. has from its beginning entailed fraud and self-deception in the name of scientific method (Gould 1981). Straining after evidence of a sort available only in the simplest experiments in high school physics does not suit real science.

It suits economics poorly enough. For better or for worse, to take a leading case, the Keynesian revolution in economics would not have happened under the modernist legislation for science. The Keynesian insights were not formulated as statistical propositions until the early 1950s, fifteen years after the bulk of younger economists had become persuaded they were true. By the early 1960s the Keynesian notions of liquidity traps and accelerator models of investment, despite repeated failures in their statistical implementations, were taught to students of economics as matters of scientific routine. Modernist methodology would have stopped all this cold in 1936: where was the evidence of an objective, controlled, and statistical kind?

Nor (I can see you forming the argument) was the monetarist counterrevolution a success in fact for modernist methodology. Modernism dominated the minds of monetarist economists by the 1960s because their leader espoused it. They had persuaded themselves that the main issues were issues of prediction and control. Yet it was not modernist certitudes that won the day for the view that money mattered. It was crude experiments and big books, by their crudeness and bigness, not the apparently modernist rituals performed in the professional journals. The Kennedy tax cut, for example, raised the Keynesians to their peak of prestige; the inflation of the 1970s brought them down again, leaving the monetarists as temporary kings of the castle. Friedman and Schwartz's big book, A *Monetary History of the United States, 1867–1960,* was another important and nonmodernist victory for monetarism. It established a correlation between money and money income, though with many exceptions to be explained by various nonmonetarist epicycles. Keynesians and other opponents of monetarism do not deny the existence of such a correlation, just its importance. The correlation is important if money causes prices. It is unimportant if prices cause money. In particular, to go beyond the usual closed-economy framework of the debate, the monetarist argument supposes that money could be controlled by the monetary authority despite the openness of the American economy to trade in goods and in money itself. To this devastating criticism of their modernism Friedman and Schwartz did not reply (the only exception is Friedman's unpersuasive comment on McCloskey and Zecher [1984] [Friedman 1984, pp. 157–62]). Yet what was telling in the debate was not the logical quality of their replies but the sheer bulk of their book, and the richness and intelligence of its arguments, however irrelevant most were to the main point. Modernist methodology had little to do with it. James Tobin the Keynesian did a review of *A Monetary History* which treated it with the great respect it deserved; taking it seriously turned the intellectual tide. Ethos did it.

A modernist methodology consistently applied, in other words, would stop advances in economics. Ask any economist. What empirical anomaly in the traditional tale inspired the new economic history of the early 1960s or the new labor economics of the early 1970s? None: it was merely a realization that the logic of economics had not exhausted itself at conventional borders. What observable implications justify the big investment of economic intellect since 1950 in mathematical general equilibrium theory? For all the modernist talk common among its theorists, none. But so what? Could applications of economics to legal questions in the style of the emergent field of law and economics rely entirely on objective evidence? No; but why would you wish to so limit the understanding? And so forth. There is nothing to be gained and much to be lost by adopting modernism in economics.

The point is itself economic. In order for an economic assertion to be tested, Ronald Coase points out, some economist must care enough about it to bother. The economist will care only when the assertion is believed by other economists—by his allies or by some significant group of his opponents. Only when enough economists believe will there be a demand for tests. Fortunately, "economists, or at any rate enough of them, do not wait to discover whether a theory's predictions are accurate before making up their minds." To wait in properly modernist style "would result in the paralysis of scientific activity" (Coase 1982, p. 14), since no one would have an incentive to choose one out of the infinite number of hypotheses for test. Even quantitative studies, Coase argues, rely heavily on prequantitative arguments founding belief, and he quotes with approval Kuhn's remark that "the road from scientific law to scientific measurement can rarely be traveled in the reverse direction" (p. 18, quoting Kuhn 1977, p. 219). The laws come from a tradition of conversation, and in physics as in economics "quantitative studies . . . are explorations with the aid of a theory" (Coase 1982, p. 17), searches for numbers with which to make specific a theory already believed on other grounds. Modernism, in other words, which denies to scientists the rhetorical devices they do in fact use, is impractical.

In 1953 the modernist fairy tale in methodology looked courageously up to date, suited to a band of revolutionaries in the mountains. By now, in part because its revolution has been successful, it looks oppressive, suited to a government in the coastal plains, squatting on the major ports and the radio station. Economists are not alone in adhering to the modernist revolution so long after its spirit has died. Perhaps it will be comforting to know that they would also not be alone if they repudiated its excesses.

10 FROM METHODOLOGY

TO RHETORIC

Any Rule-Bound Methodology
Is Objectionable

The greater objection to modernism in economics, though, is that modernism supports a rule-bound methodology. It claims to deduce laws for science from the essence of knowledge or a rational reconstruction of the history of science. It claims that the philosopher of science can tell what makes for good, useful, fruitful, progressive science. It claims that he can limit the arguments that the scientists themselves make spontaneously, casting out some as unscientific, or at best placing them firmly in the "context of discovery." The philosopher undertakes to second-guess the scientific community. In economics a rule-bound methodology claims that the rulemaker is expert in all present economic knowledge and in all future economics, too, restricting the growth of the economic conversation to make it fit a philosopher's idea of the ultimate good.

Such claims from the easy chair are hard to take seriously. Einstein remarked that "whoever undertakes to set himself up as a judge in the field of Truth and Knowledge is shipwrecked by the laughter of the gods"(1953, p. 38). The modernist methodologist is a Red Queen ("Normative argument: off with his head"), and the gods are snickering behind their hands. Any methodology that is lawmaking and limiting will have this risible effect.

The maker of rules for economic science has, of course, the noblest intentions. Like the man from the government, he is here to help you. But economists like to remark of similar cases of interference in the spontaneous order that noble intentions are no defense against laughable results. The methodologist fancies himself the judge of the practitioner. His proper business, if any, is an anarchistic one, resisting the rigidity and pretension of rules. I. A. Richards made the point about the theory of metaphor: "Its business is not to replace practice, or to tell us how to do what we cannot do already; but to protect our natural skill from the interference of unnecessarily crude views about it" (1936, p. 116).

It is regrettable that modernist methodology, or any methodology consisting of rigid precept, is crude. It is worse that it is allowed to interfere with natural skill. The custom of methodological papers in economics is to scold economists for not allowing it to interfere more. Mark Blaug's book summarizing the state of play of economic methodology in 1980, *The Methodology of Economics*, is a case in point. Its subtitle promises to tell "How Economists Explain." It might better have been "How the Young Karl Popper Explained," for it repeatedly attacks extant arguments in economics for failing to comply with the rules Popper laid down in *Logik der Forschung* in 1934. Blaug's exordium is typical of the methodologists in economics: "Economists have long been aware of the need to defend 'correct' principles of reasoning in their subject; although actual practice may bear little relationship to what is preached, the preaching is worth considering on its own ground" (Blaug 1980, p. xii). Such words flow easily from a modernist's pen. Yet it is unclear why preaching unrelated to actual rhetorical practice should be worth considering at all. Why do economists have to defend in the abstract their principles of reasoning, and before what tribunal? The methodologists—whether logical positivist or Popperian or Austrian or Marxist—should have an answer, but do not. Ancient common sense and recent philosophy of science suggest they cannot.

Blaug's peroration is frankly prescriptive, taking rules for economic speech directly from philosophy:

> What methodology can do is to provide criteria for the acceptance and rejection of research programs, setting standards that will help us to discriminate between wheat and chaff. The ultimate question we can and indeed must pose about any research program is the one made familiar by Popper: what events, if they materialize, would lead us to reject that program? A program that cannot meet that question has fallen short of the highest standards that scientific knowledge can attain. (Blaug 1980, p. 264)

It sounds grand, but Einstein's gods are rolling in the aisles. Why, the voice of pragmatism asks, should a dubious epistemological principle be a test of anything at all, much less of practice, much less the "ultimate" test? Doesn't science take place most of the time in conversations well short of the ultimate?

The operative word is "ultimate" and its numerous cousins in epistemology, such as "conceptually," "ideally," "in principle," "in the last analysis," "fundamentally," or "at the Second Coming." "Ultimately," says the epistemologist, "the only way we know is such and such." But this declaration does not persuade ordinary people and ordinary scientists. They take it as obvious that we know in many ways, not always reducible to sight or synthetic *a priori*.

The "ultimate" way is not relevant. We need intellectual nourishment here and now, not epistemological pie in the sky. The appeal of epistemological methodologists since Bacon to experimental facts as the "ultimate arbiter," for instance, will dismiss mere reflection as an idol to be cast into the flames or at least pushed off its altar. John Dewey, the voice of pragmatism, replies, "Such wholesale depreciation ignores the value inherent even in the most subjective reflection, for it takes the settled estate which is proof that thought is not needed, or that it has done its work, as if it supplied the standard for the occasions in which problems are hard upon us, and doubt is rife" (1916, p. 196f.). Dewey is here close to another friend of methodological breadth, Cardinal Newman, who hewed to broad-church reasoning. Thirty years earlier the cardinal had written that "assent on reasonings not demonstrative is too widely recognized an act to be irrational, unless man's nature is irrational, too familiar to the prudent and clearminded to be an infirmity or an extravagance" (1870, p. 150). By defending a catholicity of reasonings, of course, Dewey and Newman were not rejecting fact, or advocating the shutting down of laboratories. They were rejecting a restrictive methodism that narrows human reason to one particular kind of fact and puts most facts and most reasons beyond reasoning.

Anyone would commend the vision of scientific exploration that the best of the epistemological methodologists seem to have. It amounts to a dialectic, in the Continental sense foreign to the traditions of analytic philosophy. Dewey and Newman would have approved. Genuine exploration is brave and good. Refusing to offer hostages to evidence, though not rare even in modernist circles, is cowardly: so much you can take from the idea of falsification by evidence. Facing facts, we all agree, is good. In this modest sense we are all "empiricists." The problem comes, and the modernist shouting begins, with the words "empirical" and "evidence." Should it all be "objective," "experimental," "positive," "observable"? Can it be? I doubt it.

Something is awry with an appeal for an open intellectual society, an appeal defending itself on liberal grounds, that begins by demarcating certain ways of reasoning as forbidden and certain fields of study as meaningless. The intolerance in modernism shows in Popper's *The Open Society and Its Enemies* (1945), which firmly closed the borders of his open society to psychoanalysts and Marxists—charged with violating all manner of modernist regulations. The difficulty is that on these grounds

Popper would have to close the borders as well to a line of physicists from Galileo Galilei to the charmers of subatomic particles. During the 1890s some physicists did in fact reject atomism on the properly modernist grounds that such matters were not observable; and nowadays, as the physicist Steven Weinberg has noted (1983, pp. 9f.), no modernist would hunt for quarks. An economist wetback seized for working in such an open society would be deported summarily on the next truck (though pleading from the back his properly modernist credentials).

That adding methodological constraints to science cannot in general be wise will strike economists as obvious. Constraints, after all, constrain. The contrary notion that a rule-bound methodology is good for you has been much questioned recently by philosophers. Paul Feyerabend's demolitions of the philosophy of science and Richard Rorty's deconstructions of philosophy have left methodologists apoplectic. Rorty views the history of epistemology since Plato as an intellectual bet that did not come off: "People have, oddly enough, found something interesting to say about the essence of Force, and the definition of 'number.' They might have found something interesting to say about the essence of Truth. But in fact they haven't" (1982, p. xiv).

The founding rule of Descartes himself has been scrutinized in this way by J. A. Schuster, who concludes that Descartes's "method-talk was not abstracted from successful practice in some area of mathematics [much less physics]; it was produced by a megalomaniacal performance of operations of analogical extension upon the terms of a discourse, universal mathematics [one of Descartes's projects], which itself could not do what it was purported to do" (1983, p. 19).

The philosophers are here following antimethodological findings from other fields. In particular the sociology and history of science since 1962 or so have left the old rules of methodology looking unpersuasive. The sociologists and historians took to discovering what actually happened in science, favoring what happened over the Astounding Stories retailed in the opening chapters of science books. By this simple device the methodological claims of modernism have been rejected, repeatedly. It can be tried in economics, as we've seen.

Methodology Is Middle Management

If it were not so damaging to common sense, Methodology, strutting around issuing orders to working scientists, would only be funny. In economics it stands in the middle of a meta-economical hierarchy from shop floor to boardroom. At the bottom is method with a small *m*, ever humble and helpful, about which no reasonable person would complain or even joke much. It tells an economist what to do when the data have been selected in a particular sort of biased way or what to do when it is hard to think of reasons for price and quantity to change in a certain market. It tells, rather badly, how to write scientific prose; and it tells, rather well, how to grasp a situation in which profits remain to be earned by new entrants. It tells how to avoid the shop-floor mistakes of statistical significance. Following Joan Robinson, economists call these their box of tools. The tools are economic theory in its verbal and mathematical forms, statistical theory and practice, familiarity with certain accounting conventions and statistical sources, and a background of stylized historical fact and worldly experience. The use of such tools to fashion sturdy little arguments is the metier of the economist, the economist's method.

Far above method with a small *m*, at the peak of the scholarly enterprise, stand the conversational norms of civilization. The German philosopher Jürgen Habermas and his tradition call these *Sprachethik* (1973, p. 110). Don't lie; pay attention; don't sneer; cooperate; don't shout; let other people talk; be open-minded; explain yourself when asked; don't resort to violence or conspiracy in aid of your ideas. We cannot imagine good conversation or good intellectual life deficient in these. They are the rules, the "conversational implicatures" as the linguists put it, adopted by the act of joining a conversation, whether among economists about how to manage the economy or between parents about how to manage the teenager. Socratic dialogue—at any rate when his interlocutors are permitted to say something besides "So it would seem, Socrates"—has been the model of intellectual discourse. We do not always follow the model, but that's not a reason to abandon it as a norm. Unlike the norms of modernism it makes sense. The worst academic sin is not to be illogical or badly informed but to exhibit cynical disregard for the norms of scholarly conversation.

Between the top and the bottom, a middle manager in a green suit, below the cool majesty of *Sprachethik* and above the workaday utility of method with a small *m*, stands Methodology. Because it cannot claim the specificity of practical advice to economists, or to the lovelorn, it is not method. Because it does not claim the generality of how to speak well in our culture, or in economics, it is not *Sprachethik*. It claims instead to be a universalization from particular sciences to a science of science in general. What makes Methodology comical is what usually makes the bourgeois gentilhomme comical. The joke is his dual position, at once master and servant, inclined therefore to hypocrisy and doubletalk, 'umble and yet pompous.

The schools of economics have each their comical attachments to methodology. A Marxist economic Methodology, for example, has rules such as:

The history of all hitherto existing society is the history of class struggle.
Use statistics, which are scientific.
Beware of remarks infected by false consciousness.

Neoclassical Methodology, the dominant one in the English-speaking world, says among other things:

The history of all hitherto existing society is the history of interactions among selfish individuals.
Use statistics, which are scientific.
Beware of remarks that are nonfalsifiable or nonobservable.

Austrian methodology says,

The history of all hitherto existing society is the history of interactions among selfish individuals.
Use statistics gingerly if at all, for they are transitory figments.
Beware of remarks that do not accord with Austrian Methodological precepts.

Similar rules pertain to other modern schools, or to more subtly divided subschools among them. They share the strange Cartesian notion that practice according to the whatever-it-is below *Sprachethik* and above plain method is possible, and will yield a harvest of truth.

Most defenses of methodology get what force they have by borrowing prestige from *Sprachethik* or utility from method. The reply, for instance, that "you *must* have a Methodology hidden *somewhere*" is true in practice only if the methodology pretends to be a practical rule of method, and is true in morality only if it takes over the moral rules of *Sprachethik*. The point is that it is a poor thing when out on its own.

In practice Methodology serves chiefly to demarcate Us from Them, demarcating science from nonscience. Once the modernists have founded a Bantustan for nonsciences such as astrology, psychoanalysis, acupuncture, nutritional medicine, Marxist economics, spoonbending, or anything else they do not wish to discuss, they can get on with the business at hand with a clear head. Methodology and its corollary, the Demarcation Problem (What is Science? How is It to be distinguished from nonscience?), are ways of stopping conversation by limiting conversation to people on our side of the demarcation line.

The replies to such scepticism about the uses of Methodology and epistemology have been unpersuasive. Indeed, it has not usually been thought necessary to stoop so low as persuasion. The many traditional philosophers and the few remaining historians of science working by the old rules join in a prolonged if somewhat nervous sneer. Early in his penetrating exploration of the limits of analysis, Stanley Rosen observes that an appreciation of its limits is "not yet strong enough to prevent the typical practitioner of analytical philosophy from succumbing to the temptation of confusing irony for a refutation of opposing views." He remarks that the very "strengths of the analytical movement . . . have led to a general failure to understand the rhetorical nature of its own justification" (1980, p. xiii).

Various attempts have been made to rescue some residue of thinking about methodology. An economist, Bruce Caldwell, has contributed to the attempt, in his treatment in 1982 of the history of methodology in economics, *Beyond Positivism: Economic Methodology in the 19th Century*. Caldwell advocates methodological pluralism, as does Lawrence Boland, another economist, in his *The Foundations of Economic Method* (1982). These economists and others intend to carry on the conversation about the essence of Truth that Rorty finds so lacking in promise, albeit with a novel spirit of toleration and balance. You begin to wonder whether people can in fact keep their toleration and balance for long in a conversation about my Truth and thine. As Rorty might say, they haven't yet.

Good Science Is Good Conversation

What distinguishes good from bad in learned discourse, then, is not the adoption of a particular methodology, but the earnest and intelligent attempt to contribute to a conversation. This is the oldest of philosophical doctrines. Plato was, as Cicero said, the best orator when making merry of orators, and his Socrates was the first and best conversationalist from the pen of a man trying to end conversation. The best modern statement is Michael Oakeshott's: "As civilized human beings, we are the inheritors, neither of an inquiry about ourselves and the world, nor of an accumulating body of information, but of a conversation begun in the primeval forest and extended and made more articulate in the course of centuries. Education, properly speaking, is an initiation . . . in which we acquire the intellectual and moral habits appropriate to conversation" (1933, pp. 198–99).

Literal conversation is of course not the whole point, though part of it. In a broader sense, Cicero conversed with Aristotle and Marx with Adam Smith. True, one must not exaggerate the enthusiasm of intellectuals for real conversation. The lack of interest in what that idiot Jones has to say makes much intellectual dispute puerile. Durkheim and Weber were contemporaries at the birth of sociology, worked on similar subjects, and contributed largely to networks of conversation in their fields, yet neither so much as mentioned the other (Lepienes 1983). But such stories, like the passions about Jones, are felt to be violations of the intellectual *Sprachethik*.

The notion of a conversation gives an answer to the demand for standards of persuasiveness. You recognize with ease when a conversation in one's own field is working well. Most economists would agree, for instance, that at present the conversation about game theory is not working well, after some early promise. Abstract general equilibrium, likewise, suffered a sharp decline from a brief period of brilliance. On the other hand, no economist familiar with the situation would doubt that the conversation in economic history improved radically from the 1950s to the 1960s, and continues at this higher level.

The conversations overlap enough to make you almost as sure about neighboring fields: examining the overlap is what editors, referees, and members of research panels do. The overlaps of the overlaps, as Polanyi once observed, keep all honest if some try to be. Q.E.D.: the overlapping conversations provide the standards. It is a market argument. There is no need for philosophical lawmaking or methodological regulation to keep the economy of intellect running just fine.

Amelie Oksenberg Rorty writes that what is crucial is "our ability to engage in continuous conversation, testing one another, discovering our hidden presuppositions, changing our minds because we have listened to the voices of our fellows. Lunatics also change their minds, but their minds change with the tides of the moon and not because they have listened, really listened, to their friends' questions and objections" (1983, p. 562). It's a woman's view as well, this listening. We can pray for such a character of argument in economics. Perhaps when economists are disburdened of their philosophical baggage and begin to look at how they converse—really converse—it will be so.

Rhetoric Is a Better Way to Understand Science

A way to get out of the modernist maze is to pick up that thread long separated from science: rhetoric. Rhetoric does not deal with Truth directly; it deals with conversation. It is a literary way of examining conversation, the conversation of economists and mathematicians as much as of poets and novelists. It can be used as I have shown for a literary criticism of science. The humanistic tradition in Western civilization, in other words, can be used to understand the scientific tradition.

The literary, epistemological, and methodological strands of the new rhetoric have not yet combined into one cord. They belong together, in a study of how scholars speak, a rhetoric of inquiry. On the eve of the Cartesian revolution the French philosopher and educational reformer Peter Ramus (fl. 1550) brought to completion a medieval tendency to relegate rhetoric to mere eloquence, leaving logic in charge of all reasons. In some of the textbooks that Descartes himself read as a boy the merely probable argument was thus subordinated to the indubitable argument. Hostile to classical rhetoric, such a reorganization of the liberal arts was well suited to the Cartesian program to put knowledge on foundations built by philosophy and mathematics.

Although the best minds followed it, believing for little reason that only mathematical argument was grounded, the program failed. Probable argument was in the meantime kept subordinate to certitude. Even statistics, the science of uncertainty, sought indubitable foundations, resisting at various times the rhetoric of Bayes and Wald. In Rorty's words, following Dewey, the search for the foundations of knowledge by Descartes, Locke, Hume, Kant, Russell, and Carnap was "the triumph of the quest for certainty over the quest for wisdom" (Rorty 1979, p. 61; cf. Dewey 1929, pp. 33, 227). To reinstate rhetoric properly understood is to reinstate wider and wiser reasoning.

Other Sciences Have Rhetorics

For all its claims to the scientific priesthood, then, economics is different from the man in the street's image of science, as economists recognize uneasily. But economists should be glad that their subject fits poorly with this image. It fits well with the New Rhetoric, as do studies long foreign to economics, such as the study of literature or politics or law. Economists, especially neoclassical economists, will sometimes claim that their field is syllogistic, producing from "axioms" a series of "observable implications" by way of lengthy chains of reasoning. Their master Alfred Marshall said long ago that this is poor description and bad advice. Economics actually uses "short, stout links," in Marshall's phrase, or, in Aristotle's way, short and informal syllogisms. Economics, in other words, is not a Science in the way we came to understand that word in high school.

But neither, really, are other sciences. Economists can relax. Other sciences, even the other mathematical sciences, are rhetorical. Mathematics, to take the queen herself, seems to an outsider to be the limiting example of objectivity, explicitness, and demonstrability. Surely here only Truth counts, not human words. A long line of intellectuals has believed that here is bedrock, the ultimate authority. Yet standards of mathematical demonstration change, as the example of Euler in Chapter 4 hints. The last seventy years have been a disappointment to followers of David Hilbert, who intended to put mathematics on timeless and indubitable foundations. The historian of mathematics Morris Kline wrote that "it is now apparent that the concept of a universally accepted, infallible body of reasoning—the majestic mathematics of 1800 and the pride of man—is a grand illusion." Or again: "There is no rigorous definition of rigor. A proof is accepted if it obtains the endorsement of the leading specialists of the time and employs the principles that are fashionable at the moment. But no standard is universally acceptable today" (Kline 1980, pp. 6, 315).

Kline's point does not apply to the broad interior of mathematics, about which no one has serious doubts, but to its frontiers. An instance is the controversy some time ago about a computerized proof of the four-color proposition (the proposition that maps can be drawn without ambiguity in four colors only, unproven since Moebius noticed it in 1840). The question was whether a calculation that could be done only by an electronic computer and not ever by a human mind could play a part in a "proof." The rhetoric of proof was in question.

Kline's opinions are not widely accepted by mathematicians. Apparently more popular are those of Philip J. Davis and Reuben Hersh, whose book *The Mathematical Experience* (1981) was described in the *American Mathematical Monthly* as "one of the masterpieces of our age." Yet Davis and Hersh speak of the crisis of confidence in modern mathematical philosophy in terms nearly identical to Kline's. In the work of the Ideal Mathematician, they say, "the line between complete and incomplete proof is always somewhat fuzzy, and often controversial" (p. 34; cf. p. 40). They quote Solomon Feferman, who writes, "It is also clear that the search for ultimate foundations via formal systems has failed to arrive at any convincing conclusion" (p. 357). Without using the word, Davis and Hersh argue that what is required is a rhetoric of mathematics:

> The dominant style of Anglo-American philosophy . . . tends to perpetuate identification of the philosophy of mathematics with logic and the study of formal systems. From this standpoint, a

> problem of principal concern to the mathematician becomes
> totally invisible. This is the problem of giving a philosophical
> account . . . of preformal mathematics . . . , including an exami-
> nation of how [it] relates to and is affected by formalization. . . .
> Informal mathematics is mathematics. Formalization is only an
> abstract possibility which no one would want or be able actually
> to carry out. (pp. 344, 349)

Real proofs "are established by 'consensus of the qualified'" and are
"not checkable . . . by any mathematician not privy to the gestalt, the
mode of thought in the particular field. It may take generations to detect
an error" (p. 354; cf. Davis and Hersh 1987). Compare again Cardinal
Newman's, *A Grammar of Assent* (1870): "Strange as it may seem, this
contrast between inference [that is, formal demonstration] and assent is
exemplified even in the province of mathematics. Argument is not always able to command our assent, even though demonstrative. I am
not speaking of short and lucid demonstrations; but of long and intri-
cate mathematical investigations" (ch. 6, sec. 1, item 6). Newman, who
had studied mathematics at Oxford, was in a position to know—
admitting that in 1816 mathematics had not yet embarked on the program of rigor that climaxed in Hilbert's school.

At the end of the Hilbertian experiment, Davis and Hersh assert,

> The actual experience of all schools—and the actual daily
> experience of mathematicians—shows that mathematical truth,
> like other kinds of truth, is fallible and corrigible. It is reasonable
> to propose a different task for mathematical philosophy, not to
> seek indubitable truth, but to give an account of mathematical
> knowledge as it really is—fallible, corrigible, tentative, and
> evolving, as is every other kind of human knowledge. (1981,
> p. 406)

Not much in this line has been done, though one astounding book has
shown, as I have noted, what can be: Imre Lakatos's *Proofs and Refutations: The Logic of Mathematical Discovery* (1976), which gives a detailed
account of the rhetoric of the Descartes-Euler theorem on polyhedra.
The book is a model for how the historian of thought might pursue the
rhetoric of knowledge. Lakatos makes clear that mathematicians do not
"prove" theorems for ever and ever. They temporarily satisfy their interlocutors in a conversation.

It seems, then, that some problems facing even mathematics on its
frontiers are problems of rhetoric, problems in "the art of probing what
men believe they ought to believe," as Booth put it. Similar points can

be made about other sciences, such as paleontology or paleoanthropology or experimental psychology, as I have shown (and see Landau 1987, which discusses how aesthetic decisions about narrative determine the story of the descent from the trees).

You can make similar remarks even of physics, the favorite of those who seek a prescription for real, objective, positive, predictive science. The axiomatic, austere rhetoric that is supposed to characterize physics does not in fact characterize it well. Theoretical physicists know less formal mathematics than do mathematical economists, a peculiar reversal of the natural order of things.

A rhetoric of economics does not entail a Santa Monica approach to science ("Hey, man, how do you feel about the law of demand today?"). Were economists to give up their quaint modernism and open themselves officially to a wider range of discourse, they would not need to abandon data or mathematics or precision. They would merely agree to examine their language in action and converse more politely with others in the conversations of humanity.

Mark Perlman, in a review of Terence Hutchison's revival of modernism in economics, put it well: "The essential methodological question is what does it take to persuade oneself or others of the validity of an idea? . . . [Economists] are unwilling to ask themselves the key question, 'What methods must I use in order to persuade an audience?' Economists' self-perception is as of 'en expert.' But economists are not experts; they are basically persuaders" (1978, pp. 582f.). As are we all, we scientists, mathematicians, and economists together.

11 ANTI-ANTI-RHETORIC

The Alternative to Modernism
Is Not Irrationalism

It will I hope be plausible by now that the "objectivity" of economics is exaggerated and, what is more important, overrated. The studies of rhetoric show, as Polanyi put it (1966, p. 62), that economic knowledge depends little on "a scientific rationalism that would permit us to believe only explicit statements based on tangible data and derived from these by a formal inference, open to repeated testing." A rhetoric of economics exposes what most economists know anyway about the richness and complexity of economic argument but will not state openly and will not examine explicitly.

The invitation to rhetoric is not, I emphasize, an invitation to "replace careful analysis with rhetoric," or to abandon mathematics in favor of name-calling or flowery language. The good rhetorician loves care, precision, explicitness, and economy in argument as much as the next person. Since she has thought more carefully and explicitly than most people have about the place of such virtues in a larger system of scholarly values, she may even love them more. A rhetorical approach to economic texts is machine-building, not machine-breaking. It is not an invitation to irrationality in argument. Quite the contrary. It is an invitation to leave the irrationality of an artificially narrowed range of argument and to move to the rationality of arguing like human beings. It brings out into the open the arguing that economists do anyway—in the dark, for they must do it somewhere, and the various official rhetorics leave them benighted.

The charge of irrationalism comes easily to the lips of methodological authoritarians. Their notion is that reasoning outside the constricted epistemology of modernism is no reasoning at all. Mark Blaug, for instance, charges that Paul Feyerabend's book *Against Method* "amounts to replacing the philosophy of science by the philosophy of flower power" (1980, p. 44). Feyerabend's flamboyance commonly attracts such remarks. Yet Stephen Toulmin and Michael Polanyi are nothing if not sweetly reasonable; Blaug lumps them with Feyerabend and attacks the Feyerabend-flavored whole. On a higher level of philosophical sophistication, Imre Lakatos's *Methodology of Scientific Research Programmes* repeatedly tars Polanyi, Kuhn, and Feyerabend with "irrationalism" (e.g., Lakatos 1978, pp. 1:9n. 1, 76n. 6, 91n. 1, 130, and 130n. 3), emphasizing their sometimes aggressively expressed case against rigid rationalism and ignoring their moderately expressed case for wider rationality. The tactic is an old one. Richard Rorty notes that "the charges of 'relativism' and 'irrationalism' once leveled against Dewey [were] merely the mindless defensive reflexes of the philosophical tradition which he attacked" (1979, p. 13; cf. Rorty 1982, ch. 9). The brave resolve taken up by the opponents of Dewey, Polanyi, Kuhn, and the rest is "if the choice is between science and irrationality, I'm for science." But that's not the choice.

Yet doubt still remains. If we agree that rhetoric of various sorts plays a part in economic persuasion, and look on economic argument with a literary eye, are we not abandoning science to its enemies? Will not scientific questions come to be decided by politics or whim? Is not the routine of scientific methodology a wall against irrational and authoritarian threats to inquiry? Are not the barbarians at the gates?

The fear is a surprisingly old and persistent one. In classical times it was part of the debate between philosophy and rhetoric, evident in the unsympathetic way in which the Sophists are portrayed in Plato's dialogues. Cicero viewed himself as bringing the two together, disciplining rhetoric's tendency to become empty advocacy and trope on the one hand and disciplining philosophy's tendency to become useless and inhuman speculation on the other. The classical problem was that rhetoric was a powerful device easily diverted to evil ends, the atomic power of the classical world, and like atomic power, the subject of much worrying about its proliferation.

The classical solution was to insist that the orator be good as well as clever: Cato defined him as *"vir bonus dicendi peritus,"* the good man skilled at speaking, a Ciceronian ideal as well. Quintilian, a century after Cicero, said that "he who would be an orator must not only seem to be a good man, but cannot *be* an orator unless he is a good man" (*De Oratore* 12.1.3). We are accustomed by modernist presuppositions to talk of "good and bad rhetoric," contrasting Adlai Stevenson's splendid little jokes, say, with Joe McCarthy's vituperation. But it is people, not intellectual devices, that are good or bad. Good science demands good scientists—that is to say, moral, honest, hard-working scientists—not good methodologies. Rhetoric is merely a tool, no bad thing in itself. Or rather, it is the box of tools for persuasion taken together, available to persuaders good and bad. No surprise, then, that the classical world believed it took a *"vir (mulierque) bonus"* to use the tools right, just as ca-bala is not to be studied until those years of goodness beyond forty.

The classical worry about the power of rhetoric nonetheless looks quaint to moderns, who know well enough that regressions, comput-ers, experiments, or any of the now canonized methods of persuasion can be used to deceive. The charge of deceit is commonly leveled at sta-tistics, for instance, especially at the statistics most accessible to lay peo-ple, the statistical chart. It was a devil's invention of the late eighteenth century. Edward Tufte notes that "for many people the first word that comes to mind when they think about statistical charts is 'lie.' No doubt some graphics do distort the underlying data. But data graphics are no different from words in this regard, for any means of communication can be used to deceive" (1983, p. 53). So said Aristotle:

> And if it be objected that one who uses such power of speech unjustly might do great harm, *that* is a charge which may be made in common against all good things except virtue, and above all against the things that are most useful. It is plain that it is the function of one and the same art to discern the real and the apparent means of persuasion, just as it is the function of dialectic [that is, deductive, "compelling" reasoning] to discern the real and the apparent syllogism. *(Rhetoric* 1.1.1355b.3.14)

There is nothing intrinsic in analogies, appeals to authority, arguments from contraries, or other recognizable pieces of classical rhetoric that make them more subject to evil misuse than the more obviously mod-ern methods. You can only note with regret that the Greeks and Ro-mans were more sensitive to the possibility of misuse and less hypno-tized by the claims of method to moral neutrality.

The suspicion of rhetoric is as old as philosophy itself: we cannot use mere plausibility because an eloquent speaker could fool us:

Socrates: And he who possesses the art [of rhetoric] can make the same thing appear to the same people just, now unjust, at will?

Phaedrus: To be sure.

(Phaedrus 261d)

We need something, it has been said, besides the mere social fact that an argument proved persuasive.

To such an objection the answers, then, are two. Science and other epistemologically pure methods can also be used to lie. Our defense must be to discourage lying, not to discourage a certain class of talk. Sec-ondly, talk against talk is self-refuting. The person making it appeals to a social, nonepistemological standard of persuasiveness by the very act of trying to persuade someone that mere persuasion is not enough.

The Political Arguments for Methodology Are Weak

In 1938 Terence Hutchison, a British economist sophisticated in the conversations of the Vienna School, could bring its positivism to economics with this justification: "The most sinister phenomenon of recent decades for the true scientist, and indeed to Western civilization as a whole, may be said to be the growth of Pseudo-Science no longer confined to hole-and-corner cranks . . . but organized in comprehensive, militant and persecuting mass-creeds. [Testability is] the only principle or distinction practically adoptable which will keep science separate from pseudoscience" (1938, pp. 10–11).

Such a rhetoric has been popular since then, with parallels in many fields. Fascism arose, somehow, from Hegel and Nietzsche. In America it arose, somehow, from the pragmatists in philosophy (Peirce, James, Dewey) or the regionalists in painting (Missouri's Thomas Hart Benton, for example, or Iowa's Grant Wood), both disdained by the European avant garde. The historian Peter Novick, in his astonishing book on the rhetoric of history in the United States, *That Noble Dream: The "Objectivity Question" and the American Historical Profession* (1988), observes that "as early as 1923 Bertrand Russell had made a connection between the pragmatic theory of truth and rigged trials in the Soviet Union [in 1937, as a matter of fact, the American pragmatist John Dewey chaired a retrial of Trotsky; see Spitzer 1990]. In a 1935 discussion of the ancestry of fascism he made it clear that doubts about the existence of objective truth figured prominently in that genealogy" (Novick 1988, p. 289).

In 1938 Hutchison was attacking of course the pseudoscience of racism. Lately the philosopher of science Alexander Rosenberg has seconded Hutchison's identification of positivism with antifascism (Rosenberg 1992, p. 33). What the latter-day positivists have failed to notice is that the pseudoscience of racism was itself a product of early (neo-)positivism. The political analysis of Hutchison and his generation, echoed in rearguard actions by neo-neo-positivists nowadays, was always weak on the evidence, but especially so because the positivists themselves, most prominently the brilliant British statistician Karl Pearson, devised the pseudosciences of which Hutchison speaks—eugenics, for example, and racial anthropology, the positive sciences of the extermination camps. Listen to Pearson in the neopositivist bible, *The Grammar of Science:*

> From a bad stock can come only bad offspring. . . . [H]is offspring
> will still be born with the old taint. . . . What we need is a check
> to the fertility of the inferior stocks, and this can only arise with
> new social habits and new conceptions of the social and the
> antisocial in conduct. . . . Now this conclusion of Weismann's
> [*Essays on Heredity and Kindred Biological Problems*, trans. 1889]—
> if it be valid, and all we can say at present is that the arguments
> in favour of it are remarkably strong—radically affects our
> judgment on the moral conduct of the individual, and on the
> duties of the state and society towards their degenerate
> members. . . . The "philosophical" method can never lead to a
> real theory of morals. Strange as it may seem, the laboratory
> experiments of a biologist may have greater weight than all
> the theories of the state from Plato to Hegel! (Pearson 1900,
> pp. 26–28)

And later, "It is a false view of human solidarity, which regrets that a capable and stalwart race of white men should advocate replacing a dark-skinned tribe which can neither utilise its land for the full benefit of mankind nor contribute its quota to the common stock of human knowledge" (p. 369). On grounds of cost and benefit he draws back a little from the implications: "This sentence must not be taken to justify a brutalising destruction of human life. . . . The anti-social effects of such a mode of accelerating the survival of the fittest may go far to destroy the preponderating fitness of the survivor" (p. 369n). And yet—and yet: "At the same time, there is cause for human satisfaction in the replacement of the aborigines throughout America and Australia by white races of far higher civilisation."

Stephen Jay Gould notes that Pearson's inaugural paper in his new journal *Annals of Eugenics* (1925), an attack on Jewish migration to Britain, met the highest scientific standards of the day, alas (Gould 1984, p. 296). Most scientists were racists, as were most other people before the end. The racist narrative was of course common among educated people from the 1880s to the 1940s. The economist Alfred Marshall, for example, explaining David Ricardo's method (so un-English in its abstraction, thought Marshall, Ricardo's ancestors being Sephardic Jews), noted that "Nearly every branch of the Semitic race has had some special genius for dealing with abstraction" (Marshall 1920, p. 761n; Appendix B, p. 5).

Commonplace though they were, it is a mistake to think of such remarks as unscientific or pseudoscientific, that is, as something we can avoid merely by Being Scientific—factual or logical as against metaphorical and narrative. Karl Pearson and Alfred Marshall were among the handful of leading scientists of their generation. Science does not protect us from all nonsense, only some. Science is human speech, too. If we do not realize that science uses metaphors and tells stories now as it did in 1900 and 1938 we are going to do worse than make fools of ourselves. In 1933 the leading British journal of science, *Nature*, approved of a new law which "will command the appreciative attention of all who are interested in the controlled and deliberate improvement of human stock" (Mackenzie 1981, p. 44). What new law? That just instituted by the Nazis in Germany to sterilize those suffering from congenital feeblemindedness, manic depressive insanity, schizophrenia, hereditary epilepsy, hereditary St. Vitus's dance, hereditary blindness and deafness, hereditary bodily malformation, and habitual alcoholism.

A day at Auschwitz does not put one in mind of the learned discourses of Hegel or Nietzsche, least of all the down-to-earth pragmatism of Dewey or James. It puts one in mind of factories and laboratories and record-keeping, the measuring of boiled skulls and the testing of human tolerance for freezing water, positive science. I am not claiming that positivists are fascists or that science leads to totalitarianism (the eugenists in Britain, for example, for the most part edged away from Nazi racial theories in the 1930s; cf. Mackenzie 1981, p. 45). I am claiming merely that positivists or the other believers in a religion of Science cannot in all fairness make such charges against everyone they disagree with, as they have a notable tendency to do. It is their most common rhetorical turn. The trick of charging that anyone who does not agree with a particularly narrow version of French rationalism or British empiricism is an "irrationalist" (Stove 1982) and is therefore in cahoots with Hitler and Mussolini needs to be dropped: it sticks to the bringers of the charge.

It has arisen again in the case of Paul de Man, a Belgian professor of literature at Yale who annoyed cultural conservatives and was therefore vilified after his death by the many profound students of literature at *The New York Times*. De Man in his youth had flirted briefly with fascist ideas of culture in a few newspaper columns among hundreds he wrote at the height of Hitler's European prestige. The truth about Nazism and the Holocaust is that they came from Western civilization, from its best as from its worst, from academic positivism itself as much as from Valley-Girl irrationalism (cf. Bakan 1967, p. 166). The point is one of the proper obsessions of the literary critic George Steiner. In *Language and Silence* he quotes a Jewish victim of the camps noting in wonder that the Germans were highly educated, a people of the book. Steiner comments, "That the book might well be Goethe or Rilke remains a truth so vital yet outrageous that we try to spit it out" (1967, p. 162). A startlingly high percentage of the officers in the SS had advanced degrees in the humanities. And it was not difficult to find doctors to run experiments in working people to death.

The same is true on the left, with the additional point that the theory of Stalinism was literally old-style positivism, the centralizing rationalism of early nineteenth-century intellectuals, on which the mid–twentieth century paid the interest compounded. The positivists have long been accustomed to shouting angrily that open discourse leads to totalitarianism. Perhaps their anger assuages a wordless guilt. Positivism claims noisily to contribute to freedom, but tends to stride beyond freedom and dignity.

The methodological conservative believes that people will behave frightfully badly if not tamed by a religious belief or a literary canon or a scientific methodology. The notion has little to support it from intellectual history. Good and bad behavior have coexisted with loose and rigid rules of methodology in various times from Abraham to Goebbels. Richard Crosman, though using the word "anarchy" inexactly, attacks in such terms E. D. Hirsch's defense of a conservative canon of literature: "Amazingly enough, all we need to do to rigorously disprove the entire argument of Hirsch's book is to demonstrate that anarchy [by which he means chaos] does not necessarily result from 'subjectivism' and 'relativism'" (Crosman 1980, p. 159). You can doubt that Hirsch is quite such a sitting duck as this, yet agree that the virtues of a methodology or a canon are doubtful.

Gerald Graff (1983, pp. 604f.) argues forcefully that literary theories do not have specific "political implications." He wishes to "get beyond the whole dubious project of attaching specific political implications to theories independent of the way they operate in concrete social practice. A theory such as interpretive objectivism doesn't 'imply' any single politics. Making political judgments and classifications of theories requires an adequate analysis of social practices. Is there any reason to think current literary critics possess such an analysis?" Judging from the level of political analysis in, say, Terry Eagleton's *Literary Theory* (1983), you would have to answer, No.

In an essay called "Anti-Anti-Relativism" Clifford Geertz has argued that the fear that chaos will come from abandoning rigid methodologies is unreasonable: "There may be some genuine nihilists out there, along Rodeo Drive or around Times Square," he says, "but I doubt very many have become such as a result of an excessive sensitivity to the claims of other cultures. Anti-relativism has largely concocted the anxiety it lives from" (1984). And Richard Rorty says the same in his essay "Relativism" (1984a). All of these literary and social scientific and philosophic people are making the same point, an obvious one by now but apparently still worth making: be of good cheer, for it is real politics, not professors' politics, that leads to chaos, or to the revolution.

An irrational fear that Western intellectual life is about to be overrun by nihilists grips many people. It amounts to a reaction to the 1960s among people like Daniel Bell, who are unaware or unimpressed that the 1960s actually did liberate women and gays and blacks and others. They are driven by their fear to the advocate Objectivity, Demarcation, and other regimens said to be good for toughening, such as birching and dips in the river on New Year's Day. They were not always so devoted to the strenuous life. The Second World War and the Cold War helped do it. American historians in the 1940s and early 1950s, for instance, forswore their faith in relativism and took up an icy if unexamined Objectivity (Novick 1988). It was a premeditated act of ideology. The war against fascist and communist dictatorships, they as much as said, would be won or lost in the seminar room.

The point is that these political arguments against an openly rhetorical history or biology or economics are notably weak and unargued. The alternative to blindered methodologies of modernism is not a mob warring against itself but a body of enlightened thinkers engaging in earnest conversation in which they know what rhetorics they use. Perhaps the thinkers would be more enlightened and more earnest when freed to make arguments that actually bore on the scientific questions at issue.

We Wish to Make Plausible Statements, Whether "Scientific" or Not

The other objection to an openly rhetorical economics is not so pessimistic as the fear that the barbarians are at the gates. It is the sunny view that scientific knowledge of a modernist sort may be hard to achieve, even impossible, yet all will be well if we strive in our poor way to reach it. We should, it is said, have a standard of Truth beyond rhetoric. We should aspire to more than "mere" persuasion.

A spatial metaphor is involved. The cheerful methodologist divides all possible propositions about the world into objective and subjective, positive and normative, scientific and humanistic, hard and soft, as in Figure 3. He supposes the world comes neatly divided along the line of demarcation. (The diagram and the idea are Booth's [1974a, p. 17], but the idea has been expressed to me by many economists. It is beautifully elaborated, and used as a tool for feminist thinking, by Julie Nelson [1995].) The scientist's job is not to decide whether propositions are useful for understanding and for changing the world but to classify them into one or the other half, scientific or nonscientific, and to bring as many as possible into the scientific half.

scientific		humanistic
fact		value
truth		opinion
objective		subjective
positive	The	normative
rigorous	Demarcation	intuitive
precise	Line	vague
things		words
cognition		feeling
hard		soft
yang		yin
male		female

Figure 3. The Task of Science Is to Move the Line

But why? What would be the point of such an exercise? Whole teams of philosophical surveyors have sweated long over the placement of a demarcation line between scientific and other propositions, worrying for instance whether astrology can be demarcated from astronomy; it was the chief activity of the positivist movement for a century. It is unclear why they troubled themselves. The trouble is considerable. Kepler, for example, was a serious astrologer, Newton was a serious alchemist, and many modern scientists take seriously the claims of the paranormal, which causes much trouble for a view *a priori* that the word "serious" cannot be spoken together with "astrology" and "alchemy" and "paranormal."

We have fallen in love with the problem of finding out where God drew the boundary dividing scientific from nonscientific thinking. But there is no reason to believe that the term "scientific" occurred in God's blueprint of the universe. People are persuaded of things in many ways, as I've shown for economic persuasion in detail. It is not clear why they should labor at drawing lines on mental maps between one way and another.

Modernists have long faced the embarrassment that metaphor, case study, upbringing, authority, introspection, simplicity, symmetry, fashion, theology, and politics apparently serve to persuade scientists as well as they do other folk, and have dealt with the embarrassment by labeling these the "context of discovery." The way scientists discover hypotheses has been held to be distinct from the "context of justification," namely, justifications of a modernist sort. Thomas Kuhn's autobiographical reflections on the matter can stand for the puzzlement in recent years about this ploy: "Having been weaned intellectually on these distinctions and others like them, I could scarcely be more aware of their import and force. For many years I took them to be about the nature of knowledge, and . . . yet my attempts to apply them, even *grosso modo*, to the actual situations in which knowledge is gained, accepted, and assimilated have made them seem extraordinarily problematic" (Kuhn 1970, p. 9).

The claim of the modernist methodologist is that "ultimately" all knowledge in science can be brought into the hard, objective side of the dichotomy. Consequently, in certifying propositions as really scientific there is great emphasis placed on *"conceivable* falsification" and *"some future* test." The apparent standard is the modernist one that we must find plausible only the things we cannot possibly doubt. Yet even this peculiar standard is not in fact applied: a conceivable but practically impossible test takes over the prestige of the real test, free of its labor.

The silent substitution of a conceivable test left to the future for a present test left undone needs to be challenged. You are not doing science merely because you have promised ultimately to do it. The substitution is identical to the step taken in the "new welfare economics" of the 1940s. Economists wished to equate as morally similar *actual* compensation of those hurt during a Pareto optimal move with a *hypothetical* compensation not actually paid, as in the Hicks-Kaldor test. It was said that if conceivably we could compensate unemployed auto workers out of the gain from freer trade with Japan, then we should go ahead with freer trade. We do not actually have to pay the compensation.

The point is that you can't tell whether an assertion is persuasive by knowing from which side of the scientific/humanistic dichotomy it came. You can tell whether it is persuasive only by thinking about it and talking about it with other thoughtful people. Not all regression analyses are more persuasive than all moral arguments; not all controlled experiments are more persuasive than all introspections. People should not discriminate against propositions on the basis of epistemological origin. There are some subjective, soft, vague propositions that are more persuasive than some objective, hard, precise propositions. The economist is more persuaded that she will buy less oil when its price doubles than that the age of the universe is sixteen billion years. She might even be more persuaded of it than she is that the earth goes around the sun. She has the astronomical facts only from the testimony of people she trusts, a reliable though not of course infallible source of useful persuasions. The economic fact she has from looking into herself and seeing it sitting there smiling out at her. As we have seen, it is not because the law of demand has predicted well or has passed some statistical test that it is believed—although such further tests are not to be scorned. The "scientific" character of the tests is irrelevant.

It may be claimed in reply, and often is, that people can agree on precisely what a regression coefficient means but cannot agree precisely on the character of their introspection. This is false: people can converse on the character of their introspections, and do so habitually—about their aesthetic reactions, say, to a painting by Brueghel or a theory by Lucas. The conversations often reach conclusions as precise as human talk can. But even if it were true that regression is more precise, this would not be a good argument for economists to abandon introspection in economics. Introspections, even if imprecise, can be better than regression estimates infected with misspecifications and errors in the variables. That the regression uses numbers, precise as they look, is irrelevant. To speak precisely, precision means low variance of estimation (and we know what's wrong with that); but if the estimate is greatly biased, it will tell precisely nothing.

Saying merely that an argument is "scientific" by some narrow canon does not say much. We know that the stealing of strips of land and sheaves of grain troubled the villager of medieval England. One way we know it is the confession of Avarice in *Piers Plowman:*

> If I go to the plough, I pinch so narrow
> That a foot's land or a furrow to fetch I would
> Of my next neighbor, take of his earth;
> And if I reap, overreach, or give advice to him that reap
> To seize for me with his sickle what I never sowed.
> (Langland, passus 13, lines 370–75)

Another is a properly scientific count of the percentage of cases in the manorial court dealing with strip and sheaf stealing, with due regard to what we know of the frailties of the statistics (McCloskey 1991). There is no need to choose between the qualitative and the quantitative evidence: an intelligent rhetoric of economic history would give privilege to neither. Both have some weight, the one on account of the artistic excellence of the poem (a great poet sees well) and the other on account of the apparent definiteness of the offense (one case, one strip, usually). In view of our difficulty in saying much about the world, such catholicity in argument seems sensible.

An extreme case unnecessary for the argument here will make the point. You are more strongly persuaded that it is wrong to murder than that inflation is always and everywhere a monetary phenomenon. This is not to say that similar techniques of persuasion will be applicable to both propositions. It says merely that each within its field, and each therefore subject to the methods of honest persuasion appropriate to that field, the one achieves a greater certitude than the other.

To deny the comparison is to deny that reason and the partial certitude it can bring applies to nonscientific subjects, a common but unreasonable position. There is no reason why specifically "scientific" persuasiveness (well, actually pseudoscientific: "at the .05 level the coefficient on M in a regression of prices of 30 countries over 30 years is insignificantly different from 1.0") should take over the whole of persuasiveness, leaving moral persuasiveness incomparably inferior to it. Arguments like "murder violates the reasonable moral premise that we should not force other people to be means to our ends" or "from behind a prenatal veil of ignorance of which side of the murderer's revolver we would be after birth we would enact laws against murder" are persuasive in comparable units. Not always, but sometimes, they are more persuasive, better, more probable (Toulmin 1958, p. 34). Frank Knight, whose thinking is congenial to this rhetorical approach, made a similar point in similar words (1940, p. 164). Of the basic postulates of economics, attested by "sympathetic introspection," he said, "We surely 'know' these propositions better, more confidently and certainly, than we know the truth of any statement about any concrete physical fact or event . . . and fully as certainly as we know the truth of any axiom of mathematics."

We believe and act on what persuades us—not what persuades a majority of a badly chosen jury, but what persuades well-educated participants in the conversations of our civilization and of our field. To attempt to go beyond persuasive reasoning is to let epistemology limit reasonable persuasion.

The Philosophical Objections to Rhetoric Are Not Persuasive

Against this stands the ancient notion that we are all in pursuit of Truth—as against lower-case truths, such as the temperature in Iowa City this afternoon or the quality of the president's judgment in foreign affairs. The pursuit of Truth is said to be very different from mere persuasion. Yet when set beside the actual behavior of scientists and scholars the notion looks strange.

The strangeness is not that the scientists and scholars in fact pursue Falsehood. They do not. They pursue other things, but things which have only an incidental relation with Truth. They do so not because they are inferior to philosophers in moral fiber but because they are human. Truth-pursuing is a poor theory of human motivation and non-operational as a moral imperative. The human scientists pursue persuasiveness, prettiness, the resolution of puzzlement, the conquest of recalcitrant details, the feeling of a job well done, and the honor and income of office: as Nelson Goodman says, they pursue "varieties of rightness other than truth" (1983, p. 105). It must be borne in mind that it is only a philosophical doctrine that we pursue Truth.

The philosophical doctrine is not so decisively True, furthermore, that it should be allowed to overwhelm our common sense in the matter of how much weight to place on rhetoric. The very idea of Truth—with a capital T, something beyond what is merely persuasive to all concerned—is a fifth wheel, inoperative except that it occasionally comes loose and hits a bystander. If we decide that the quantity theory of money or the marginal productivity theory of distribution is persuasive, interesting, useful, reasonable, appealing, acceptable, we do not also need to know that it is *True*. Its persuasiveness, interest, usefulness, and so forth come from particular arguments: "Marginal productivity theory, for one thing, is a consequence of rationality in the hiring of inputs" (and we think highly of rationality). "The quantity equation, for one thing, is a simple framework for macroeconomics" (and we think highly of simplicity).

These are particular arguments, good or bad. After making them, there is no point in asking a last, summarizing question: "Well, is it True?" It's whatever it is—persuasive, interesting, useful, and so forth. The particulars suggest answerable rhetorical questions that might matter, such as what exactly the use of the fact is or to whom exactly it is persuasive. There is no reason to search for a general quality called Truth, which answers only the unanswerable question "What is it that is in the mind of God?" Such and such and so and so accord with a human checklist of arguments persuasive to humans. That is all ye need to know.

The usual way of rebutting such an argument is to say that one *must* have a theory of truth, an Epistemology. Recall the argument that one *must* have a Methodology. How can you talk without one? (A light bulb goes on in the mind of the speaker.) Indeed, talking *against* epistemology is *itself* epistemological talk—talk *about* epistemology, which therefore *does* exist. (People who think they have discovered a neat philosophical argument favor italics.) Willard Quine calls the argument Plato's Beard, in honor of the man who got most famously tangled in it: "Nonbeing must in some sense be [or, in the italic style, *be*], otherwise what is it [or what *is* it] that there is not?" (Quine 1948, pp. 2f.). With it, he points out, you can prove the existence of nonbeings such as Pegasus, pigs with wings, and, here, epistemology: that is to say, the existence of an actual referent for any reference in the language. The point is a *reductio ad absurdum*. And if the reduction were not considered absurd, it would still not imply that serious people should spend much time thinking about the referent in question. The serious issues are rhetorical—how we become persuaded, in the actual case at hand—not epistemological.

Epistemology, as we have seen, has had its uses, and many uplifting sermons have been heard on pursuing Truth. They are more uplifting, to be sure, when the threat to the values thus celebrated is genuine: the preacher of the gospel facing death in the jungle looks more courageous than the same man thundering in Wiltshire to a congregation of shepherds and military wives. The defenders of truth and rationality in the West have a habit of using the rhetoric of danger without really facing it. Listen to Lawrence Stone, that best of historians and worst of methodologists, issuing a call to arms from the letters column of *Harper's*: "Today, we need to stand shoulder to shoulder against the growing army of enemies of rationality. By that I mean the followers of the fashionable cult of absolute relativism, emerging from philosophy, linguistics, semiotics, and deconstructionism. These . . . tend to deny the possibility of accurate communication by the use of language, the force of logical deduction, and the very existence of truth and falsehood" (Stone 1984, p. 5).

But the most serious minds doubt the very existence of Truth, capital-T, if it is construed as something standing there in the absolute, waiting to be observed by the lone scientist or historian. Nelson Goodman, no enemy of rationality, writes, "The scientist who supposes that he is singlemindedly dedicated to the search for truth deceives himself. He seeks system, simplicity, scope; and when satisfied on these scores he tailors truth to fit. He as much decrees and discovers the laws he sets forth, as much designs and discerns the patterns he delineates" (1978, p. 18). Nor was Frank Knight prone to semiological fevers. Yet in his review of Hutchison's positivism in economics he declared, with many reasonable people since Gorgias of Liontini: "Testing observations is chiefly . . . a social activity or phenomenon. This fact makes all knowledge of the world of sense observation . . . itself a social activity. A conscious, critical social consensus is of the essence of the idea of objectivity or truth" (1940, p. 156). These sober people, and many more, agree that Truth is a fifth wheel and persuasion social.

A specialization of the argument that we pursue Truth is that we pursue Logic. This, too, is questionable. In questioning it, again I do not mean to imply that it would be better to become illogical. Formal logic is fine, within its limits. What goes wrong is that formal logic is treated sometimes as all of reason. The impulse to treat it this way shows up especially in lists of fallacies. Fallacy-mongering reveals a legislative attitude toward method. It is no surprise that Jeremy Bentham, confident of his ability to legislate for others in matters of method as in matters of education, prisons, and government, had compiled from his notes *The Book of Fallacies* (1824). David Hackett Fischer's book *Historians' Fallacies* (1970) has such a flaw: it takes as "fallacious" the many arguments that may be merely supporting, if by themselves inconclusive.

Elementary texts on logic exhibit this older attitude, that a form of words that cannot be fitted into a valid syllogism is to be judged fallacious—which is to say, bad argument. Irving Copi's fifth edition of his *Introduction to Logic* (1978), for instance, praises Fischer's zeal in rooting out fully 112 different forms of fallacious heresy in the works of historians, and then turns to attack as "fallacies" (pp. 87, 91) the argument from authority, from the character of one's opponent, from equal ignorance, and many other arguments used daily by scientists, by historians, by judges (as Copi notes without realizing the significance), and, most significant of all, by philosophers themselves. His Chapter 3, "Informal Fallacies," deals with such errors. A later chapter, "Analogy and Probable Inference," is strictly segregated, as is customary in philosophical exposition, from reasoning that is properly syllogistic (and therefore "demonstrative," "necessary," and so forth). There Copi admits charmingly that of course "most of our own everyday inferences are by analogy," presumably also the philosopher's own. He does not consider the possibility that his everyday deductions may also be analogies. L. Susan Stebbing's little book on logic, first published in 1943 and reissued since to successive generations of British students of philosophy, takes an even firmer stand against arguments merely persuasive to all concerned: "We can *know* our conclusions to be true only when we *know* both that the premises are true and that they imply the conclusion. For this purpose we *reason*" (1943, p. 160). Observe the force of her italics here, a bit of yelling in the cause of reason. She goes on to inveigh against "the orator," whose aim, she believes, "is to induce belief at all costs" and whose "appeal is not to reason but to uncontrolled emotion, not to considerations logically relevant but to prejudice."

It is notable that these logicians, committed presumably to the serious study of reason, do not exhibit serious understanding of rhetoric and its history. Copi sneers at rhetoric (pp. 75, 242), though he does admit (p. 255) that there were "older times when logic and rhetoric were more closely connected than they are today." Stebbing is less tolerant, though she first wrote in the decade in which rhetoric touched its nadir, and may be excused for using a little uncontrolled emotion and prejudice in defense of even a narrow idea of reasoning.

It is less excusable, though, that in narrow terms the defenses of narrowness are circular (the fallacy *petitio principii*). The rhetorical device is to use words like "true" or "correct" or "sound" or "what we know" (let us abandon "valid" for whatever uses the logician wishes to put it) to mean "obeying all the laws of a narrow logic as laid down by the local fallacymongerer" (Stebbing 1943, p. 161; Copi 1978, p. 87). Since the conclusion has been assumed, by definition, it is no trick to reduce truth, correctness, soundness, and what we know to formal logic of a syllogistic sort, casting out the rest as fallacy. This is the procedure in J. L. Mackie's article "Fallacies" in *The Encyclopedia of Philosophy* (1967). Here the deduction of "ought" from "is" is described flatly as "an error exposed by Hume, but still frequently committed" (p. 178). In the past few decades, for instance, it has been frequently committed by Willard Quine, John Searle, J. L. Austin, and other notorious advocates of fallacy. It has taken a long time for Cardinal Newman's reasoned complaint, written in 1841 (1870, p. 90), to become a common opinion among philosophers themselves: "Logicians are more set on concluding rightly, than on right conclusions."

Anti-Modernism Is Nice

The larger issue reaches well beyond technical philosophy, and beyond the philosophical misapprehensions of economists. The issue is modernism, economics being merely one field ready to shed it. Modernism was worth trying. But it didn't work. For unpersuasive reasons it has confined psychologists (until recently) to theories that do not use the unconscious mind and has confined economists (until recently) to theories that do not use psychology. Perhaps it is time to stop.

An economist who thinks so, and wishes a broader and more cogent conversation to begin in economics, does not have to join the antimodernists in everything they do. The antimodernists have been trying to revive certain writers long neglected, especially in the English-speaking world, who would not have accepted the modernist/scientistic orthodoxy as defined around 1950. These include such *bêtes noires* as the sophists, Cicero, scholastic philosophy, and Hegel. More recently they include the American pragmatists, long out of philosophical fashion, whose work was once viewed as an amusing but after all rather crude approximation to what was done properly in Vienna or Cambridge; of whom you might say,

> I write them out in a verse:
> James and Dewey and Peirce.
> Sweetness and light enough,
> Mathematically not up to snuff.

The antimodernists themselves are as alarming as their heroes: they have included Continental philosophers such as Heidegger, Habermas, Adorno, Foucault, and other alarming people; certain unconventional observers of science (Polanyi, Bronowski); renegade analytic philosophers such as Stephen Toulmin and Richard Rorty; social scientists using nonquantitative methods (from Freud to Piaget and Fraser to Geertz); sociologists, philosophers, and historians of science after Thomas Kuhn; and, most alarming of all, literary critics in profusion.

An attack on the narrowness of modernist rhetoric in economics does not depend on accepting such folk as allies. Richard Rorty has named them "the new fuzzies" (1984a), a term of affection (for he is one), evoking Winnie ille Pu discoursing on philosophy. In our actual practice in daily life and thought, though, we are all fuzzies, even we economists, however glinty and Darth Vaderish we think we are made by mastery of the identification problem and the Kuhn-Tucker conditions.

Rhetoric Is Good for You

The thinking about thinking that suits antimodernism is rhetoric. Rhetoric is not a new methodology. It is antimethodology. It points out what we actually do, what seems to persuade us, and why. At the end of his treatment of the rhetoric of analytic philosophy Stanley Rosen declared that his argument

> is not offered as a new theory or how to philosophize, but
> as an account of what we actually do. The positive task of the
> philosopher is to fecundate his analytic skills with dreams, and
> to discipline his dreams with analysis. I cannot provide him with
> a manual of rules and regulations governing this activity. There
> are no rules and regulations for being reasonable, and certainly
> no rules and regulations for dreaming reasonable dreams. (1980,
> p. 260)

To repeat: "There are no rules and regulations for being reasonable." Being reasonable is weighing and considering all reasons, not merely the reasons that some methodology or epistemology or logic claims to be stations of the cross along the one path to Justified True Belief. A methodology that claims the historical dialectic or the hypotheticode-ductive model or phenomenology or historical *verstehen* or any one style of giving reasons to be The One is probably unreasonable. The reasonable rhetorician cannot write down his rules. They are numberless, because they cover all reasons, and bromidic, because they cover all circumstances. Above all, they change. The rhetorician demands a cheerful, mature, and sober clientele that can bear to face a world of hap without a drink in hand.

The modernist pedlar, on the other hand, makes large claims, and the rubes gather. If you will but be a modernist, says he to the amazed economists gathering at the tent, and scientistic and whatever else is current, following its rules, you will be a good economist, my friend, whether or not you are honest or imaginative or good. There's nothing to it, my lad.

Little wonder that youths in science are drunk with methodology: "Ale, man, ale's the stuff to drink / For fellows whom it hurts to think / . . . / And faith, 'tis pleasant till 'tis past: / The mischief is that 'twill not last." You can understand the attraction of methodological formulas immediately potable. A textual critic equipped with the formula "the more sincere text is the better" or an economist with "the statistically significant coefficient should be retained" is ready for work. That his work will be wrong bothers him less than that he will not get the stuff out at all unless he possesses, as he is inclined to say, *some* Methodology. Output, man, output's the stuff to get, / So deans and chairmen will not fret.

The ironic vocabulary of science reflects an uneasiness about taking methodology as against taking thought: the scientist speaks of "turning the crank" or "grinding it out." Taking thought would seem better than crank-turning, and a rhetorical criticism of economics is an invitation to take thought. What, you ask yourself in a rhetorical manner, is the root metaphor in my work? Do I really have evidence for its aptness? I have appealed to an authority here: is it a good one? There my formal language claims the Objectivity of Science: is the point I'm making really up to it? Here I am making a quantitative argument: what are my conversational standards of bigness? Should I simulate the results mathematically, to show that they have quantitative bite? I appeal to "theoretical reasons" in this argument: do I mean pretty diagrams? In what way exactly are they pretty? I depend heavily on introspection for that point: how can I increase my confidence that my audience has the same introspection? I appeal to symmetry at this point: have I appealed symmetrically? Is there another symmetry I might as well impose, too? What role do definitions play in my argument? How can I refine my appeal to the argument a fortiori? Rhetorical criticism is an invitation to take thought but not, to repeat, a formula for good thinking.

The very economics of the matter, to make the now familiar argument *ad hominem*, makes such formulas impossible. A scholar in possession of a scholarly formula more specific than Work and Pray would be a scientific millionaire. Scientific millionaires are not common. Methodology claims prescience in scientific affairs. The difficulty with prescience is that it is exactly "pre-science"—that is, knowing things before they are known, a contradiction. Methodology entails this contradiction. It pretends to know how to achieve knowledge before the knowledge to be achieved is in place. Life is not so easy. Even anarchists in methodology face this difficulty if they propose actual policies for science. No one can know what the scientific future will bring: it may be that the centralized, bureaucratized, methodized science that threatens to make the scientists into crank-turners, despite the evidence from the history of science that progress in science is seldom advanced and often retarded by such a structure, is just the ticket for the twenty-first century. Reasonable arguments can be made on both sides. The historical evidence is merely one strong argument among others, not the end of the conversation.

The best you can do, then, is to recommend what is good for science now, and leave the future to the gods. What is good for science now, to recur to an earlier theme, is good scientists, in most meanings of "good." A rhetorical criticism of economics can perhaps make economists more modest, tolerant, and self-aware, and improve one of the conversations of humanity.

12 SINCE RHETORIC

PROSPECTS FOR A

SCIENTIFIC ECONOMICS

Well, has it worked? Since the first edition in 1985, and before it the philosophically oriented paper in 1983, have economists paid attention?

No. Most economists have reckoned from the title of the book that Aunt Deirdre "advocates" rhetoric, as "against" mathematics. Or else maybe she is ripping aside a veil, showing economics to be Not Science, Merely Literature. Or maybe she's just nuts. After all, in 1995 we got another piece of evidence "consistent with" that Hypothesis.

I admit I get annoyed when the first question out of someone's mouth after they've read a piece of mine is, "How have economists reacted?" What annoys me is that it sounds like the questioner wants to get his opinions from a public opinion poll, instead of weighing and considering what I have said. It is the duty of professors to think for themselves, and to weigh and consider rhetorically and philosophically the thoughts of people who claim to be thinking. If more professors did their duty, rhetorical scandals like statistical significance or positive economics or modernist architecture would not go on and on as they do.

The appeal to the herd of independent minds annoys. It reminds me of the attitude in progressive circles at the University of Massachusetts at the time of the Tienanmen Square demonstrations in 1989. The tanks had just stopped democracy in China, and we had watched it happen on Channel 3 with Dan Rather. What to think? Anyone who thought for herself knew what to think: What a *horrible* thing to do! Down with the dictators! But the progressives hesitated. As one of them explained to a friend of mine: I have to see what the editorials say. I have to get the line. After all, socialism is Good, and China is socialist. How have politically correct people reacted?

But the curiosity about how people have reacted to *The Rhetoric of Economics* is not always so craven as the Massachusetts progressives. I

187

have done a weird thing (all right: two weird things). Economics is a "conservative" field, at least by comparison with anthropology and performance art. Good Lord, how have *those* stiffs reacted?

As I say, to the book (not to the other weird thing) they have reacted imperfectly from my point of view. True, the book was widely and favorably noticed. I hope you yourself noticed and were impressed. But even its friends kept getting it wrong in ways that let them go on as before. A wonderful review by Bob Heilbroner in the *New York Review of Books,* for example, said, This is nice, but after all it's just about Style, not Substance. Oh, Bob, Bob. When am I going to persuade you that style *is* substance, you master of style? Bob Solow from another ideological direction had the same idea and evokes from me the same response. Oh, Bob, Bob. The number of economists who have understood the book and then acted on the understanding in print is to my knowledge small: Arjo Klamer first (he in fact discovered the point independently in his Ph.D. dissertation at Duke), Jack Amariglio, John Davis, Jerry Evensky, Willie Henderson, Don Lavoie, Hans Lind, William Milberg. Not a middle-of-the-road neoclassical establishment figure among them. And anyway not many of any description.

I am calm about this. Really I am. I strike some people as arrogant, though more so in my former gender than now, I hope. But truly I am as modest a lady as anyone could wish, very sweet and unassuming. I would never assume in particular that people who do not read my books or do not understand them or do not agree with them are fools and knaves. Well, some are, and I sometimes feel impelled to say so. That's nasty: I shouldn't. But I really do not expect people to agree with me. People haven't agreed with me as a soft Marxist, as a social engineering transport economist, as a quantitative economic historian, as a Chicago School economist, as a neoinstitutionalist, as a libertarian, as a global monetarist, as a free market feminist. No wonder they don't agree with me as a rhetorician of science.

Of course, like most people, I do assume that those folks are wrong and I am right. (And in sober truth—can I confide in you as a friend?— I *am* right.) But no matter. I learned the hard way, over and over and over again, that most people are not open to persuasion to what is right. It's a pity that it is as true of the average professor carrying *The New York Times* as it is of your local Bubba carrying a six-pack, but there you are. It just goes to show that rhetoric is about something serious. Science doesn't work by people handing each other platters filled with Results and Findings to be gobbled up like cocktail canapés. As Schopenhauer once said, "It is quite natural that we should adopt a defensive and negative attitude towards every new opinion concerning something on which we have already an opinion of our own. For it forces its way as an enemy into the previously closed system of our own convictions, shatters the calm of mind we have attained through this system, demands renewed efforts of us and declares our former efforts to have been in vain" (Schopenhauer 1851 [1970] No. 19, p. 124). Thomas Kuhn said the same thing and showed it working in the rhetorical history of science.

I think the first edition and my later writings made a space in economics for thinking about the conversation. But it's still a very small space. Economists are still unaware of how they talk. I failed. Oh well, keep trying.

The results of the rhetorical unawareness of economists, I have realized more and more, are unspeakably sad. A lot of good work gets done in economics, new facts and new ideas. Economists are not stupid or lazy, not at all. I love the field. I belong to the mainstream and would float happily in it if it made a bit of sense. But the mainstream of normal science in economics, I'm afraid, has become a boys' game in a sandbox. It has become silly.

In two usages especially, as I've argued, the field since the 1940s has become so silly that nothing scientific can be expected until it gets over them: blackboard economics and statistical significance. The one is the gift of the Math Department, the other of the Statistics Department. As I have said, no one could reasonably object to mathematics and statistics in economics. But in the Department of Mathematics and the Department of Statistics the outputs are not scientific findings. They are theorems about mathematical objects and statistical tests. Unfortunately the economists have not followed the fields like physics and engineering, which *use* results from the two departments in question without taking over their theorem-proving intellectual values (I go into this in more detail in *Knowledge and Persuasion in Economics*, [1994, chs. 9–13]). In physics and engineering people are interested in how a theory matters in the world, and they have good ways of finding out, chiefly observation and simulation (not statistical significance). By contrast, nothing scientific comes from the theorems from the departments of Mathematics or Statistics or Economics, for the good reasons that (1) the set of theorems is practically unbounded and (2) statistical significance has practically nothing to do with scientific significance. In practical terms what is published in academic journals of economics is so irrelevant to the way real scientific persuasion goes on that I can by now only sit and moan quietly. Please, *please*, boys: let's get out of the sandbox. Let's start having a serious scientific rhetoric.

I once had a trans-Atlantic flight seated beside a young economist who must qualify as the most barbarous scholar I have ever met. That's a stiff competition. He told me that his Scientific duty was to sit at his computer all day long. (Much as I do, I must admit, writing; but I've read a book or two.) What he meant is that he did not need to read anything or talk to any businessperson or even copy down government statistics. All he needed to do to be a modern economist was to run regression equations, searching for statistical significance, in standard data sets, already collected and committed to machine-readable form. Although I am pretty sure that the young man, now not quite so young, still has nothing but contempt for the values of actual science and scholarship that I espouse here, I do feel sorry for him and worry what will happen when he discovers that his life has been wasted. I look at the boys playing in the sandbox like a doting aunt and worry: Oh, boys, it is *so* foolish what you have allowed yourself to specialize in playing; please, *please* start caring about the world and its very interesting economy; you are going to feel *very* unhappy this evening when you go home and think over what you have accomplished. It's not the young man's fault that he is a barbarian. He was taught to be one in a fine graduate program by nameable modernist econometricians, positive economists, and methodologists with whom I am personally acquainted. By their fruits ye shall know them.

If I had my wish about how this second edition would be used it would be that every graduate student in economics would read it and reflect, to avoid an unscientific barbarism. In my day Koopmans's *Three Essays on the State of Economic Science* (1957) was The Book. It was, I realize now, an appalling production, outlining the fraudulent truce between econometrics and mathematical theory that has dominated economics since 1957. We all read it and thought it very fine. My book is partly an anti-Koopmans.

The cynical and perhaps realistic view is that nothing would actually change in economics if the graduate students read the second edition of my book. Certainly you should never underestimate the conservatism of science. Geologists fought for decades against plate tectonics (I was perhaps the last person in the United States to be educated in the old geology, by conservatives at Harvard contemptuous of the crazy notion that the continents fitted into each other). As George Stigler, America's leading vulgar Marxist, never tired of arguing, the status quo usually has lots of money and power to back it. A narrow, ignorant, antihumanistic, unscientific economics is easier to run than anything better. Look at how popular the old way is with political scientists, for example, who have made themselves into departments of third-rate economists, the leading econowannabes of academic life. Why, it's economics.

No, it's only a modernist economics briefly regnant in the mid–

twentieth century, as obsolete as the architecture of the 1950s. I think the cynical view is wrong. I think if the graduate students reflected they could in ten years remake economics into a serious science and a serious moral philosophy, such as it was with Adam Smith, say.

But the graduate students are frightened. In 1990 Arjo Klamer and David Colander showed just how frightened in their book *The Making of an Economist*. That is certainly a book every graduate student in economics, actual or prospective, must read.

I would like above all with my book to encourage the graduate students, to help them overcome their careerist fears. I can make the argument on wholly prudential grounds. A cute blackboard argument is that in choosing graduate school you have chosen a low-income option anyway. You could have gone to law school or business school, and being smart and hardworking you would have done well. But you wanted to be an economist, perhaps a professor of economics. Having chosen that lower income stream it is inconsistent to distort your intellectual life in fear of . . . a lower income steam. Be courageous. You've chosen to be so anyway: you might as well get credit for it.

Yes, I know. The cute blackboard argument is not very persuasive. But haven't I been saying that? A more serious argument is empirical. It is the case now that graduate students who actually discover something about the economic world—instead of writing three theoretical essays in search of a theme—and find it out in ways that sidestep the killing field of statistical significance (by gathering utterly new facts, for example) get better jobs. Look around. You'll find it's so. Even the older boys playing in the sandbox know instinctively when someone shows up with serious scientific intent. They try to hire her. When I was a graduate student most Ph.D. dissertations were empirical, and because inverting even a 10-by-10 matrix was difficult in 1965 the empirical work was actually about the world, not game-playing with statistical significance. Then gradually the dissertations all became theoretical. Even when they were called "empirical" they were exercises in imaginary worlds undisciplined by the overwhelming question: How Big is Big? Or, sadly, they fell for the idea that statistical significance tells. Now they are shifting back. On prudential grounds, my dears, be courageous. If you just get up and walk out of the sandbox, insisting on learning about the economic world and thinking hard about what you have learned in light of the history of economic ideas since Smith, you will prosper.

But the most serious argument I can make has nothing to do with prudence. It therefore contradicts the economics of Jeremy Bentham and George Stigler and Paul Samuelson and says, No, identity matters, too. Another way of saying it is that virtues aside from Prudence matter. Courage, Temperance, Justice, Love. If you ever read Adam Smith's other book, *The Theory of Moral Sentiments*, you will find an articulation of the five virtues that puts the Prudence of *The Wealth of Nations* in its proper context.

If we will be who we are, take our courage, and use it, we can change economics. People sometimes ask me how my views of economics have changed since I became a woman. It's not been long, and I am, goodness knows, nothing like an expert at Being a Woman. In some important ways I never will be, alas. Still, I see some differences. The virtue of Love, it seems to me, belongs in any serious science of economics, and radically changes even the studies of Prudence. The boys' games seem to me now to be even sillier than I had thought. A few other things, and more to come, I expect.

But what I mainly learned is that a life must be itself, and in a rich, free country like ours it can be. Do this (no, no, I don't mean change gender unless you *have* to: it's *very* inconvenient!). Be courageous and be yourself. People do not come into economics mainly because they like the sandbox games at present taking place in the field. Some do; but not most people. Most people want to change the world or make a scientific contribution. With such noble goals the first thing to do is to break through the phony rhetoric of modern economics and bring economics, that glorious conversation since Adam Smith, back into the conversation of humankind.

Please, my dears, please.

BIBLIOGRAPHY

INDEX

BIBLIOGRAPHY

Works Cited Other than on the Rhetoric of Economics

This first of three lists gives some of the works cited in the text, not a bibliography of any one subject or a list of works consulted. There are two other lists. I think the inconvenience of splitting the citations between three lists—this one, then a Bibliography on the Rhetoric of Economics Except for Reviews, and then Reviews of *The Rhetoric of Economics*—is outweighed by advantages: with the other two lists the reader can see ostensibly what a "rhetoric of economics" might be, and can judge the (small) impact of the first edition.

Akerlof, George A., and W. T. Dickens. 1982. "The Economic Consequences of Cognitive Dissonance." *American Economic Review* 72 (June): 307–19.

Alchian, Armen. 1950. "Uncertainty, Evolution, and Economic Theory." *Journal of Political Economy* 58 (June): 211–21.

Aristotle. *Rhetoric.* Trans. George A. Kennedy. New York: Oxford University Press, 1991.

Arrow, Kenneth. 1959. "Decision Theory and the Choice of a Level of Significance for the *t*-Test." In Ingram Olkin et al., eds., *Contributions to Probability and Statistics: Essays in Honor of Harold Hotelling.* Stanford, Calif.: Stanford University Press.

Austen, Jane. 1818. *Persuasion.* New York: Houghton Mifflin, 1965.

Austin, J. L. 1955. *How to Do Things with Words.* 2d ed. J. O. Urmson and M. Sbisà, eds. Cambridge: Harvard University Press.

Bakan, David. 1966. "The Test of Significance in Psychological Research." *Psychological Bulletin* 66 (December): 423–37. Reprinted in Bernhardt Lieberman, ed., *Contemporary Problems in Statistics: A Book of Readings for the Behavioral Sciences.* New York: Oxford University Press, 1971.

Bakan, David. 1967. *On Method: Toward a Reconstruction of Psychological Method.* San Francisco: Jossey-Bass.

Barfield, Owen. 1947. "Poetic Diction and Legal Fiction." Reprinted in Max Black, ed., *The Importance of Language,* pp. 51–71. Englewood Cliffs, N.J.: Prentice Hall, 1962.

Barnes, Barry, and David Edge, eds. 1982. *Science in Context: Readings in the Sociology of Science.* Cambridge, Mass.: M.I.T. Press.

Barthes, Roland. 1960. "Authors and Writers," in his *Critical Essays* (trans. 1972). Reprinted in S. Sontag, ed., *A Barthes Reader.* New York: Hill and Wang, 1982.

Bibliography

Battaglio, Raymond C., et al. 1981. "Commodity Choice Behavior with Pigeons as Subjects." *Journal of Political Economy* 84 (February): 116–51.

Bauer, Peter. 1984. *Reality and Rhetoric: Studies in the Economics of Development.* Cambridge, Mass.: Harvard University Press.

Bazerman, Charles. 1981. "What Written Knowledge Does: Three Examples of Academic Discourse." *Philosophy of the Social Sciences* 11 (September): 361–87.

Bazerman, Charles. 1983. "Scientific Writing as a Social Act: A Review of the Literature of the Sociology of Science." In Paul Anderson and John Brockmann, eds., *New Essays in Scientific and Technical Communications: Theory, Research, and Practice.* Farmingdale, N.Y.: Baywood.

Bazerman, Charles. 1984. "The Modern Evolution of the Experimental Report in Physics: Spectroscopic Articles in *Physical Review, 1893–1980.*" *Social Studies of Science* 14: 163–96.

Bazerman, Charles. 1988. *Shaping Written Knowledge: The Genre and Activity of the Experimental Article in Science.* Rhetoric of the Human Sciences series. Madison: University of Wisconsin Press.

Bazerman, Charles, and James Paradis, eds. 1991. *The Textual Dynamics of the Professions.* Rhetoric of the Human Sciences series. Madison: University of Wisconsin Press.

Becker, Gary S., and George J. Stigler. 1977. "De Gustibus Non Est Disputandum." *American Economic Review* 67 (March): 76–90.

Bentham, Jeremy. 1824. *The Book of Fallacies, from Unfinished Papers.* London: Hunt.

Black, Max, ed. 1962a. *The Importance of Language.* Englewood Cliffs, N.J.: Prentice-Hall.

Black, Max. 1962b. *Models and Metaphors: Studies in Language and Philosophy.* Ithaca, N.Y.: Cornell University Press.

Blaug, Mark. 1980. *The Methodology of Economics; or, How Economists Explain.* Cambridge: Cambridge University Press.

Boland, Lawrence A. 1979. "A Critique of Friedman's Critics." *Journal of Economic Literature* 17 (June): 503–22.

Boland, Lawrence A. 1982. *The Foundations of Economic Method.* London: Allen and Unwin.

Booth, Wayne C. 1961. *The Rhetoric of Fiction.* Chicago: University of Chicago Press.

Booth, Wayne C. 1974a. *Modern Dogma and the Rhetoric of Assent.* Chicago: University of Chicago Press.

Booth, Wayne C. 1974b. *A Rhetoric of Irony.* Chicago: University of Chicago Press.

Booth, Wayne C. 1979. *Critical Understanding: The Powers and Limits of Pluralism.* Chicago: University of Chicago Press.

Bordo, Michael D., and Anna J. Schwartz, eds. 1984. *A Retrospective on the Classical Gold Standard, 1821–1931.* Chicago: University of Chicago Press.

Borel, Armand. 1983. "Mathematics: Art and Science." *Mathematical Intelligencer* 5, no. 4: 9–17.

Boring, Edwin G. 1919. "Mathematical Versus Scientific Significance." *Psychological Bulletin* 16 (October): 335–38.

Boulding, Kenneth. 1975. *Ecodynamics: A New Theory of Societal Evolution.* Beverly Hills, Calif.: Sage.

Braudel, Fernand, and Frank Spooner. 1967. "Prices in Europe from 1450 to 1750." In E. A. Rich and C. H. Wilson, eds., *The Cambridge Economic History of Europe,* vol. 4. Cambridge: Cambridge University Press.

Bronowski, Jacob. 1965. *Science and Human Values.* Rev. ed. New York: Harper and Row.

Bruns, Gerald L. 1984. "The Problem of Figuration in Antiquity." In G. Shapiro and A. Sica, eds., *Hermeneutics: Questions and Prospects,* pp. 147–164. Amherst: University of Massachusetts Press.

Burke, Kenneth. 1945. *A Grammar of Motives.* Berkeley: University of California Press, 1969.

Burke, Kenneth. 1950. *A Rhetoric of Motives.* Berkeley: University of California Press, 1969.

Burke, Kenneth. 1961. *The Rhetoric of Religion: Studies in Logology.* Berkeley: University of Califomia Press, 1970.

Burke, Kenneth. 1968. "Interaction: Dramatism." In *The International Encyclopedia of the Social Sciences.* New York: Macmillan.

Caldwell, Bruce. 1982. *Beyond Positivism: Economic Methodology in the 19th Century.* London: Allen and Unwin.

Campbell, John Angus. 1987. "Charles Darwin: Rhetorician of Science." In John Nelson, et al., eds., *Rhetoric of the Human Sciences,* pp. 69–86. Madison: University of Wisconsin Press.

Case, K. E., and R. J. Shiller. 1989. "The Efficiency of the Market for Single-Family Homes." *American Economic Review* 79 (March).

Cheung, Steven N. S. 1973. "The Fable of the Bees." *Journal of Law and Economics* 16 (April): 11–33.

Cicero, Marcus Tulius. 45 B.C. *De Divinatione.* In W. A. Falconer, ed. and trans., *De Senectute, de Amicitia, de Divinatione.* Cambridge, Mass.: Harvard University Press, 1938.

Cicero, Marcus Tullius. *De Oratore.* Trans. E. W. Sutton. Vol. 1. Cambridge, Mass.: Harvard University Press, 1942.

Coase, Ronald H. 1937. "The Nature of the Firm." *Economica* 4 (November): 386–405. Reprinted in Coase 1988a, to which reference is made.

Coase, Ronald H. 1960. "The Problem of Social Cost." *Journal of Law and Economics* 3 (1960): 1–44. Reprinted in Coase 1988a, to which reference is made.

Coase, Ronald H. 1974. "The Lighthouse in Economics." *Journal of Law and Economics* 17 (October): 357–376. Reprinted in Coase 1988a.

Coase, Ronald H. 1982. "How Should Economists Choose?" G. Warren Nutter Lecture in Political Economy. Washington, D.C.: American Enterprise Institute.

Coase, Ronald H. 1988a. *The Firm, the Market, and the Law.* Chicago: University of Chicago Press.

Bibliography

Coase, Ronald H. 1988b. "The Nature of the Firm: Origin." *Journal of Law, Economics, and Organization* 4 (Spring): 3–17.

Coase, Ronald H. 1988c. "The Nature of the Firm: Meaning." *Journal of Law, Economics, and Organization* 4 (Spring): 19–32.

Coase, Ronald H. 1988d. "The Nature of the Firm: Influence." *Journal of Law, Economics, and Organization* 4 (Spring): 33–47.

Cochrane, John H. 1989. "The Sensitivity of Tests of the Intertemporal Allocation of Consumption to Near Rational Alternatives." *American Economic Review* 79 (June): 319–37.

Cohen, Kalman, and Richard Cyert. 1975. *Theory of the Firm.* 2d ed. Englewood Cliffs, N.J.: Prentice-Hall.

Collins, Harry M. 1985. *Changing Order: Replication and Induction in Scientific Practice.* Beverly Hills, Calif.: Sage.

Commager, Steele. 1965. "Notes on Some Poems of Catullus." *Harvard Studies in Classical Philology* 70: 83–110.

Cooley, T. F., and S. F. LeRoy. 1981. "Identification and Estimation of Money Demand." *American Economic Review* 71 (December): 825–44.

Copi, Irving. 1978. *Introduction to Logic.* 5th ed. New York: Macmillan.

Corbett, Edward P. J. 1971. *Classical Rhetoric for the Modern Student,* 3d ed. New York: Oxford University Press.

Crain, Robert. 1984. Quoted in Ellen K. Coughlin, "Social Scientists' Research on School Desegregation: Mountains of Data, but Nothing That Everybody Agrees On." *Chronicle of Higher Education* (May 16): 12.

Crosman, Richard. 1980. "Do Readers Make Meaning?" In Susan R. Suleiman and Inge Crosman, eds., *The Reader in the Text: Essays on Audience and Interpretation,* pp. 149–64. Princeton, N.J.: Princeton University Press.

Crowley, Sharon. 1994. *Ancient Rhetorics for Contemporary Students.* Boston: Allyn and Bacon.

Davies, G. R. 1989. "The Quantity Theory and Recent Statistical Studies." *Journal of Political Economy.*

Davis, Lance. 1965. "The Investment Market, 1870–1914: The Evolution of a National Market." *Journal of Economic History* 25 (September): 355–99.

Davis, Philip J., and Reuben Hersh. 1981. *The Mathematical Experience.* Boston: Houghton Mifflin.

Davis, Philip J., and Reuben Hersh. 1987. "Mathematics and Rhetoric." In John Nelson et al., eds., *The Rhetoric of the Human Sciences.* Madison: University of Wisconsin Press.

Debreu, Gerard. 1984. "Economic Theory in the Mathematical Mode." *American Economic Review* 74 (June): 267–78.

Debreu, Gerard. 1991. "The Mathematization of Economic Theory." *American Economic Review* 81 (March): 1–7.

DeGroot, Morris H. 1975. *Probability and Statistics.* Reading: Addison-Wesley, 1989.

Denton, Frank T. 1988. "The Significance of Significance: Rhetorical Aspects of Statistical Hypothesis Testing in Economics." In Arjo Klamer, D.N. McCloskey, and Robert M. Solow, eds, *The Consequences of Economic Rhetoric,* pp. 163–83. New York: Cambridge University Press.

Dettmer, Helena. 1983. *Horace: A Study in Structure.* Altertumswissenschaftliche Texte und Studien, Bd. 12. Hildensheim, West Germany: Olms.

Dettmer, Helena. 1984a. "The Design of the Catullan Corpus." Manuscript, Department of Classics, University of Iowa.

Dewey, John. 1916. *Essays in Experimental Logic.* New York: Dover.

Dewey, John. 1929. *The Quest for Certainty: A Study of the Relation of Knowledge and Action.* New York: Putnam, 1960.

Dudley-Evans, T., and W. Henderson. 1987. "Changes in the Economics Article." Department of Extramural Studies, University of Birmingham, England.

Duhem, Pierre. 1906. *The Aim and Structure of Physical Theory.* Princeton, N.J.: Princeton University Press, 1954.

Eagleton, Terry. 1983. *Literary Theory: An Introduction.* Minneapolis: University of Minnesota Press.

Einstein, Albert. 1953. "Aphorisms for Leo Baeck." Reprinted in *Ideas and Opinions.* New York: Dell, 1973.

Elster, Jon. 1979. *Ulysses and the Sirens: Studies in Rationality and Irrationality.* Cambridge: Cambridge University Press.

Feyerabend, Paul. 1975. *Against Method: Outline of an Anarchistic Theory of Knowledge.* London: Verso, 1978.

Feyerabend, Paul. 1978. *Science in a Free Society.* London: New Left Books.

Finley, M. I. 1973. *The Ancient Economy.* London: Chatto and Windus.

Finocchiaro, Maurice. 1980. *Galileo and the Art of Reasoning: Rhetorical Foundations of Logic and Scientific Method.* Dordrecht and Boston: Reidel.

Fischer, David Hackett. 1970. *Historians' Fallacies.* New York: Harper and Row.

Fish, Stanley. 1980. *Is There a Text in This Class? The Authority of Interpretive Communities.* Cambridge, Mass.: Harvard University Press.

Fisher, Irving. 1930. *The Theory of Interest.* New York: Macmillan.

Fisher, R. A. 1925. *Statistical Methods for Research Workers.* Edinburgh: Oliver and Boyd.

Fishlow, Albert. 1965. *American Railroads and the Transformation of the Antebellum Economy.* Cambridge, Mass.: Harvard University Press.

Fleck, Ludwick. 1935. *Genesis and Development of a Scientific Fact.* Chicago: University of Chicago Press, 1979.

Flory, Marleen Boudreau. 1983. "Semantics and Symbioses: How to Write an Article to Impress Your Peers." *Chronicle of Higher Education* (January 26).

Fogel, Robert W. 1960. *The Union Pacific Railroad: A Case in Premature Enterprise.* Baltimore: Johns Hopkins University Press.

Fogel, Robert W. 1962. "A Quantitative Approach to the Study of Railroads in American Economic Growth: A Report of Some Preliminary Findings." *Journal of Economic History* 22 (June): 163–97.

Fogel, Robert W. 1964. *Railroads and American Economic Growth: Essays in Econometric History.* Baltimore: Johns Hopkins University Press.

Fogel, Robert W. 1979. "Notes on the Social Saving Controversy." *Journal of Economic History* 39 (March): 1–54.

Fogel, Robert W., and G. R. Elton. 1983. *Which Road to the Past? Two Views of History.* New Haven, Conn.: Yale University Press.

200

Bibliography

Frank, Robert. 1988. *Passions Within Reason.* New York: Norton.

Fraser, D. A. S. 1958. *Statistics: An Introduction.* New York: Wiley.

Freedman, David, Robert Pisani, and Roger Purves. 1978. *Statistics.* New York: Norton.

Frenkel, Jacob. 1978. "Purchasing Power Parity: Doctrinal Perspectives and Evidence from the 1920s." *Journal of International Economics* 8 (May): 169–91.

Friedman, Milton. 1953. "The Methodology of Positive Economics." In *Essays in Positive Economics.* Chicago: University of Chicago Press.

Friedman, Milton. 1975. *An Economist's Protest.* 2d ed. Glen Ridge, N.J.: Thomas Horton and Daughters.

Friedman, Milton. 1984. "Comment [on McCloskey and Zecher 1984]." In Michael D. Bordo and Anna J. Schwartz, eds., *A Retrospective on the Classical Gold Standard, 1821–1931.* Chicago: University of Chicago Press and National Bureau of Economic Research.

Friedman, Milton, and Anna J. Schwartz. 1963. *A Monetary History of the United States, 1867–1960.* Princeton, N.J.: Princeton University Press.

Frye, Northrop. 1957. *An Anatomy of Criticism.* New York: Atheneum, 1967.

Gardner, John. 1978. *On Moral Fiction.* New York: Basic Books.

Geertz, Clifford. 1984. "Anti-Anti-Relativism." *American Anthropologist* 86 (June): 263–78.

Geison, Gerald L. 1995. *The Private Science of Louis Pasteur.* Princeton, N.J.: Princeton University Press.

Genberg, A. Hans. 1976. "Aspects of the Monetary Approach to the Balance-of-Payments Theory: An Empirical Study of Sweden." In Jacob A. Frenkel and Harry G. Johnson, eds., *The Monetary Approach to the Balance of Payments.* London: Allen and Unwin.

Georgescu-Roegen, Nicholas. 1975. *Entropy, Law, and the Economic Process.* Cambridge, Mass.: Harvard University Press.

Gibson, Walker. 1950. "Authors, Speakers, Readers, and Mock Readers." *College English* 11 (February): 265–69. Reprinted in Jane P. Thompkins, ed., *Reader-Response Criticism: From Formalism to Post-Structuralism.* Baltimore: Johns Hopkins University Press, 1980.

Glymour, Clark. 1980. *Theory and Evidence.* Princeton, N.J.: Princeton University Press.

Goldberger, Arthur S. 1991. *A Course in Econometrics.* Cambridge, Mass.: Harvard University Press.

Goodman, Nelson. 1978. *Ways of Worldmaking.* Indianapolis: Hackett.

Goodman, Nelson. 1983. "Notes on the Well-Made World." *Erkenutnis* 19: 99–107.

Gould, Stephen Jay. 1977. *Ever Since Darwin.* New York: Norton.

Gould, Stephen Jay. 1981. *The Mismeasure of Man.* New York: Norton.

Gould, Stephen Jay. 1984. *Hen's Teeth and Horse's Toes: Further Reflections in Natural History.* New York: Norton.

Graff, Gerald. 1983. "The Pseudo-Politics of Interpretation." *Critical Inquiry* 9 (March): 597–610.

Granger, Clive W. J. 1994. "A Review of Some Recent Textbooks of Econometrics," *Journal of Economic Literature* 32, no. 1 (March): 115–22.

Griffith, John G. 1968. "A Taxonomic Study of the Manuscript Tradition of Juvenal." *Museum Helveticum* 25 (April): 101–38.

Griliches, Zvi. 1976. "Automobile Prices Revisited: Extensions of the Hedonic Hypothesis." In N. E. Terleckyj, ed., *Household Production and Consumption.* Studies in Income and Wealth, vol. 40. New York: National Bureau of Economics Research.

Griliches, Zvi, and Michael D. Intriligator, eds. 1983, 1984, 1986. *Handbook of Econometrics.* Vols. I, II, and II. Amsterdam: North-Holland.

Habermas, Jürgen. 1973. *Legitimation Crisis.* Trans. T. McCarthy. Boston: Beacon Press, 1975.

Hausman, Daniel. 1981. *Capital, Profits, and Prices: An Essay in the Philosophy of Economics.* New York: Columbia University Press.

Hawke, Gary. 1970. *Railways and Economic Growth in England and Wales, 1840– 1870.* Oxford: Oxford University Press.

Heckman, J. J., and B. S. Payner. 1989. "Determining the Impact of Antidiscrimination Policy on the Economic Status of Blacks: A Study of South Carolina." *American Economic Review* 79 (March): 138–77.

Heinzelmann, Kurt. 1980. *The Economics of the Imagination.* Amherst: University of Massachusetts Press.

Hesse, Mary. 1963. *Models and Analogies in Science.* South Bend, Ind.: University of Notre Dame Press.

Hexter, J. H. 1971. "The Rhetoric of History." In *Doing History.* Bloomington: Indiana University Press.

Hicks, J. R. 1939. *Value and Capital.* Oxford: Oxford University Press.

Hirsch, Abraham, and Neil de Marchi. 1990. *Milton Friedman: Economics in Theory and Practice.* Ann Arbor: University of Michigan Press.

Hirschman, Albert. 1970. *Exit, Voice, and Loyalty.* Cambridge, Mass.: Harvard University Press.

Hirschman, Albert. 1984. "Against Parsimony: Three Easy Ways of Complicating Some Categories of Economic Discourse." *American Economic Review* 74 (May): 89–96.

Hoel, Paul G. 1954. *Introduction to Mathematical Statistics.* New York: John Wiley.

Hogben, Lancelot. 1968. *Statistical Theory: The Relationship of Probability, Credibility, and Error.* New York: Norton.

Horsburgh, H. J. N. 1958. "Philosophers against Metaphor." *Philosophical Quarterly* 8 (July): 231–45.

Housman, A. E. 1922. "The Application of Thought to Textual Criticism." In J. Diggle and F. R. D. Goodyear, eds., *The Classical Papers of A. E. Housman,* vol. 3, pp. 1058–69. Cambridge: Cambridge University Press, 1961.

Houthakker, Hendrick, and Lance Taylor. 1970. *Consumer Demand in the United States: Analysis and Projections, with Applications to Other Countries.* 2d ed. Cambridge, Mass.: Harvard University Press.

Howitt, Peter, and Hans-Werner Sinn. 1989. "Gradual Reform of Capital Income Taxation." *American Economic Review* 79 (March): 106–24.

Hume, David. 1748. *An Enquiry Concerning Human Understanding.* Oxford: Oxford University Press, 1975.

Bibliography

Hutchison, Terence. 1938. *The Significance and Basic Postulates of Economic Theory.* 2d ed. New York: Kelley, 1960.

Iser, Wolfgang. 1980. "The Interaction Between Text and Reader." In Susan R. Suleiman and Inge Crosman, eds., *The Reader in the Text,* pp. 106–19. Princeton, N.J.: Princeton University Press.

James, William. 1907. "Pragmatism's Conception of Truth." In Alburey Castell, ed., *Essays in Pragmatism by William James,* pp. 159–76. New York: Hafner, 1948.

Johnston, John. 1972. *Econometric Methods.* 2d ed. New York: McGraw-Hill.

Johnston, John. 1984. *Econometric Methods.* 3d ed. New York: McGraw-Hill.

Jones, G. T. 1933. *Increasing Returns.* Cambridge: Cambridge University Press.

Jonsen, Albert R., and Stephen Toulmin. 1988. *The Abuse of Casuistry: A History of Moral Reasoning.* Berkeley: University of California Press.

Kelvin, William Thompson, Lord. 1883. "Electrical Units of Measurement." In *Popular Lectures and Addresses,* vol. 1. London, 1888–1889.

Kendall, M. G., and A. Stuart. 1951. *Advanced Theory of Statistics.* Vol. 2. 3d ed. London: Griffin.

Kennedy, George A. 1984. *New Testament Interpretation Through Rhetorical Criticism.* Chapel Hill: University of North Carolina Press.

Kennedy, Peter. 1985. *A Guide to Econometrics.* 2d ed. Cambridge, Mass.: M.I.T Press.

Klamer, Arjo. 1987. "As if Economists and Their Subjects Were Rational . . ." In John Nelson et al., eds. *Rhetoric of the Human Sciences,* pp. 163–83. Madison: University of Wisconsin Press.

Klamer, Arjo. 1991. "The Advent of Modernism in Economics." Manuscript. Department of Economics, George Washington University, Washington, D.C.

Klamer, Arjo, and David C. Colander. 1990. *The Making of an Economist.* Boulder: Westview.

Klamer, Arjo, and Thomas C. Leonard. 1994. "So What's an Economic Metaphor?" In Philip Mirowski, ed., *Natural Images in Economic Thought,* pp. 20–51. Cambridge: Cambridge University Press.

Klamer, Arjo, and D. N. McCloskey. 1992. "Accounting as the Master Metaphor of Economics." *The European Accounting Review* 1 (May): 145–60.

Klein, Lawrence. 1985. *Economic Theory and Econometrics.* Jaime Marquez, ed. London: Blackwell.

Kline, Morris. 1980. *Mathematics: The Loss of Certainty.* New York: Oxford University Press.

Kmenta, Jan. 1971. *Elements of Econometrics.* New York: Macmillan.

Knight, Frank. 1940. "'What is Truth' in Economics?" [review of Hutchison 1938] *Journal of Political Economy* 48 (February): 1–32. Reprinted in *On the History and Method of Economics: Selected Essays.* Chicago: University of Chicago Press, 1963, to which reference is made.

Koopmans, Tjalling. 1957. *Three Essays on the State of Economic Science.* New York: McGraw-Hill.

Kornai, Janos. 1983. "The Health of Nations: Reflections on the Analogy Between Mecial Science and Economics." *Kyklos* 36: 191–212.

Kravis, I. B., and R. E. Lipsey. 1978. "Price Behavior in the Light of Balance-of-Payments Theories." *Journal of International Economics* 8 (May): 193–246.

Krugman, P. R. 1978. "Purchasing Power Parity and Exchange Rates: Another Look at the Evidence." *Journal of International Economics* 8 (August): 397–407.

Kruskal, William. 1968 (revised 1978). "Significance, Tests of." In *International Encyclopedia of Statistics*. New York: Macmillan.

Kruskal, William. 1978. "Formulas, Numbers, Words: Statistics in Prose." *The American Scholar* 47 (Spring): 223–29. Reprinted in D. Fiske, ed., *New Directions for Methodology in Social and Behavioral Sciences*. San Francisco: Jossey-Bass, 1981, to which reference is made.

Kuhn, Thomas. 1970. *The Structure of Scientific Revolutions*. 2d ed. Chicago: University of Chicago Press.

Kuhn, Thomas. 1977. *The Essential Tension: Selected Studies in Scientific Tradition and Change*. Chicago: University of Chicago Press.

Kurtz, A. K., and H. A. Edgerton, eds. 1939. *Statistical Dictionary of Terms and Symbols*. New York: Wiley.

Lakatos, Imre. 1976. *Proofs and Refutations: The Logic of Mathematical Discovery*. Vol. 1. Cambridge: Cambridge University Press.

Lakatos, Imre. 1978. *Methodology of Scientific Research Programmes*. Cambridge: Cambridge University Press.

Landes, David. 1969. *The Unbound Prometheus: Technological Change and Industrial Development in Western Europe from 1750 to the Present*. Cambridge: Cambridge University Press. (Reprinting, with additions, his book-length essay, "Technological Change and Development in Western Europe, 1750–1914." In *Cambridge Economic History of Europe*. Vol. VI. Cambridge: Cambridge University Press, 1965.)

Lanham, Richard. 1991. *A Handlist of Rhetorical Terms*. 2d ed. Berkeley: University of California Press.

Lanham, Richard A. 1994. *The Electronic Word: Democracy, Technology, and the Arts*. Chicago: University of Chicago Press.

Lavoie, Don C., ed. 1990. *Economics and Hermeneutics*. London: Routledge.

Leamer, Edward. 1978. *Specification Searches: Ad Hoc Inferences with Nonexperimental Data*. New York: Wiley.

Leamer, Edward. 1983. "Let's Take the Con Out of Econometrics." *American Economic Review* 73 (March): 31–43.

Lentricchia, Frank, and Thomas McLaughlin, eds. 1990. *Critical Terms for Literary Study*. Chicago: University of Chicago Press.

Leontief, W. 1982. "Letter: Academic Economics." *Science* 217: 104, 107.

Lepienes, Wolf. 1983.Manuscript on the history of sociology. Institute for Advanced Study, Princeton University, Princeton, N.J.

Levi, Edward. 1948. *An Introduction to Legal Reasoning*. Chicago: University of Chicago Press, 1967.

Lewis, C. S. 1939. "Buspels and Flansferes: A Semantic Nightmare." In *Rehabilitations and Other Essays*. Reprinted in Max Black, ed., *The Importance of Language*. Englewood Cliffs, N.J.: Prentice Hall, 1962.

Bibliography

Lewis, T., and D. E. M. Sappington. 1989. "Inflexible Rules in Incentive Problems." *American Economic Review* 79 (March): 69–84.

Lieberman, Bernhardt. 1971. *Contemporary Problems in Statistics: A Book of Readings for the Behavioral Sciences.* New York: Oxford University Press.

Lucas, Robert E., Jr., and Thomas J. Sargent, eds. 1981. *Rational Expectations and Econometric Practice.* Vol. 1. Minneapolis: University of Minnesota Press.

Machlup, Fritz. 1955. "The Problem of Verification in Economics." *Southern Economic Journal* 22 (July): 1–21.

Mackenzie, Donald A. 1981. *Statistics in Britain, 1865–1930: The Social Construction of Scientific Knowledge.* Edinburgh: Edinburgh University Press.

Mackie, J. L. 1967. "Fallacies." In *The Encyclopedia of Philosophy.* New York: Macmillan.

Maddala, G. S., C. R. Rao, and H. D. Vinod, eds. 1993. *Handbook of Statistics,* Vol. 11. Amsterdam: North Holland.

Marshall, Alfred. 1920. *Principles of Economics.* London: Macmillan.

Martin, Wallace. 1986. *Recent Theories of Narrative.* Ithaca, N.Y.: Cornell University Press.

Masica, Colin. 1976. *Defining a Linguistic Area: South Asia.* Chicago: University of Chicago Press.

McClelland, Peter. 1975. *Causal Explanation and Model Building in History, Economics, and the New Economic History.* Ithaca, N.Y.: Cornell University Press.

McCloskey, D. N. 1985. *The Applied Theory of Price.* 2d ed. New York: Macmillan.

McCloskey, D. N. 1990. *If You're So Smart: The Narrative of Economic Expertise.* University of Chicago Press.

McCloskey, D. N. 1991. "The Prudent Peasant: New Findings on Open Fields." *Journal of Economic History* 51 (June): 343–55.

McCloskey, D. N. 1994. *Knowledge and Persuasion in Economics.* Cambridge: Cambridge University Press.

McCloskey, D. N. 1997a. *The Vices of Economists; The Virtues of the Bourgeoisie.* Amsterdam and Ann Arbor: University of Amsterdam Press and University of Michigan Press.

McCloskey, D. N. 1997b. "The Good Old Coase Theorem and the Good Old Chicago School: Comment on the Medema-Zerbe Paper." In Steven Medema, ed., *Coasean Economics: The New Institutional Economics and Law and Economics.* Boston: Kluwer.

McCloskey, D. N., and J. Richard Zecher. 1976. "How the Gold Standard Worked, 1880–1913." In Jacob A. Frenkel and Harry G. Johnson, eds., *The Monetary Approach to the Balance of Payments.* London: Allen and Unwin.

McCloskey, D. N., and J. Richard Zecher. 1984. "The Success of Purchasing Power Parity." In Michael D. Bordo and Anna J. Schwartz, eds., *A Retrospective on the Classical Gold Standard, 1821–1931.* Chicago: University of Chicago Press and National Bureau of Economic Research.

McCloskey, D. N., and Stephen Ziliak. 1996. "The Standard Error of Regression." *Journal of Economic Literature* 34 (March): 97–114.

McCrea, W. H. 1983. "Review of Allaby and Lovelock, *The Great Extinction.*" *Times Literary Supplement* (July 19).

Mechling, Elizabeth Walker, and Jay Mechling. 1983. "Sweet Talk: The Moral Rhetoric Against Sugar." *Central States Speech Journal* 34 (Spring): 19–32.

Millis, Harry A. 1935. "The Union in Industry: Some Observations on the Theory of Collective Bargaining." *American Economic Review* 25 (March 1935): 1–13.

Mises, Ludwig von. 1949. *Human Action.* New Haven: Yale University Press.

Mood, A. F., and F. A. Graybill. 1963. *Introduction to the Theory of Statistics.* 2d ed. New York: McGraw-Hill.

Mood, Alexander M. 1950. *Introduction to the Theory of Statistics.* New York: McGraw-Hill.

Moore, David S., and George P. McCabe. 1993. *Introduction to the Practice of Statistics.* New York: W. H. Freeman.

Morgenstern, Oskar. 1963. *On the Accuracy of Economic Observations.* 2d ed. Princeton, N.J.: Princeton University Press.

Morrison, Denton E., and Ramon E. Henkel. 1969. "Significance Tests Reconsidered." *American Sociologist* 4 (May): 131–40. Reprinted in Morrison and Henkel 1970, to which reference is made.

Morrison, Denton E., and Ramon E. Henkel. 1970. *The Significance Test Controversy: A Reader.* Chicago: Aldine.

Mosteller, Frederick, and John W. Tukey. 1977. *Data Analysis and Regression.* Reading, Mass.: Addison-Wesley.

Mulkay, Michael. 1985. *The Word and the World: Explorations in the Form of Sociological Analysis.* Winchester, Mass.: Allen and Unwin.

Muth, John F. 1961. "Rational Expectations and the Theory of Price Movements." *Econometrica* 29 (July): 315–35. Reprinted in Arnold Zellner, ed., *Readings in Economic Statistics and Econometrics,* pp. 536–56. Boston: Little, Brown, 1968.

Nelson, John. 1983. "Models, Statistics, and Other Tropes of Politics; or, Whatever Happened to Argument in Political Science?" In D. Zarefsky, M. O. Sillars, and J. Rhodes, eds., *Argument in Transition: Proceedings of the Third Summer Conference on Argumentation.* Annandale, Va.: Speech Communication Association.

Nelson, John, Allan Megill, and D. N. McCloskey, eds. 1987. *The Rhetoric of the Human Sciences: Language and Argument in Scholarship and Public Affairs.* Rhetoric of the Human Sciences series. Madison: University of Wisconsin Press.

Nelson, Julie. 1995. *Feminism, Objectivity and Economics.* London: Routledge.

Newman, John Henry, Cardinal. 1870. *An Essay in Aid of a Grammar of Assent.* New York: Image, 1955.

Neyman, Jerzy, and E. S. Pearson. 1933. "On the Problem of the Most Efficient Tests of Statistical Hypotheses." *Philosophical Transactions of the Royal Society,* ser. A, 231: 289–337.

Nicholas, Stephen. 1982. "Total Factor Productivity Growth and the Revision of

Post-1870 British Economic History." *Economic History Review* 2d ser. 25 (February): 83–98.

Nicholas, Stephen. 1985. "British Economic Performance and Total Factor Productivity Growth, 1870–1940." *Economic History Review* 2d ser. 38 (November): 576–82.

Novick, Peter. 1988. *That Noble Dream: The "Objectivity Question" and the American Historical Profession.* Cambridge: Cambridge University Press.

Oakeshott, Michael. 1933. "Poetry as a Voice in the Conversation of Mankind." In *Experience and Its Modes.* Reprinted in *Rationalism in Politics.* New York: Basic Books, 1962.

Olson, Mancur, Jr. 1965. *The Logic of Collective Action.* Cambridge, Mass.: Harvard University Press.

Ortony, Andrew, ed. 1979. *Metaphor and Thought.* Cambridge: Cambridge University Press.

Palmer, Leonard R. 1954. *The Latin Language.* London: Faber and Faber.

Palmer, Leonard R. 1972. *Descriptive and Comparative Linguistics: A Critical Introduction.* New York: Crane, Russak.

Passmore, John. 1961. *Philosophical Reasoning.* 2d ed. London: Duckworth, 1970.

Passmore, John. 1966. *A Hundred Years of Philosophy.* 2d ed. London: Penguin.

Passmore, John. 1967. "Logical Positivism." In *The Encyclopedia of Philosophy.* New York: Macmillan.

Pearson, Karl. 1892. *The Grammar of Science.* 2d ed. London: Black, 1900.

Pearson, Karl. 1911. "Probability That Two Independent Distributions of Frequency Are Really Samples from the Same Population." *Biometrika* 8.

Perelman, Chaim, and Lucy Olbrechts-Tyteca. 1958. *The New Rhetoric: A Treatise on Argumentation.* Trans. John Wilkinson and Purcell Weaver. South Bend, Ind.: University of Notre Dame Press, 1969.

Perlman, Mark. 1978. "Review of Hutchison's *Knowledge and Ignorance in Economics.*" *Journal of Economic Literature* 16 (June): 582–85.

Plato. *Phaedrus.* Trans. H. N. Fowler. Cambridge, Mass.: Harvard University Press, 1914.

Polanyi, Michael. 1962. *Personal Knowledge: Towards a Post-Critical Philosophy.* Chicago: University of Chicago Press.

Polanyi, Michael. 1966. *The Tacit Dimension.* Garden City, N.Y.: Doubleday.

Polya, George. 1954. *Induction and Analogy in Mathematics.* Vol. 1 of *Mathematics and Plausible Reasoning.* Princeton, N.J.: Princeton University Press.

Popper, Karl. 1934. *The Logic of Scientific Discovery.* English trans. New York: Harper, 1968.

Popper, Karl. 1945. *The Open Society and Its Enemies.* London: Routledge.

Popper, Karl. 1976. *Unended Quest: An Intellectual Autobiography.* London: Collins.

Posner, Richard A. 1972. *Economic Analysis of Law.* Boston: Little, Brown.

Posner, Richard A. 1988. *Law and Literature: A Misunderstood Relation.* Cambridge, Mass.: Harvard University Press.

Prince, Gerald. 1973. *A Grammar of Stories.* Paris: Mouton.

Quine, Willard. 1948. "On What There Is." *Review of Metaphysics* 2 (September):

21–38. Reprinted in *From a Logical Point of View*. 2d ed. Cambridge, Mass.: Harvard University Press, 1961, to which reference is made.

Quine, Willard. 1951. "Two Dogmas of Empiricism." *Philosophical Review* 51 (January): 20–43. Reprinted in *From a Logical Point of View*. 2d ed. Cambridge, Mass.: Harvard University Press, 1961.

Quintilian, Marcus F. *Institutio Oratoria*. Trans. H. E. Butler. Cambridge, Mass.: Harvard University Press, 1920.

Rabinowitz, Peter J. 1968. "'What's Hecuba to Us?' The Audience's Experience of Literary Borrowing." In Susan R. Suleiman and Inge Crosman, eds., *The Reader in the Text*, pp. 241–63. Princeton, N.J.: Princeton University Press, 1980.

Reynolds, L. D., and N. G. Wilson, 1974. *Scribes and Scholars: A Guide to the Transmission of Greek and Latin Literature*. 2d ed. Oxford: Oxford University Press.

Richards, I. A. 1925. *Principles of Literary Criticism*. New York: Harcourt Brace Jovanovich.

Richards, I. A. 1936. *The Philosophy of Rhetoric*. New York: Oxford University Press.

Richardson, J. D. 1978. "Some Empirical Evidence on Commodity Arbitrage and the Law of One Price." *Journal of International Economics* 8 (May): 341–51.

Robinson, William. 1893. *Forensic Oratory: A Manual for Advocates*. Boston: Little, Brown.

Roll, Richard, and Stephen Ross. 1980. "An Empirical Investigation of the Arbitrage Pricing Theory." *Journal of Finance* 35 (December): 1073–1103.

Root-Bernstein, Robert. 1983. "Mendel and Methodology." *History of Science* 21 (September): 275–95.

Rorty, Amelie Oksenberg. 1983. "Experiments in Philosophic Genre: Descartes' *Meditations*." *Critical Inquiry* 9 (March): 545–65.

Rorty, Richard. 1979. *Philosophy and the Mirror of Nature*. Princeton, N.J.: Princeton University Press.

Rorty, Richard. 1982. *The Consequences of Pragmatism: Essays*. Minneapolis: University of Minnesota Press.

Rorty, Richard. 1984a. "Relativism." Manuscript, University of Virginia.

Rosen, Stanley. 1980. *The Limits of Analysis*. New York: Basic Books.

Rosenberg, Alexander. 1976. *Microeconomic Laws: A Philosophical Analysis*. Pittsburgh: Pittsburgh University Press.

Rosenberg, Alexander. 1992. *Economics—Mathematical Politics or Science of Diminishing Returns?* Chicago: University of Chicago Press.

Rosenblatt, Louise M. 1978. *The Reader, the Text, the Poem: The Transactional Theory of the Literary Work*. Carbondale: Southern Illinois University Press.

Rossetti, Jane. 1990. "Deconstructing Robert Lucas." In Warren J. Samuels, ed., *Economics as Discourse*, pp. 225–43. London: Kluwer Academic.

Rossetti, Jane. 1992. "Deconstruction, Rhetoric, and Economics." In Neil de Marchi, ed., *The Post-Popperian Methodology of Economics: Recovering Practice*, pp. 211–34. Boston: Kluwer and Neijhoff.

Bibliography

Ruskin, John. 1851–1853. *The Stones of Venice.* 3 Vols. New York: Peter Fenelon Collier, 1890.

Ruthven, K. K. 1979. *Critical Assumptions.* Cambridge: Cambridge University Press.

Samuelson, Paul A. 1947. *Foundations of Economic Analysis.* Cambridge, Mass.: Harvard University Press.

Saussure, F. de. 1915. *Course in General Linguistics.* Trans. Roy Harris. London: Duckworth, 1983.

Schelling, Thomas. 1978. *Micromotives and Macrobehavior.* New York: Norton.

Schoepenhauer, Arthur. 1857. *Essays and Aphorisms.* Trans. R. J. Hollingdale. Harmondsworth: Penguin, 1970.

Schuster, J. A. 1983. "The Developmental and Structural Demystification of Descartes' Method: A Case Study in the Construction of Scientific Discourse." Manuscript, University of Wollongong, N.S.W., Australia.

Scitovsky, Tibor. 1976. *The Joyless Economy.* New York: Oxford University Press.

Scott, Elizabeth. 1953. "Testing Hypotheses." In R. J. Trumpler and H. F. Weaver, eds., *Statistical Astronomy.* New York: Dover, 1963.

Scott, Robert. 1967. "On Viewing Rhetoric as Epistemic." *Central States Speech Journal* 18 (February): 9–17.

Searle, John. 1969. *Speech Acts: An Essay in the Philosophy of Language.* Cambridge: Cambridge University Press.

Sharpe, William. 1970. *Portfolio Theory* and *Capital Markets.* New York: McGraw-Hill.

Shell, Marc. 1978. *The Economy of Literature.* Baltimore: Johns Hopkins University Press.

Smith, Adam. 1776. *An Inquiry into the Nature and Causes of the Wealth of Nations.* R. H. Campbell, A. S. Skinner, and W. B. Todd, eds. 2 Vols. Indianapolis: Liberty Classics, 1981.

Smith, Adam. 1790. *The Theory of Moral Sentiments.* D. D. Raphael and A. L. Macfie, eds. Indianapolis: Liberty Classics, 1982.

Solow, Robert. 1957. "Technical Change and the Aggregate Production Function." *Review of Economics and Statistics* 39 (August): 312–20. Reprinted in Arnold Zellner, ed., *Readings in Economic Statistics and Econometrics,* Boston: Little, Brown, 1968.

Spitzer, Alan B. 1990. "John Dewey, the 'Trial' of Leon Trotsky and the Search for Historical Truth." *History and Theory* 29, no. 1: 16–37.

Stebbing, L. Susan. 1943. *A Modern Elementary Logic.* 5th ed. Revised by C. W. K. Mundle. London: Methuen, 1965.

Steiner, George. 1967. *Language and Silence: Essays on Language, Literature, and the Inhuman.* New York: Atheneum, 1982.

Steiner, Mark. 1975. *Mathematical Knowledge.* Ithaca, N.Y.: Cornell University Press.

Stigler, George J. 1966. *The Theory of Price.* 3d ed. New York: Macmillan.

Stigler, Stephen M. 1978. "Francis Ysidro Edgeworth, Statistician." *Journal of the Royal Statistical Society,* ser. A, 141: 187–313.

Stigler, Stephen M. 1986. *The History of Statistics: The Measurement of Uncertainty Before 1900.* Cambridge, Mass.: Harvard University Press.

Stone, Lawrence. 1984. Letter. *Harper's* (June).

Stove, David. 1982. *Popper and After: Four Modern Irrationalists.* Oxford: Pergamon.

Suleiman, Susan R., and Inge Crosman, eds. 1980. *The Reader in the Text: Essays on Audience and Interpretation.* Princeton, N.J.: Princeton University Press.

Summerson, John. 1963. *The Classical Language of Architecture.* Cambridge, Mass.: M.I.T. Press.

Syme, Ronald, 1956. "Piso and Veranius in Catullus." *Classica and Mediaevalia* 17: 129–34.

Thurow, Lester. 1985. *The Zero-Sum Solution: Building a World-Class American Economy.* New York: Simon and Schuster.

Todorov, Tzvetan. 1975. "Reading as Construction." In Susan R. Suleiman and Inge Crosman, eds., *The Reader in the Text,* pp. 67–82. Princeton, N.J.: Princeton University Press, 1980.

Toulmin, Stephen. 1958. *The Uses of Argument.* Cambridge: Cambridge University Press.

Tufte, Edward R. 1983. *The Visual Display of Quantitative Information.* Cheshire, Conn.: Graphics Press.

Wald, Abraham. 1939. "Contributions to the Theory of Statistical Estimation and Testing Hypotheses." *Annals of Mathematical Statistics* 10 (December): 299–326.

Wallis, W. Allen, and Harry V. Roberts. 1956. *Statistics: A New Approach.* New York: Macmillan.

Ward, Benjamin. 1972. *What's Wrong with Economics?* New York: Basic Books.

Warner, Martin. 1989. *Philosophical Finesse: Studies in the Art of Rational Persuasion.* Oxford: Clarendon.

Webster, Glenn, Ada Jacox, and Beverly Baldwin. 1981. "Nursing Theory and the Ghost of the Received View." In Joanne Comi McCloskey and Helen Grace, eds., *Current Issues in Nursing,* pp. 16–35. Boston: Blackwell Scientific.

Weinberg, Steven. 1983. "Beautiful Theories." Revision of the Second Annual Gordon Mills Lecture on Science and the Humanities, University of Texas, April 5, 1983.

Whately, Richard. 1846. *Elements of Rhetoric.* Reprint of 7th ed. Carbondale: University of Illinois Press, 1963.

White, Hayden. 1973. *Metahistory: The Historical Imagination in Nineteenth Century Europe.* Baltimore: Johns Hopkins University Press.

White, Hayden. 1981. "The Value of Narrativity in the Representation of Reality." In W. J. T. Mitchell, ed. *On Narrative,* pp. 1–24. Chicago: University of Chicago Press.

Williamson, Jeffrey. 1974. *Late Nineteenth-Century American Development: A General Equilibrium History.* Cambridge: Cambridge University Press.

Willis, James. 1972. *Latin Textual Criticism.* Urbana: University of Illinois Press.

Wonnacott, Ronald J., and Thomas H. Wonnacott. 1982. *Statistics: Discovering Its Power.* New York: Wiley.

Woolf, Virginia. 1925. *The Common Reader. First Series.* New York: Harcourt Brace Jovanovich, 1953.

Yule, G. U., and M. Greenwood. 1915. "The Statistics of Anti-Typhoid and Anti-

Cholera Inoculation and the Interpretation of Such Statistics in General." *Proceedings of the Royal Society of Medicine*, 8.

Zeckhauser, Richard, and Edith Stokey. 1978. *A Primer for Policy Analysis*. New York: Norton.

Zellner, Arnold, ed. 1968. *Readings in Economic Statistics and Econometrics*. Boston: Little, Brown.

The Rhetoric of Economics, Other than Reviews of *The Rhetoric of Economics*

Amariglio, Jack. 1984. "Epistemology, Literary Theory, and Neoclassical Economics." Unpublished paper, Department of Economics, Merrimack College, Andover, Mass.

Amariglio, Jack. 1988. "The Body, Economic Discourse, and Power: An Economist's Introduction to Foucault." *History of Political Economy* 20: 583–613.

Amariglio, Jack, Stephen Resnick, and Richard Wolff. 1990. "Division and Difference in the 'Discipline' of Economics." *Critical Inquiry* 17 (Autumn): 108–37.

Andvig, Jens-Christoph. 1991. "Verbalism and Definitions in Interwar Theoretical Macroeconomics." *History of Political Economy* 23 (Fall): 431–55.

Arrington, C. Edward. 1990. "Comment on Benton." In Warren J. Samuels, ed., *Economics as Discourse*, pp. 90–100. London: Kluwer Academic.

Ashmore, Malcolm, Michael Mulkay, and Trevor Pinch. 1989. *Health and Efficiency: A Sociology of Health Economics*. Philadelphia: Open University Press.

Backhouse, Roger, Tony Dudley-Evans, and Willie Henderson, eds. 1993. *Economics and Language*. London: Routledge.

Backhouse, Roger, Tony Dudley-Evans, and Willie Henderson. 1993. "Exploring the Language and Rhetoric of Economics." In Backhouse, Dudley-Evans, and Henderson 1993, pp. 1–20.

Bazerman, Charles. 1993. "Money Talks: The Rhetorical Project of *The Wealth of Nations*." In Backhouse, Dudley-Evans, and Henderson 1993, pp. 173–99.

Berger, Lawrence A. 1990. "Self-Interpretation, Attention, and Language: Implications for Economics of Charles Taylor's Hermeneutics." In Don C. Lavoie, ed., *Economics and Hermeneutics*, pp. 262–84. London: Routledge.

Brown, Vivienne. 1993. "Decanonizing Discourses: Textual Analysis and the History of Economic Thought." In Backhouse, Dudley-Evans, and Henderson 1993, pp. 64–84.

Brown, Vivienne. 1994. *Adam Smith's Discourse*. London: Routledge.

Collins, H. M. 1991. "History and Sociology of Science and History and Methodology of Economics." In Neil de Marchi and Mark Blaug, eds., *Appraising Economic Theories: Studies in the Methodology of Research Programs*, pp. 492–98. Aldershot, England: Elgar.

Cosgel, Metin. 1990. "Rhetoric in the Economy: Consumption and Audience." Manuscript, Department of Economics, University of Connecticut.

Cosgel, Metin, and Arjo Klamer. 1990. "Entrepreneurship as Discourse." Manuscript, Departments of Economics, University of Connecticut/George Washington University.

Davis, John B. 1990. "Comment on Rossetti's 'Deconstructing Robert Lucas.'" In Warren J. Samuels, ed., *Economics as Discourse*, pp. 244–50. London: Kluwer Academic.

Dudley-Evans, Tony, and Willie Henderson. 1987. "Changes in the Economics Article." Department of Extramural Studies, University of Birmingham, England.

Dudley-Evans, Tony, and Willie Henderson, eds. 1990. *The Language of Economics: The Analysis of Economic Discourse*. ELT Documents No. 134. Oxford: Modern English Publications.

Elshtain, Jean Bethke. 1987. "Feminist Political Rhetoric and Women's Studies." In John Nelson et al., eds., *Rhetoric of the Human Sciences*, pp. 319–40. Madison: University of Wisconsin Press.

Fish, Stanley. 1988. "Comments from Outside Economics." In Arjo Klamer et al., eds., *Consequences of Economic Rhetoric*, pp. 21–30. New York: Cambridge University Press.

Folbre, Nancy, and Heidi Hartmann. 1988. "The Rhetoric of Self-Interest: Ideology and Gender in Economic Theory." In Arjo Klamer et al., eds., *Consequences of Economic Rhetoric*, pp. 184–203. New York: Cambridge University Press.

Frey, Bruno S., Werner W. Pommerehne, Friedrich Schneider, and Guy Gilbert. 1984. "Consensus and Dissension among Economists: An Empirical Inquiry." *American Economic Review* 74 (December): 986–94.

Galbraith, John Kenneth. 1978. "Writing, Typing, and Economics." *Atlantic Monthly* 241 (March): 102–5.

George, David. 1990. "The Rhetoric of Economics Texts." *Journal of Economic Issues* 24 (September): 861–78.

Heinzelmann, Kurt. 1980. *The Economics of the Imagination*. Amherst: University of Massachusetts Press.

Henderson, Willie. 1982. "Metaphor in Economics." *Economics* (Winter): 147–53.

Henderson, Willie. 1993. "The Problem of Edgeworth's Style." In Roger Backhouse, Tony Dudley-Evans, and Willie Henderson, eds., *Economics and Langauge*, pp. 200–222. London: Routledge.

Henderson, Willie, and A. Hewings. 1987. *Reading Economics: How Text Helps or Hinders*. British National Bibliography Research Fund Report No. 28, British Library Publications Sales Unit, Boston Spa, West Yorkshire.

Henderson, Willie, and A. Hewings. 1988. "Entering the Hypothetical World: Assume, Suppose, Consider, and Take as Signals in Economics Text." Department of Extramural Studies, University of Birmingham, England.

Henderson, Willie, Tony Dudley-Evans, and Roger Backhouse, eds. 1993. *Economics and Language*. London: Routledge.

Hewings, Ann, and Willie Henderson. 1987. "A Link Between Genre and Schemata: A Case Study of Economics Text." *English Language Research Journal* 1: 156–75.

Bibliography

Hirschman, Albert O. 1991. *The Rhetoric of Reaction: Perversity, Futility, Jeopardy.* Cambridge: Harvard University Press.

Kearl, J. R., Clayne Pope, Gordon Whiting, and Larry Wimmer. 1979. "A Confusion of Economists?" *American Economic Review* 69 (May): 28–37.

Klamer, Arjo. 1983. *Conversations with Economists: New Classical Economists and Opponents Speak Out on the Current Controversy in Macroeconomics.* Totawa, N.J.: Rowman and Allanheld.

Klamer, Arjo. 1984. "Levels of Discourse in New Classical Economics." *History of Political Economy* 16 (Summer): 263–90.

Klamer, Arjo. 1987. "As if Economists and Their Subjects Were Rational . . ." In John Nelson et al., eds., *Rhetoric of the Human Sciences*, pp. 163–83. Madison: University of Wisconsin Press.

Klamer, Arjo. 1988a. "Economics as Discourse." In Neil de Marchi, ed., *The Popperian Legacy in Economics*, pp. 259–78. Cambridge: Cambridge University Press.

Klamer, Arjo. 1988b. "Negotiating a New Conversation about Economics." In Klamer et al. 1988, pp. 265–79.

Klamer, Arjo. 1990a. "The Textbook Presentation of Economic Discourse." In Warren J. Samuels, ed., *Economics as Discourse*, pp. 129–54. London: Kluwer Academics.

Klamer, Arjo. 1990b. "Towards the Native's Point of View: The Difficulty of Changing the Conversation." In Don C. Lavoie, ed., *Economics and Hermeneutics*, pp. 19–33. London: Routledge.

Klamer, Arjo. 1991. "The Advent of Modernism in Economics." Manuscript, Department of Economics, George Washington University, Washington, D.C.

Klamer, Arjo. ed. 1997. *The Value of Art.* Amsterdam: Amsterdam University Press.

Klamer, Arjo, and David C. Colander. 1990. *The Making of an Economist.* Boulder: Westview.

Klamer, Arjo, and Thomas C. Leonard. 1994. "So What's an Economic Metaphor?" In Philip Mirowski, ed., *Natural Images in Economic Thought*, pp. 20–51. Cambridge: Cambridge University Press.

Klamer, Arjo, and D. N. McCloskey. 1988. "Economics in the Human Conversation." In Arjo Klamer et al., eds., *Consequences of Economic Rhetoric*, pp. 3–20. New York: Cambridge University Press.

Klamer, Arjo, and D. N. McCloskey. 1989. "The Rhetoric of Disagreement." *Rethinking Marxism* 2 (Fall): 140–61.

Klamer, Arjo, and D. N. McCloskey. 1992. "Accounting as the Master Metaphor of Economics." *The European Accounting Review* 1 (May): 145–60.

Klamer, Arjo, and D. N. McCloskey. 1995. "One-Quarter of GDP is Persuasion." *American Economic Review* 92 (May): 191–95.

Klamer, Arjo, D. N. McCloskey, and Robert M. Solow, eds. 1988. *The Consequences of Economic Rhetoric.* New York: Cambridge University Press.

Kornai, Janos. 1983. "The Health of Nations: Reflections on the Analogy Between Medical Science and Economics." *Kyklos* 36: 191–212.

Lavoie, Don C., ed. 1990. *Economics and Hermeneutics.* London: Routledge.

Lind, Hans. 1992. "A Case Study of Normal Research in Theoretical Economics." *Economics and Philosophy* 8 (April): 83–102.

Mäki, Uskali. 1993. "Two Philosophies of the Rhetoric of Economics." In Roger Backhouse, Tony Dudley-Evans, and Willie Henderson, eds., *Economics and Language*, pp. 23–50. London: Routledge.

Maris, Bernard. 1990. *Des Économistes au-dessus de Tout Soupçon*. Paris: Albin Michel.

Mayer, Thomas. 1993. *Truth Versus Precision in Economics*. Aldershot, England: Edward Elgar.

McCloskey, D. N. 1983. "The Rhetoric of Economics." *Journal of Economic Literature* 31 (June): 482–517.

McCloskey, D. N. 1985a. "Economical Writing." *Economic Inquiry* 24 (April): 187–222.

McCloskey, D. N. 1985b. "The Loss Function Has Been Mislaid: The Rhetoric of Significance Tests." *American Economic Review* 75 (May): 201–5.

McCloskey, D. N. 1985c. *The Rhetoric of Economics*. Madison: University of Wisconsin Press.

McCloskey, D. N. 1986. *The Writing of Economics*. New York: Macmillan.

McCloskey, D. N. 1988a. "The Rhetoric of Law and Economics." *Michigan Law Review* 86 (February): 752–67.

McCloskey, D. N. 1988b. "Thick and Thin Methodologies in the History of Economic Thought." In Neil de Marchi, ed., *The Popperian Legacy in Economics*, pp. 245–57. Cambridge: Cambridge University Press.

McCloskey, D. N. 1990a. "Agon and Ag Ec: Style of Persuasion in Agricultural Economics." *American Journal of Agricultural Economics* 72 (December): 1124–30.

McCloskey, D. N. 1990b. *If You're So Smart: The Narrative of Economic Expertise*. Chicago: University of Chicago Press.

McCloskey, D. N. 1991a. "The Essential Rhetoric of Law, Literature, and Liberty." *Critical Review* 5 (Spring): 203–23.

McCloskey, D. N. 1991b. "Voodoo Economics: Some Scarcities of Magic." *Poetics Today* 12 (Winter): 287–300.

McCloskey, D. N. 1993a. "In Defense of Rhetoric: The Rhetorical Tradition in the West." *Common Knowledge* 1, no. 3.

McCloskey, D. N. 1993b. "The Lawyerly Rhetoric of Coase's 'The Theory of the Firm.'" *Journal of Corporate Law* 18 (Winter): 423–39.

McCloskey, D. N. 1993c. "Some Consequences of a Conjective Economics." In Julie Nelson and Marianne Ferber, eds., *Beyond Economic Man: Feminism and Economics*. Chicago: University of Chicago Press.

McCloskey, D. N. 1994. *Knowledge and Persuasion in Economics*. Cambridge: Cambridge University Press.

McCloskey, D. N. 1997a. "The Good Old Coase Theorem and the Good Old Chicago School: Comment on the Medema-Zerbe Paper." In Steven Medema, ed., *Coasean Economics: The New Institutional Economics and Law and Economics*. Boston: Kluwer.

McCloskey, D. N. 1997b. *The Vices of Economists; The Virtues of the Bourgeoisie*.

Amsterdam and Ann Arbor: University of Amsterdam Press and University of Michigan Press.

McCloskey, D. N., and John Nelson. 1990. "The Rhetoric of Political Economy." In J. H. Nichols, Jr., and C. Wright, eds., *Political Economy to Economics—And Back?*, pp. 155–74. San Francisco: Institute for Contemporary Studies Press.

Mehta, Judith. 1993. "Meaning in the Context of Bargaining Games—Narratives in Opposition." In Roger Backhouse, Tony Dudley-Evans, and Willie Henderson, eds., *Economics and Language*, pp. 85–99. London: Routledge.

Milberg, William. 1988. "The Language of Economics: Deconstructing the Neoclassical Texts." *Social Concepts* 4, no. 2: 33–57.

Milberg, William. 1991. "Marxism, Post-Structuralism, and the Discourse of Economics." *Rethinking Marxism* 4, no. 2: 93–104.

Milberg, William. 1992. "The Rhetoric of Policy Relevance in International Economics. "Manuscript, Department of Economics, New School for Social Research, New York.

Milberg, William, and Bruce A. Pietrykowski. 1990. "Realism, Relativism and the Importance of Rhetoric for Marxist Economics." Manuscript, Department of Economics, New School for Social Research, New York.

Miller, Carolyn R. 1990. "The Rhetoric of Decision Science, or Herbert A. Simon Says." In Herbert Simons, ed., *The Rhetorical Turn*, pp. 162–84. Chicago: University of Chicago Press.

Mirowski, Philip. 1989. *More Heat than Light: Economics as Social Physics, Physics as Nature's Economics.* Cambridge: Cambridge University Press.

Mirowski, Philip. 1994. *Natural Images in Economic Thought.* Cambridge: Cambridge University Press.

Nelson, Julie. 1995. *Feminism, Objectivity and Economics.* London: Routledge.

Perlman, Mark. 1978. "Review of Hutchison's *Knowledge and Ignorance in Economics.*" *Journal of Economic Literature* 16 (June): 582–85.

Resnick, Stephen, and Richard Wolff. 1988. "Marxian Theory and the Rhetoric of Economics." In Arjo Klamer et al., eds., *Consequences of Economic Rhetoric*, pp. 47–63. New York: Cambridge University Press.

Rossetti, Jane. 1990. "Deconstructing Robert Lucas." In Samuels 1990, pp. 225–43.

Rossetti, Jane. 1992. "Deconstruction, Rhetoric, and Economics." In Neil de Marchi, ed., *The Post-Popperian Methodology of Economics: Recovering Practice*, pp. 211–34. Boston: Kluwer and Neijhoff.

Salant, Walter. 1969. "Writing and Reading in Economics." *Journal of Political Economy* 77 (July–August): 545–58.

Samuels, Warren J., ed. 1990. *Economics as Discourse: An Analysis of the Language of Economists.* London: Kluwer Academic.

Schimdt, Christian. 1985. *La Sémantique Économique en Question.* Paris: Calmann-Levy.

Summers, Lawrence. 1991. "The Scientific Illusion of Empirical Economics." *Scandinavian Journal of Economics* 93, no. 2: 27–39.

Swales, John M. 1993. "The Paradox of Value: Six Treatments in Search of a

Reader." In Roger Backhouse, Tony Dudley-Evans, and Willie Henderson, eds., *Economics and Language*, pp. 223–39. London: Routledge.

Tribe, Keith. 1978. *Land, Labour and Economic Discourse*. London: Routledge and Kegan Paul.

Weintraub, E. Roy. 1991. *Stabilizing Dynamics: Constructing Economic Knowledge*. Cambridge: Cambridge University Press.

Reviews of the First Edition

"Reviews" mean here all direct responses to *The Rhetoric of Economics* and some of my other works on rhetoric.

Backhouse, Roger E. 1993. "Rhetoric and Methodology." In R. F. Hébert, ed., *Perspectives in the History of Economic Thought*. Aldershot, England: Edward Elgar.

Bellofiore, Riccardo. 1988. "Retorica ed economia." *Economia Politica* 5 (December): 417–63.

Bicchieri, Cristina. 1988. "Should a Scientist Abstain from Metaphor?" In Arjo Klamer et al. eds., *Consequences of Economic Rhetoric*, pp. 100–114. New York: Cambridge University Press.

Blaug, Mark. 1987. "Methodology with a Small m." *Critical Review* 1 (Spring): 1–5.

Boettke, Peter J. 1988. "Storytelling and the Human Sciences." *Market Process* 6 (Fall): 4–7.

Bonello, Frank J. 1987. "Review of *The Rhetoric of Economics*." *Social Science Quarterly* 68 (March): 209–10.

Bornemann, Alfred H. 1987. "Review of *The Rhetoric of Economics*." *Kyklos* 40, no. 1: 128–29.

Butos, William. 1987. "Rhetoric and Rationality: A Review Essay of McCloskey's *The Rhetoric of Economics*." *Eastern Economic Journal* 13 (July–Sept): 295–304.

Caldwell, Bruce J., and A. W. Coats. 1984. "The Rhetoric of Economists: A Comment on McCloskey." *Journal of Economic Literature* 22 (June): 575–78.

Coates, John. 1986. "Review of *The Rhetoric of Economics*." *Times Literary Supplement* (August 1).

Coats, A. W. 1987. "Comment on McCloskey." *Eastern Economic Journal* 13 (July–Sept): 305–7.

Coats, A. W. 1988. "Economic Rhetoric: The Social and Historical Context." In Arjo Klamer et al., eds., *Consequences of Economic Rhetoric*, pp. 64–84. New York: Cambridge University Press.

Davis, John B. 1990a. "Comments on the Rhetoric Project in Methodology." *Methodus* 2 (June): 38–39.

Davis, John B. 1990b. "Rorty's Contribution to McCloskey's Understanding of Conversation as the Methodology of Economics." *Research in the History of Thought and Methodology* 7: 73–85.

Bibliography

Dyer, Alan W. 1988. "Economic Theory as an Art Form (Rhetoric vs. Semiotics)." *Journal of Economic Issues* 22 (March): 157–66.

Evensky, Jerry. 1992. "Ethics and the Classical Liberal Tradition in Economics." *History of Political Economy* 24 (Spring): 61–77.

Galbraith, James. 1988. "The Grammar of Political Economy." In Arjo Klamer et al., eds., *Consequences of Economic Rhetoric,* pp. 221–39. New York: Cambridge University Press.

Gerrard, Bill. 1990. "On Matters Methodological in Economics." *Journal of Economic Surveys* 4, no. 2: 197–219.

Gordon, David. 1991. "Review of McCloskey's *If You're So Smart.*" *Review of Austrian Economics* 5 no. 2: 123–27.

Graziano, Loretta. 1987. "Review of *The Rhetoric of Economics.*" *Et Cetera* 44 (Winter): 417–20.

Hahn, Frank. 1987. "Review of *The Rhetoric of Economics.*" *Journal of Economic Literature* 25 (March): 110–11.

Hammond, J. Daniel. 1990. "McCloskey's Modernism and Friedman's Methodology: A Case Study with New Evidence." *Review of Social Economy* 48 (Summer): 158–71.

Hands, D. Wade. 1991. "Review of *The Consequences of Economic Rhetoric.*" *Journal of Economic Literature* 29 (March): 85–87.

Hausman, Daniel M., and Michael S. McPherson. 1987. "Standards." *Economics and Philosophy* 4 (June): 1–7.

Heilbroner, Robert. 1986. "The Murky Economists." *New York Review of Books* (April 24). Reprinted with revisions in Arjo Klamer et al., eds. *Consequences of Economic Rhetoric,* pp. 38–43. New York: Cambridge University Press, 1988.

Hollis, Martin. 1985. "The Emperor's Newest Clothes." *Economics and Philosophy* 1: 128–33.

Hoppe, Hans-Hermann. 1989. "In Defense of Extreme Rationalism: Thoughts on Donald McCloskey's *The Rhetoric of Economics.*" *Review of Austrian Economics* 3: 179–214.

Kaufer, David S. 1986. "Review of *The Rhetoric of Economics.*" *Clio* 15 (Spring): 330–33.

Keohane, Robert. 1988. "The Rhetoric of Economics as Viewed by a Student of Politics." In Klamer et al. 1988, pp. 240–46.

Klamer, Arjo. 1986. "Review of *The Rhetoric of Economics.*" *Quarterly Journal of Speech* 72 (November): 469–72.

Klamer, Arjo, D. N. McCloskey, and Robert M. Solow, ed. 1988. *The Consequences of Economic Rhetoric.* New York: Cambridge University Press.

Kregel, J. A. 1987. "Review of *The Rhetoric of Economics.*" *Economic Journal* 97 (March): 278–80

Kuttner, Robert. 1985. "The Poverty of Economics." *Atlantic* 255: 74–80; reply by McCloskey in Letters of the next edition.

Mäki, Uskali. 1988a. "How to Combine Rhetoric and Realism in the Methodology of Economics." *Economics and Philosophy* 4 (April): 89–109.

Mäki, Uskali. 1988b. "Realism, Economics, and Rhetoric: A Rejoinder to Mc-Closkey." *Economics and Philosophy* 4 (April): 167–69.

Mäki, Uskali. 1993. "Two Philosophies of the Rhetoric of Economics." In Roger Backhouse, Tony Dudley-Evans, and Willie Henderson, eds., *Economics and Language*, pp. 23–50. London: Routledge.

McPherson, Michael. 1987. "Review of *The Rhetoric of Economics*." *Journal of Economic History* 47 (June): 596–98

Munz, Peter. 1990. "The Rhetoric of Rhetoric." *Journal of the History of Ideas* 51 (January–March): 121–42.

Palmer, Tom G. 1986–1987. "An Economist Looks at His Science." *Humane Studies Review* 4 (Winter): 1, 12–13.

Rappaport, Steven. 1988a. "Arguments, Truth, and Economic Methodology: A Rejoinder to McCloskey. *Economics and Philosophy* 4 (April): 170–72.

Rappaport, Steven. 1988b. "Economic Methodology: Rhetoric or Epistemology?" *Economics and Philosophy* 4 (April): 110–28.

Rhoads, Steven E. 1987. "Review of *The Rhetoric of Economics*." *American Political Science Review* 81 (March): 338–39.

Romano, Carlin. 1987 "Review of *The Rhetoric of Economics*." *Philadelphia Inquirer* (March 22): S2.

Rosenberg, Alexander. 1988a. "Economics Is Too Important to Be Left to the Rhetoricians." *Economics and Philosophy* 4 (April): 129–49.

Rosenberg, Alexander. 1988b. "Rhetoric Is Not Important Enough for Economists to Bother About." *Economics and Philosophy* 4 (April): 173–75.

Ruccio, David F. 1987. "Review of *The Rhetoric of Economics*." *American Journal of Sociology* 93 (November): 723–25.

Samuels, Warren J. 1984. "Comments on McCloskey on Methodology and Rhetoric." *Research in the History of Thought and Methodology* 2: 207–10.

Tribe, Keith. 1986. "Review of *The Rhetoric of Economics*." *Manchester School of Economic and Social Studies* 54 (December): 447–48.

Vaubel, Roland. 1988. "Review of *The Rhetoric of Economics*." *Economic History Review* 41 (May): 340–42.

Waller, William T., Jr., and Linda R. Robertson. 1990. "Why Johnny (Ph.D. Economics) Can't Read: A Rhetorical Analysis of Thorstein Veblen and a Response to Donald McCloskey." *Journal of Economic Issues* 24 (December): 1027–44.

Warsh, David. 1993. "Trust-Buster in the Idea Business." In *Economic Principals*. New York: Free Press.

Webly, Simon. 1987. "Review of *The Rhetoric of Economics*." *International Affairs* 63 (Summer): 489–90.

Wolff, Richard, and Stephen Resnick. 1988. "Rhetoric, Economics, and Marxian Theories." In Arjo Klamer et al., eds. *Consequences of Economic Rhetoric*. New York: Cambridge University Press.

INDEX

RHETORIC OF THE HUMAN SCIENCES

Lying Down Together: Law, Metaphor and Theology
Milner S. Ball

Shaping Written Knowledge: The Genre and Activity
of the Experimental Article in Science
Charles Bazerman

Textual Dynamics of the Professions: Historical and
Contemporary Studies of Writing in Professional
Communities
Charles Bazerman and James Paradis, editors

Politics and Ambiguity
William E. Connolly

The Rhetoric of Reason: Writing and the
Attractions of Argument
James Crosswhite

Philosophy, Rhetoric, and the End of Knowledge:
The Coming of Science and Technology Studies
Steve Fuller

Machiavelli and the History of Prudence
Eugene Garver

Language and Historical Representation: Getting
the Story Crooked
Hans Kellner

The Rhetoric of Economics
Donald N. McCloskey

The Rhetoric of Economics, Second Edition
Deirdre N. McCloskey

synchronic/diachronic "rhetoric" (29-30)
↓ ⌐
instrumental *constitutive*

Therapeutic Discourse and Socratic Dialogue:
A Cultural Critique
Tullio Maranhão

The Rhetoric of the Human Sciences: Language and
Argument in Scholarship and Public Affairs
John S. Nelson, Allan Megill, and
Donald N. McCloskey, editors

Tropes of Politics: Science,Theory, Rhetoric, Action
John S. Nelson

What's Left? The Ecole Normale Supérieure and
the Right
Diane Rubenstein

Understanding Scientific Prose
Jack Selzer, editor

The Politics of Representation: Writing Practices
in Biography, Photography, and Policy Analysis
Michael J. Shapiro

Hayden White —
irony and the
"problematical
nature of
language" (51)

The Legacy of Kenneth Burke
Herbert Simons and Trevor Melia, editors

The Unspeakable: Discourse, Dialogue, and Rhetoric
in the Postmodern World
Stephen A. Tyler

Heracles' Bow: Essays on the Rhetoric and the
Poetics of the Law
James Boyd White